THE FALSE PROPHET

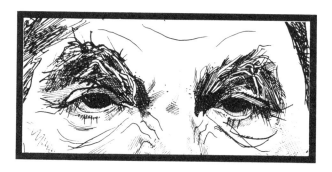

RABBI MEIR KAHANE

FROM FBI INFORMANT TO KNESSET MEMBER

Robert I. Friedman

LAWRENCE HILL BOOKS

Library of Congress Cataloging-in-Publication Data
Friedman, Robert I., 1950-
  The false prophet : Rabbi Meir Kahane—from FBI informant to
Knesset member/Robert I. Friedman.—1st ed.
    p. cm.
  ISBN 1-55652-078-6 : $19.95
  1. Kahane, Meir. 2. Israel. Knesset—Biography. 3. Rabbis-United
States—Biography. 4. Revisionist Zionists—Biography. 5. Israel—
Politics and government. I. Title.
DS126.6.K2F75   1990
324.25694'08'092—dc20
[B]   89-26973
                                                                  CIP

Cover drawing by David Levine. Reprinted with
permission from *The New York Review of Books.*©1986,
Nyrev, Inc.

Printed in the United States of America
First edition
First printing
Published by Lawrence Hill Books, Brooklyn, New York
An imprint of Chicago Review Press, Incorporated
814 North Franklin Street
Chicago, Illinois 60610
ISBN 1-55652-078-6

To Christine, who wouldn't let me quit.

Drawing by David Levine.
Reprinted with permission from
The New York Review of Books.
Copyright ©1986, Nyrev, Inc.

CONTENTS

PROLOGUE
The False Prophet

~~~~~~

I first met Rabbi Meir Kahane in December 1979, at his Jerusalem headquarters, a cramped, airless office in an upper-class section of the city. He calls it the Museum of the Potential Holocaust. The "museum" was filled with Nazi flags and anti-Semitic literature that he had clipped from American hate-group publications and pasted on display boards. At the time, Kahane was a political pariah. His followers in Israel consisted of no more than a few dozen teenagers who had belonged to the Jewish Defense League (JDL) in America. "Numbers aren't important," Kahane told me. "How many Maccabees fought the Greeks?"

While Kahane admitted that his movement in Israel was small, he said that it was growing—especially in Kiryat Arba, the sprawling, ultranationalist Jewish settlement on the West Bank, where he kept a second home, and in the Sephardic slums of Jerusalem and Tel Aviv, where he was fast becoming a folk hero to youth who were attracted to his fiercely-held, anti-establishment views, as well as to his uncompromising hatred of the Arabs.

It struck me on that first encounter that Kahane was a man obsessed with sex and violence. He chattered incessantly about Arab men sleeping with Jewish women. He claimed, for instance, that English-speaking Arab men often tried to pass themselves off as Jews to unsuspecting American Jewish women studying at the Hebrew University in Jerusalem. He had recently spent an entire day, he told me, plastering the university cafeteria and dormitories with flyers that warned coeds to check their dates' identity cards before jumping into bed with them.

As far as Kahane was concerned, no Jew in Israel, man, woman, or child, was safe as long as there was a single Arab in the country. Just that morning, he told me, he had read a report in the Hebrew press about a Jew who had been pulled from a taxicab and beaten up by a gang of West Bank Arabs. He confided that he would stage a "reprisal mission" on the guilty Arabs' village the next day. He invited me to come along.

There were ten of Kahane's followers on the "mission"—three Israelis of Moroccan origin, two recent Russian immigrants, and five Americans; most were in their late teens or early twenties. "We are going to pay the Arabs back for beating up a Jew here yesterday," said twenty-eight-year-old, Brooklyn-born Chaim Shimon, as Kahane deftly maneuvered his yellow Ford van through Jerusalem traffic. "Arabs often attack Jews in Israel," he continued, "but Jews are afraid to fight back. The Israeli superman is a media myth. The country needs us to defend them."

The van stopped in front of an Israeli police roadblock outside Beit Safafa, a prosperous Arab suburb near East Jerusalem. Apparently, the police had been tipped off to Kahane's plan.

"Go and do what you have to do," Kahane ordered the young men in the van as he jumped from the driver's seat. "I'll deal with this!"

Kahane strode toward the knot of police in riot gear with a clear look of manifest destiny in his eyes. Dressed in a sun-faded green army parka, gray pants, and combat boots, with a yarmulke pinned to his thinning black hair, he was a vision of a modern-day warrior-priest ready for battle. While Kahane engaged the police in a noisy conversation, his "boys" drove through the suburb to look for Arab prey.

After a short drive, the burly young Moroccan driver spotted a lone Arab. The man was perhaps fifty. His face was gnarled and stained copperbrown from years in the sun. The Jews attacked with their fists so swiftly that his black eyes were quiet and unbelieving as he was pummeled to the ground. The group returned quickly to the van.

"It served the bastard right!" Shimon sneered as we drove away. Bearded and wearing a yarmulke, Shimon recalled that he had been riding his bike through Prospect Park in Brooklyn several years earlier when he was jumped by a gang of young Blacks. He was attacked, he said, solely because he was a Jew. A few days later he joined the JDL.

"I wanted to feel proud and unafraid," he told me. "I had heard of Rabbi Kahane and had read some of his work. I decided to get involved with the JDL—like 'riding shotgun' in predominantly Black neighborhoods to protect the remaining old Jews. But anti-Semitism in America got too intense. I came to Israel to be with the rabbi and to fulfill the Torah's commandments."

The van lurched as it turned the corner. Although it was winter the sun was warm. The driver wound down the window and called out to a group of middle-aged Arab workers lounging against the peeling, whitewashed wall of a cafe.

"Hey, Mohammed," he barked in Arabic. "I'm horny! Where are all your Arab whores?"

Laughter flickered through the van.

"Arabs try to sleep with Jewish women whenever they can," Shimon said. "Like Eldridge Cleaver said in *Soul On Ice*, 'Sleeping with a white woman is the ultimate revolutionary act.' "

We drove full circle. Kahane was still at the roadblock arguing with the police. We stopped. The rabbi, who was then forty-seven, and small and thin with a darkly handsome face, stepped into the front seat and sat like a stone icon. As we climbed the highway on our way back to Jerusalem, the only sound in the van was the grinding of gears.

I visited Kahane again the next day, curious to discover if he had read a story in the morning's newspapers that said the Jew who had been pulled from the cab and beaten up, the one they had staged their assault for, had not been attacked by Arabs, as previously reported, but was actually the victim of a *Jewish* gangland assault.

Kahane's eyes twitched. He could barely control what was once a serious childhood stutter.

"I told them to stay in the van and to stay out of trouble," he muttered. "But some of them are a little crazy. It's important to have crazies in a mass movement, though. They'll do anything for you, especially when you're the first to cross the barricades."

"But the Arabs were innocent," I pointed out.

The rabbi was not impressed.

"This time the Arabs didn't do it," he growled. "But there are hundreds of unreported incidents of Arabs attacking and sexually molesting Jews. And who do you think plants bombs here—the American Boy Scouts? I don't want to live in a state where I have to worry about being blown up in the back of a bus.

"I don't blame the Arabs for hating us," the rabbi continued, warming to his subject. "This was their land—once! And no matter what the Israeli Left says, you can't buy Arab love with indoor toilets and good health care. Israeli Arabs and West Bank Arabs identify with the PLO. And they multiply like rabbits. At their rate of growth they will take over the Knesset in twenty-five years. I am not prepared to sacrifice Zionism to democracy. There is only one solution: the Arabs must leave Israel!"

I squirmed in my seat.

"Of course it's not nice. Did I say it's nice? Is it nice when Israel bombs the PLO in Lebanon and kills women and children? We have smart bombs, not nice bombs."

"How would you implement these ideas if you were the prime minister of Israel?" I asked.

"I'd go to the Arabs and tell them to leave," he replied. "I'd promise generous compensation. If they refused, I'd forcibly move them out."

"How could you do that?" I asked. "Midnight deportations in cattle cars?"

"Yes!" he declared.

Thus spoke Meir Kahane—the rabbi who took the concept of the nice Jewish boy and turned it on its head.

* * *

Even as a young man in New York, Meir Kahane was a right-wing extremist, although he strove to create the appearance of middle-class normalcy. In Laurelton, Queens in the mid-1960s, Kahane seemed to be just another obscure Orthodox rabbi giving Hebrew lessons. To his neighbors, he was a self-effacing teacher who was wonderful with children. But by his own admission, and confirmed by sources in the Justice Department, he spent many of those years leading a double life, spying on left-wing student groups for the Federal Bureau of Investigation and promoting the U.S. position on the Vietnam War in the Orthodox Jewish community for the Central Intelligence Agency.

Then, in the turbulent summer of 1968, Kahane cofounded the Jewish Defense League, declaring that it would protect Jews from anti-Semitism. The JDL emerged out of the racial tensions generated by the 1968 New York City teachers' strike, which pitted the predominantly Jewish teachers' union against militant Blacks who sought greater control of their neighborhood schools. The strike, together with Black demands for quotas for Civil Service jobs, open admission to city universities and open housing, drew thousands of Orthodox and working-class Jews from New York's outer boroughs to the JDL, which was at the forefront of the white backlash. Kahane, who was then also the associate editor of the Brooklyn-based, Orthodox Jewish weekly, *The Jewish Press*, filled the tabloid with lurid stories about anti-Semitic acts of violence by Blacks and Puerto Ricans against Jews too old and too poor to leave America's decaying inner cities. The stories further exacerbated racial tensions, while creating a pretext for Kahane to dispatch squads of armed JDL militants to "patrol" mixed Jewish-Black neighborhoods. In a few short months, the JDL had helped to polarize New York City almost beyond repair.

The JDL enjoyed considerable notoriety as an anti-Black protest group. But it achieved international celebrity when Kahane seized on an issue largely ignored by the American Jewish establishment—the plight of Soviet Jews. By 1970, the JDL's bombing and shooting attacks against Soviet embassies in the United States and Europe were so numerous that President Richard Nixon became concerned Kahane would wreck the Strategic Arms Limitations Talks. JDL violence forced the American Jewish establishment and, in turn, the U.S. government to make the free immigration of Soviet Jews a top priority. It was Kahane's crowning achievement. He gained the support of prominent labor leaders, politicians, and wealthy Jewish philanthropists. Little did they know that the JDL's guerrilla war against the Soviet Union was orchestrated by right-wing Mossad officers led by Israel's future prime minister Yitzhak Shamir.

It is not surprising that Kahane was entrusted with this sensitive mission, given his background. His father was a highly respected Brooklyn rabbi, a fervent Zionist and a member of the right-wing Revisionist movement headed by Ze'ev Jabotinsky, who was once a guest at the Kahanes' Flatbush home when Meir was a child. As a teenager Kahane was a member of Betar, the youth wing of the Revisionist movement. Together with his young colleagues, Kahane packed arms at the Hoboken, New Jersey docks to be smuggled to the right-wing Jewish underground Irgun during Israel's War of Independence.

In September 1971, Kahane moved to Israel, one step ahead of a federal indictment stemming from his JDL activities. He was lionized by the Israeli media and fought over by political parties in a way that is reminiscent of the kind of attention that Natan Sharansky received when he came to Israel from Russia. Although Kahane was invited to join Menachem Begin's right-wing Herut Party and Yosef Burg's National Religious Party, he turned both down, preferring to start his own movement. But he floundered on his own. His megalomaniacal drive, interrupted by periodic bouts of crippling depression, made it virtually impossible for him to work within a regimented, bureaucratic party structure. In America he had always managed to have a cadre of talented and disciplined people around him who kept the JDL functioning when he could not. In Israel he was increasingly a one-man act, alienating those around him. In a few short years, Kahane was a forgotten figure. His party, called Kach (this is the way), was made up a few dozen young American Jewish malcontents who specialized in terrorizing Arabs.

But in the early 1980s, as the Jewish state lurched to the Right, Kahane emerged from the margins of Israeli politics to head a mass movement essentially built around a single idea—a call to expel Israel's Arabs. It was a demand that unlocked wellsprings of support in the Jewish state because expulsion had always occupied a central—though never public—position in mainstream Zionist thinking. In 1984, Kahane was elected to the Knesset. His victory stunned the nation.

By 1988, Kahane had made extraordinary inroads into Israeli politics by mixing a volatile brew of xenophobic right-wing Jewish nationalism with an Orthodox world view that proclaims Jews are chosen to lead humanity into the Messianic era. In America, Kahane's support among Jews was equally impressive. According to a 1986 survey conducted for the American Jewish Committee by Professor Steven M. Cohen, 14 percent of American Jews professed strong sympathy for Kahane, a proportion that rose to 30 percent among the 500,000-strong Orthodox community. On the eve of the 1988 Knesset elections, with his popularity surging in response to the Palestinian uprising, Israeli pollsters predicted Kahane could win as many as 6 of the 120 Knesset seats, making him the leader of the third largest party in Israel. Fearing that development, parties on the Right and the Left joined forces and passed a law later upheld by the Israeli High Court, which barred Kahane from running for office on the grounds that his movement was racist and anti-democratic. Although back in the early 1970s Shamir and other prominent right-wing politicians in Israel had much to do with turning Kahane into a potent political phenomenon, by the late 1980s they wanted nothing more than to destroy his political career and siphon away his tens of thousands of supporters.

Although for now Kahane cannot exercise political power, Israeli polls indicate that his movement continues to thrive, undoubtedly nourished by the passions unleashed by the Palestinian uprising, or *intifada*. Kahane may have broken the taboo on publicly calling for the expulsion of Israel's Arabs, but the *intifada* gave the concept a sort of hideous urgency. Now prominent politicians on the "respectable Right," from Likud to the National Religious Party, are recommending "transfer" (the euphemism in Israel for mass expulsion) as a solution to the country's "demographic" problem.

Kahane's career has been a roller coaster ride that seems far from over. In the past, whenever it appeared that the rabbi's career had run aground, he would reemerge phoenix-like out of the tensions born of social and political upheaval. "The worse it gets for Israel the better it gets for me!" Kahane once told me.

One indication of Kahane's future path is his apparent connection to a terrorist underground in Israel that has begun to attack Israeli Jews who advocate negotiating with the Palestine Liberation Organization. Calling themselves the Sicarrim after a sect of Jewish assassins who murdered Romans and "Hellenist" Jews during the Second Temple period, they claimed credit for firebombing the homes of a number of prominent left-wing figures in 1988, including Yair Tzaban, leader of the Socialist Mapam Party, and Dan Margolit, a television journalist. In telephone calls to Israeli news organizations, people claiming to speak for the Sicarrim have said that they are members of Rabbi Kahane's Kach movement.

The original Sicarrim emerged during the first century A.D., a time when many false prophets and self-proclaimed Messiahs attracted large and fanatical followings with claims that they could overthrow the Romans and usher in the Messianic Age. The appearance of false prophets is a phenomenon that seems to recur in Jewish history whenever the community feels imperiled. Hence today in Israel, there is a burgeoning Jewish fundamentalist movement, backed by powerful right-wing politicians, calling for the annexation of the Occupied Territories as a prelude to the Biblically ordained End of Days and the Redemption of Mankind.

Long at the cutting edge of this fundamentalist movement, Kahane is driven by the politics of redemption, which he says will be hastened by ridding Israel of its Arabs. As he wrote in *Thorns in Your Eyes*, one of several anti-Arab manifestos he has published:

> The Arabs of Israel are a desecration of God's name. Their non-acceptance of Jewish sovereignty over the Land of Israel is a rejection of the sovereignty of the God of Israel and his kingdom. Removing them from the land is therefore more than a political matter. It is a religious matter, a religious obligation to wipe out the desecration of God's name. Instead of worrying about the reactions of the Gentiles if we act, we should tremble at the thought of God's wrath if we do not act. Tragedy will befall us if we do not remove the Arabs from the land, since redemption can come at once in its full glory if we do as God commands us. . . . Let us remove the Arabs from Israel and hasten the Redemption.

Although it may be unpleasant to realize that Kahane has become a significant political force in Israel, it does not help that many American Jewish leaders have preferred to keep the phenomenon of widespread support for the rabbi's views among American Jews under wraps. Denial does not spare Israel from the consequences of Kahane's politics. Rabbi Meir Kahane's life and times are a looking glass into the dark side of Israel's soul. Like bigotry of any kind, Kahaneism cannot be understood and challenged if it is shrouded in ignorance where it is free to flourish.

CHAPTER ONE
Early Years

~~~~~~

Meir Kahane was fifteen when he was arrested for the first time. In 1947, he led an attack on British Foreign Minister Ernest Bevin, who had been turning away Jewish refugee ships from Palestine. Bevin arrived on the S.S. *Queen Mary* to speak at the United Nations. As his car came down the gangplank at Pier 84, Kahane and a group of his friends from Betar, the youth wing of the Revisionist Movement, pelted it with eggs and tomatoes.

The police chased the Jewish youths, and Kahane, who often bragged about his blazing speed on the high school track team, was tackled from behind by a policeman. A photo of Kahane locked in the grip of the officer's choke hold appeared the next day in *The New York Daily News*.

Charles Kahane was shocked by his son's arrest, although he himself had often called for Jews in Palestine to take up arms against the British. "My father yelled at me when he came to bail me out," Kahane said many years later. "But I said, 'It was your fault! You taught me all this!' He never yelled at me again."

Even at that age, the family recognized Kahane for what he was. "Meir was a revolutionary from a young age," said his uncle, Rabbi Isaac Trainin, who recently retired as the director of New York's Federation of Jewish Philanthropies. As a child, Trainin said, his nephew had a "Messianic complex"— a sense that he was destined to play a historical role in the revival of the Jewish people. "After his Bar Mitzvah, I recall hearing my father say to my mother: 'You will see, Hannah, some day he will give us a lot of trouble.' "

Yet Kahane's childhood began peacefully enough as the son of a respected rabbi. "People often ask me why I formed the JDL—was it a personal trauma? No, I had an extremely pleasant life," Kahane once told me.

Martin David Kahane was delivered by caesarean section on August 1, 1932. His parents, Charles and Sonia, then lived in a quiet, middle-class neighborhood of small, well-kept, two-family brick homes in the Flatbush section of Brooklyn.

In the 1930s, the neighborhood was an amalgam of Italian and Eastern European Jewish immigrants who had recently escaped the crime and clamor of the Lower East Side in Manhattan, across the East River. Even if some of the older kids did carry razor blades in their wallets "just in case," street crime was almost unknown in that insular world. And though Kahane would one day become obsessed with anti-Semitism, during his childhood it was little more than an abstract phenomenon. "People used to sit on stoops and benches at all times of the day and night," said Allan Mallenbaum, a childhood friend of Kahane. "Nobody was afraid of crime. You never saw a Black face. The only language you heard on the street besides English was Italian and Yiddish—and you heard a lot of both. I remember walking to school down First Street, and the old Italian men would come out of their homes to give us kids candy."

Martin, who would later adopt his Hebrew name Meir, was a precocious, sickly child. At the age of four, he was operated on for a mastoid that had become infected after a botched tonsillectomy hemorrhaged—a serious matter in the days before penicillin. "For three or four days after the operation we were not allowed to go into the room," Kahane's mother, Sonia, told me in her small, neatly furnished apartment in Jerusalem, where she has lived since 1971. "We looked at him through a glass window. He kept pulling the bandages from his head. One day, his private nurse brought him the *Daily News* so that he could look at the comics. He threw it down and said, 'I'm an intelligent boy! I don't read junk! I want *The New York Times*!' The doctors couldn't get over it. He couldn't read but he could recognize the difference," she said with a mother's pride.

The young Kahane spent two weeks in the hospital convalescing, only to come home to catch whooping cough, which wracked him with spasmodic, convulsive coughing fits. His doctor feared that the attacks would reinfect the mastoid, and so three days a week for a year, the child had to have the incision behind his right ear drained.

The needle terrified him. "My brother Isaac used to hold Meir on his lap while the doctor drained the pus with a big needle," said Sonia. "Meir used to yell, 'I'll be a good boy!' 'I'll be a good boy!' He thought we were having him punished for being a bad boy."

As a young child, Kahane was dressed by his mother in knickers with high top shoes and flowered print blouses, and taken on long strolls down Ocean Parkway. Sonia recalled that passersby often mistook him for a little girl, with his long black hair curling down to his shoulders, and his thick eyelashes waving upwards.

When he grew older, Kahane spent endless hours playing stickball games and long Saturday afternoons at the candy store where debates with friends raged about their favorite baseball hero. Charles encouraged his sons to experience the world beyond the narrow confines of Orthodox Judaism. "My father knew enough about the world to recognize he had to make compromises," said Kahane's younger brother, Nachman, today an Orthodox rabbi in Jerusalem. "He let us grow up one hundred percent American."

Meir Kahane remembers these years with a fondness that borders on the sentimental. "I loved my neighborhood and my Jewish and Italian friends," Kahane reminisced to me one day. "I spent hours roaming the streets, hanging out on the corner, and playing games. I was a great baseball player. . . . I remember going to Ebbets Field to watch Dixie Walker. He used to hit these sharp, magnificent line drives off the right-field wall that were tremendous!"

Because Charles Kahane was a moderately well-paid rabbi with a large congregation, Meir never felt the privations of the Depression. Though Charles's congregation was not wealthy, the Sha'arei Tef'ilah Synagogue on West First Street was one of the most striking temples in the neighborhood with beautiful high ceilings, gold chandeliers, and elegantly carved wooden pews. On Yom Kippur the shul was packed with more than two thousand people, divided between Ashkenazi or European Jews who held their service upstairs, and Sephardic or Oriental Jews who prayed in the first-floor chapel.

As in most Orthodox households, the central event of the week was celebrating the Sabbath. Preparations began at 3:00 P.M. every Friday, when Charles summoned Meir and Nachman, who were both usually in the street playing ball. They took showers, put on suits, and joined their father on the short walk to the synagogue. Following services conducted by Charles, the boys returned home for the kiddish (prayers) and the meal. The house on West Second Street was always filled with guests. And the conversation invariably turned to the fate of the Jews in Europe and Palestine. "It was such a holy house, a wonderful, warm house," said Nachman. "It was a house of Torah, learning, the Sabbath." Several years ago Nachman returned to the house where he grew up. "I wanted to see it again. There are eight stairs leading up to the porch. I started up the stairs, but I knew I'd see a cross on the door where our *mezzuzah* had been. I turned and walked away."

Even as a child, Nachman remembers their street was lit up with colored lights on Christmas. "There was a Christmas tree in front of every pleasant, middle-class Italian home," he told me. "It was during Christmas that we Jews felt like strangers."

But if the Kahanes sometimes felt ill at ease during Christian holidays, the family also found in Flatbush a kind of peace that Sonia and Charles had only dreamed about before coming to America. Indeed, Meir Kahane's parents had grown up thousands of miles from Brooklyn, under conditions far harsher than those of their darkly gifted eldest son.

* * *

Charles Kahane was born in the village of Safed in Palestine, near the Lebanese border, in 1905, after his family had emigrated there from Galicia in 1873. His grandfather, Baruch David Kahane, journeyed to Palestine—then a miserably poor, malaria-infested backwater of the Ottoman Empire—at the behest of the Sanzer Rebbe, the head of a powerful Hasidic dynasty renowned for its mystical fervor. Baruch David, himself the scion of a prominent Hasidic family, was instructed to help rebuild Safed, which had been devastated by an earthquake. He was also entrusted with distributing money and clothing to the town's impoverished religious scholars. Most of Palestine's Jews were pious men who lived on donations from Jews in the diaspora. But Baruch David's arrival in Safed was resented by some community elders, who spread rumors that he was pocketing relief funds, prompting him to offer his resignation. "Pay no attention to empty talk," the Sanzer Rebbe wrote to Baruch David. "Great indeed is the reward of those who care for the public good of Israel, as is explained in the words of the Sages. Hence (you) should not turn (your) back on the privilege which has been granted (you) by heaven."

Safed was not only one of the four holy cities of Judaism, but it also had been a seat of Jewish mysticism and learning since the fifteenth century—a refuge for Jews seeking divine truths revealed through the secret codes and formulas found in the cabala, a body of Jewish mysticism, which if mastered is supposed to hasten the coming of the Messiah. Baruch David and his son Nachman became cabalists, spending long hours in private study with Jewish mystics.

Baruch David combined mysticism with a fervent love of Zion. Long before the birth of modern Zionism, he wrote a book called *Hibat Ha'aretz,* or *Love of the Land*. In it he expressed the importance of returning to Israel—the ancient land of the Jewish people—a return that religious Jews believe is divinely ordained. That Palestine was inhabited by a large and hostile Arab population who viewed the country as their homeland was not mentioned in the book.

During the First World War, the occupying Ottoman Turks destroyed or closed many of Palestine's great Talmud academies as they retreated from the advancing British army. As the war raged, Nachman brought his thirteen-year-old son Charles to Europe, enrolling him in a highly-regarded yeshiva (a school where Orthodox Jews study Talmud) in the Polish town of Oswiecim—near the future Nazi death camp of Auschwitz, where the Kahanes would lose most of the Eastern European branch of their family. Several years later, Charles was accepted into an even more prestigious yeshiva in Pressburg, Bratislava on the Hungarian-Polish border.

Like many of the yeshiva students who crowded the Talmud academies of Eastern Europe during the years between the world wars, Charles was penniless, surviving on handouts from the Jewish community. "It was a very hard period for my father," said Meir's younger brother, Nachman. "Yeshiva students customarily ate in the home of more well-to-do Jews. But my father was born into a very noble Hasidic family; so noble in fact that he couldn't sit at the table of a less noble family." So, Nachman says, his father ate restaurant scraps and slept on the benches of synagogues. "It made him very tough, very independent," he added. After four years of study Charles received rabbinical ordination, and in 1922, at the age of seventeen, he journeyed alone to America.

If Meir Kahane's father, Charles, was tough-minded, his mother, Sonia Trainin, was made of cast iron. Meir probably received his sense of choseness—the feeling that he was somehow superior to his fellow Jews— from his father's family. But it was from his mother's family that he inherited the chutzpah to take on the establishment. Meir inherited more than his renegade nature from the Trainins; he got their temperament. The Trainins were always unsettled and anxious. Sonia could hyperventilate about something as simple as going to a department store to buy a dress. Calamity always seemed to be just around the corner.

Certainly, Sonia grew up in volatile times. She was born in 1909 in Sizerin, Russia, some two thousand miles east of Moscow on the Volga. Her maternal grandfather was a prosperous grain merchant who supplied the Czar's army. Sonia's mother, a firebrand who spoke six languages, was arrested and nearly executed for her involvement in left-wing student politics during the aborted Revolution of 1905. Sonia's grandfather won her release with a large bribe. "Our mother was a real 'women's libber'," said Sonia's younger brother, Isaac.

Sizerin became a battleground during the Russian Revolution, changing hands between the Red and White Armies. In 1918, soldiers caught Sonia's mother buying milk on the black market. As she was being taken away, Sonia followed, pleading for her mother's life, until the soldiers relented. But a wave of vicious pogroms and the chronic food shortage soon forced the family westward. "We walked twenty miles to a boat," Sonia told me, "which we took to Samarkand." Then they caught a train to St. Petersburg where they were quarantined for six weeks in the Winter Palace with thousands of other refugees. Many died from exposure and starvation. "My mother would go to Red Square to buy potatoes, and bake them there in the snow," Sonia remembered.

The family eventually moved to Dvisnk, Latvia, where Sonia's parents had been born. Sonia entered a gymnasium and studied German and Latin. Her frenetic energy, and her lack of concern for community morals frazzled even her pugnacious younger brother. At the time, most Jewish men in Eastern Europe wore long black coats and had unkempt beards, the garb that Hasids had been wearing since the Middle Ages. Women were equally conservative. But Sonia was an emancipated Jew—one of a growing number in tradition-bound Eastern Europe who were influenced by the radical transformations wrought by the French Revolution, Napoleon, and the Industrial Age. "Sonia went to dances, did not pay too much attention to her schoolwork, and ran around with one boy after another," said Isaac Trainin. "Her behavior shocked our neighbors—all of whom were extremely pious."

Isaac recalls that the first few years in Latvia, however, were "unhappy ones." "My parents had a horrible relationship," he said. "They were constantly at each other's throats. It took a toll on all the children." To make matters worse, his father squandered most of a large inheritance on failed business ventures, plunging the family deep into debt. "Our rabbi said there was no alternative but to go to America and get a fresh start," recalled Sonia. In 1922, her father, Baruch Shalom, travelled alone to America, where after several years working in Cleveland he became a rabbi in a small Plainfield, New Jersey synagogue.

But Sonia's father had grander ambitions. Shortly after arriving in America, he organized a small band of anti-establishment Orthodox rabbis that challenged the leadership of the Union of Orthodox Rabbis of America, the country's largest rabbinical body, which regulated everything from kosher food to marriages and divorces. At the time, Orthodox Judaism in America was riven with petty disputes and personality conflicts. Some Orthodox rabbis were open to life in America while others adhered to narrow Eastern European traditions. As a boy, Isaac Trainin was taken to a convention of the Union of Orthodox Rabbis where he witnessed the head of the organization call another rabbi an "ignoramus" in front of hundreds of members.

The most serious conflicts—and scandals—revolved around the kosher food industry, which already in the 1920s was a half-billion-dollar-a-year business. The ritual slaughter and preparation of kosher meat and poultry was supervised by Orthodox rabbis, as was the manufacture of kosher food products. Corruption was rampant and disputes over kosher production and supervision often ended in bloodshed. It was during this period that Trainin's group accused the Manischewitz Company, America's largest kosher food manufacturer, of improperly following kosher dietary laws, according to one of Charles Kahane's nephews, a prominent New York rabbi. The effect was similar to a shakedown. To defuse the conflict, the company gave Trainin a lucrative job supervising food production during Passover. Soon after, Rabbi Jacob Eskolsky, a leader of Trainin's rebel rabbinical group, was kidnapped from his home and murdered, apparently by rivals in the kosher food business. It was the bitter climax of a decade-long scandal that ultimately forced New York State to tighten its regulation of the industry.

In 1928, Baruch Shalom sent for his family in Latvia. "We arrived in New York harbor on the eve of Rosh Hashona on October 4th at 3 P.M.," Sonia remembered. "The day was short but we made it home before the Sabbath."

First, however, Sonia was to have a serendipitous encounter with her future husband. Charles Kahane, her senior by five years, had come to the dock with some right-wing Zionist friends to picket British Prime Minister Ramsay MacDonald, who happened to be travelling on the ship that was bringing Sonia and her family to New York. The Zionists were pressuring the British to allow increased Jewish immigration to Palestine. "Charles noticed me in the crowd," recalled Sonia, more than sixty years after the incident. "I was wearing a navy blue suit with a white ermine collar and a little red hat. Charles walked up to my father and asked if he needed any help with the luggage. My father said to him in Yiddish, 'Who needs you here?' I hardly noticed him. I was bewildered. I wanted to go back to Latvia. I didn't know the language. I only spoke Russian and Yiddish. So what was I going to do here? I went on a three-day hunger strike."

Charles, however, had quickly adjusted to life on Manhattan's Lower East Side—a densely crowded neighborhood of narrow, dirty streets lined with tenements populated mainly by Jews newly arrived from Eastern Europe's ghettos. The first thing Charles did in America was to cut his *payis* (long side curls) and his beard. He put the clippings in an envelope and sent them to his father, who was living in Vienna. "I have no one else to keep them for me," he wrote. Then he put on an American-made suit and went to look for a job.

Charles met sixteen-year-old Bernard Bergman while searching for a place to live. In no time, according to Sonia, they were the "very best of friends." Bergman, who wore the *payis,* untamed beard, and long, black coat of the ultra-Orthodox, had emigrated from Hungary in the 1920s. He was working for his father's bootlegging business when Charles and he first met. Although he was obviously quite intelligent, Bergman neither went to school nor spoke English. "You don't learn? You don't get any education?" Charles asked his new friend in Yiddish. "I'm only two months in this country and I've already skipped four classes in public school!" Bergman's father, a rabbi, was pleased that Charles encouraged his son to study English and offered him a cot in the family's basement next to a whiskey still.

Bernard Bergman would later become one of the richest and most powerful Orthodox Jews in the world, with close ties to Israel's National Religious Party. He made his fortune from a national conglomerate of Medicaid nursing homes, where infirm patients were left unattended to soak in their own urine. *The New York Daily News* characterized the homes as warehouses where the aged were dumped to die. No doubt Bergman learned his business ethics from his parents, who not only were bootleggers, but also were convicted in 1941 of smuggling eight kilos of heroin from France in the bindings of Hebrew prayer books. "Bernard Bergman was into all kinds of dirty business," said Sonia. "He kept dead bodies in freezers in his nursing homes to collect their Social Security payments. Then, after he was indicted [in 1974 for fraud], he stood in front of television cameras and said, 'As God is my witness, I'm innocent.' " Bergman later pleaded guilty to fraud and bribery and spent one year in prison on Rikers Island.

But in the 1920s, when Bergman's parents began their illicit career, bootlegging was an upwardly mobile occupation. Speakeasies and brothels were a unique American melting pot, in which the emerging underworld, which was dominated by Jewish and Italian mobsters during the pre-war years, could rub shoulders with the elites from industry, banking and entertainment. The Jewish bootleggers became more respectable as they laundered their profits into legitimate businesses, real estate, synagogues, and later Israel. They also took over labor unions, bought politicians, cops, and newspaper publishers.

Although Charles lectured his new friend that bootlegged booze could never buy respectability, he was wrong. Several years later, Sonia said, Bernard Bergman bought a rabbinical degree from Yeshiva University.

Not long after moving into Bergman's basement, Charles spotted Sonia studying at the New York Public Library. He remembered her as the appealingly bewildered young girl that he had seen at the harbor. But he was too timid to approach her. Instead, he found out her name from a mutual friend. "The next day Charles pulled up in a cab in front of our house in Plainfield," said Isaac Trainin. As Sonia remembers it, "Charles walked into the house, and saw my father sitting in the study with a *Gemorah* [a Jewish prayer book]. 'You're the pest from the boat!' my father growled. Within a year we were married."

By the time that Charles and Sonia moved to Flatbush, he was a roly-poly man who spoke the affected English of someone who had worked hard to overcome an accent. Although neither a towering intellect nor a great scholar, he had intellectual pretensions: he had painstakingly translated *The Five Books of Moses* from Hebrew into English, which put him a cut above the average rabbi. *The New York Times* even published an article about the achievement. But that was not quite enough for him. He bought a Ph.D. degree in philosophy from a midwestern mail-order college, telling friends that he had received it from Columbia University, where he claimed to have studied three nights a week for several years, according to Isaac Trainin. He also told friends that he had a college degree in forestry, although his only real exposure to nature came on long walks through Prospect Park in Brooklyn, which he sometimes took to escape from the pressures of family life. "Nature relaxed him," said Sonia. "When the 'Wild Kingdom' was on TV on Sunday nights, you couldn't talk to him."

Sonia, on the other hand, was incapable of relaxing. Known as the neighborhood shrieker, she was an intense, nervous woman with limitless energy and a voice that could be heard by children playing several blocks away. Bright and ambitious, she says that she was accepted into New York University's pre-med program, although her father would not let her attend because the tuition was too expensive. Later, she was among the first Orthodox Jewish women in Brooklyn to learn to drive. Her green '38 Plymouth, which she and Nachman carefully washed and polished every weekend until Meir stripped the gears, became a source of power over Charles, who failed about a dozen driving tests and never got a license. "She was a frustrated housewife who had wanted to go to medical school," said a relative. "And Charles, who thought he was so superior, couldn't even drive. Sonia used to dangle the keys in front of Charles to torment him."

Sonia's needling sometimes provoked Charles into fits of rage, which he often took out on his eldest son. The family tensions inevitably had an effect on Meir. By grade school he had a severe stuttering problem. Although in public Sonia and Charles gave the impression of a warm family environment with Meir at the center, they had "a horrible marriage like my mother and father," said Isaac Trainin. "Charles screamed at and humiliated Meir constantly. He had a furious temper. I remember Charles slapping my ten-year-old brother across the face just for taking some candy. He scared the hell out of Meir and Sonia. Charles was a tyrant."

Perhaps much of the anger that Charles directed at Meir stemmed from the extremely high standards that he set for his son. Even before Meir could talk, Charles felt there was something special about this shy, sensitive child—that he was somehow put on earth by God to save the Jewish people. This may well explain why Charles encouraged his son's path to militancy and why Meir later confused Israel's fate with his own. "Maybe destiny sent him to bring redemption to his tortured people throughout the world," Charles once told a *New York Times* reporter. "May God help him he should achieve that goal." And if it ever seemed—as it often did—that young Meir was falling behind schedule in becoming the savior of his people, he was roundly ridiculed by his father.

Meir Kahane may not have liked growing up in an emotional pressure cooker, but he certainly liked the feeling that the world revolved around him. "As far as Sonia was concerned, Meir could do no wrong," said Meir's childhood friend Allan Mallenbaum, a frequent visitor in the Kahane house. "Charles also looked up to him and admired him. He was really his father's pride and joy. Not that they didn't love Nachman, but even Nachman looked up to Marty."

Ironically, when Meir finally rebelled, it was not so much against his father's authority as against what he perceived to be his imperfect practice of religion. By the time he entered college, Meir was a religious purist and an activist. Unlike Charles, who tried to accommodate congregants who strove to become 100 percent American, Meir brooked no compromise with tradition. He despaired that his father's shul had no *mehitza*, the screen that separates men from women during prayers in Orthodox synagogues. As a teenager, he was actually tossed out of B'nai Akiva, an Orthodox Jewish youth movement, partly for trying to bar men and women from dancing with each other. And as his own sense of self-importance grew, he became increasingly embarrassed by his father, who though prominent in Brooklyn, was still little more than a neighborhood rabbi. "Meir impressed me as not wanting to be just a little Orthodox rabbi," said a family friend. "He had huge ambitions."

The product of Meir Kahane's ambitions are now enshrined in his mother's modest Jerusalem apartment. In my November 1987 interview—one of the few that she has granted in the past twenty years—seventy-seven-year-old Sonia Kahane told me that her eldest son was as normal as any other exceptionally bright Jewish boy who grew up in Flatbush during the Second World War. We talked in her small, drab apartment surrounded by her son's dozen or so books with their defiant, angry titles such as *They Must Go!*, *Thorns in Your Eyes!*, and *Never Again!*. In the dining room, above the table, hung a large oil painting of Meir, his chin resting on his hand, his brown eyes moist and beckoning, the Israeli flag unfurled behind him. "Meir was a normal, healthy boy," Sonia insisted, as the late sun filtered through an open window casting her deeply wrinkled face in a soft glow. "He was an expert in ping-pong. He played basketball. I used to play handball with him until my back gave out. He had a beautiful singing voice. His teachers used to take him to the old age homes to entertain. My son is normal. It's his critics who are insane."

CHAPTER TWO
Political Awakening

On a clear, cool morning in March 1938, three Palestinian Arabs crouched in a ditch that ran parallel to the Haifa-Safed road, where they waited patiently for a carload of Jews. Shortly before 3 P.M., a taxi carrying ten Jews returning from a wedding party in Tel Aviv passed a spot near the Arab village of Sajur, between Majd el-Kurum and Rama. As the driver swerved to avoid hitting a boulder placed in the road, the Arabs sprang from their hiding place, wildly firing their British-made Enfield automatic rifles.

The massacre did not take long. Charles Kahane's sister-in-law, Ziporah Kahane, who was thirty-seven, was shot twice in the chest and died instantly. Her seventy-one-year-old mother was shot three times in the head at point-blank range. In all, six people were murdered, including a young woman who survived the gunfire but was dragged to a stony slope, where she was gang-raped and hacked to death. One-year-old Rebecca, Ziporah's daughter, was found by police buried alive under her mother's blood-soaked body.

The slaughter near Sajur village, which left five members of Charles Kahane's family dead, was one of the worst incidences of violence in the increasingly bloody struggle between Arabs and Jews in Palestine. Later that same day, unexploded bombs were found in the Jewish quarters of Jerusalem and Haifa, and two young German Jews were found murdered near Mount Scopus.

Safed's Jewish quarter, where the victims had lived, closed down as thousands of people, including Palestine's chief rabbi, attended the funeral. The Kahanes were buried in an ancient cemetery plot next to Jews who had been murdered by Arabs in the anti-Zionist pogroms of 1929 and 1936.

For days following the taxicab massacre, the Hebrew press was filled with grisly photos of the slain Jews, whipping up Jewish fury. The Palestinian press gave prominence to the murders without comment or condemnation.

Jews and Arabs had been murdering each other in Palestine for decades—and the British, who had ruled Palestine since the end of the First World War, seemed powerless to stop them. The Zionists, who began to arrive in large numbers from Eastern Europe around the turn of the twentieth century, were seeking to build a Jewish state as a refuge from nearly two thousand years of persecution. The Arabs, who had lived in Palestine for generations and had their own aspirations for self-determination, sought to stop them. In 1936, in the wake of increased Jewish emigration from Nazi Germany, the Arabs of Palestine revolted against British mandatory rule. For three years British troops fought pitched battles with Arab guerrillas, inflicting heavy casualties. By the time the rebellion was crushed, the Palestinian community was so enfeebled that it could no longer seriously challenge the Zionist quest for statehood.

The mainstream Zionist organizations, meanwhile, had shown remarkable self-restraint in the face of increasing Palestinian terrorist attacks. The Haganah, a quasi-underground Jewish self-defense force affiliated with the Jewish Agency—the Jewish provisional government in Palestine headed by David Ben-Gurion—developed a policy of restraint called *Havlaga*. However, the much smaller Irgun, the militant arm of Ze'ev Jabotinsky's Revisionist Movement, carried out acts of indiscriminate terror against Arab civilians, such as putting bombs in Arab marketplaces and on Arab buses.

Following the taxi massacre, three youths from a Jewish village near Safed ambushed an Arab civilian bus with rifles and grenades. Though miraculously no one was injured, the British authorities arrested the youths—all of whom were members of

Betar, the youth-wing of the Revisionist Movement. And to show the Arabs that Jewish terrorism would not be tolerated, the group's leader, Ben Yosef, was sentenced by a British court to hang as a convicted terrorist. As the eighteen-year-old Jew from Poland walked to the gallows, he began to sing the 'Song of Betar':

From the pit of decay and dust
Through blood and sweat
A generation will arise to us,
Proud, generous and fierce.

The hanging galvanized the Jewish community in Palestine, touching off a chain of events that radicalized Zionist policies. The Irgun launched a frenzy of indiscriminate raids against Arab civilians, in the belief that the only alternative to an iron fist was appeasement, which, in the words of one of their leaders, Menachem Begin, would lead to "the peace of the graveyard." The Haganah, abandoning its policy of restraint, also began to retaliate against Arabs who had attacked Jewish targets.

The large Kahane clan in Palestine, meanwhile, split into pro-Irgun and pro-Haganah factions. Moshe Kahane, whose mother was killed in the taxi massacre, joined the Irgun and became a high-ranking intelligence officer in Jerusalem, where he later helped plan the 1946 terrorist bombing of British headquarters at the King David Hotel, in which ninety-one died and forty-five were injured.

Mordechai Kahane, who had been in Tel Aviv when his wife, Ziporah, was killed in the massacre, journeyed to New York. He moved into the Kahane home in Flatbush, where he lived off and on for many years, working as a professional fundraiser for Jewish institutions, haunted by his wife's murder until he died.

There is no question that the massacre in Palestine traumatized the Kahane family in Brooklyn. "I think this is the time Meir developed a hatred of the Arabs," Sonia told me. That is hardly surprising, since Mordechai and Charles talked about the massacre frequently at the Sabbath table. The only antidote to Arab terror, the men declared, was Jewish counter-terror. Even though Meir was then just a child, he was transfixed by his father's tales of Jewish heroism and Arab cruelty in Palestine. "Charles imbued Meir with a sense of Jewish pride in every aspect," said Mordechai's brother, Moshe, the former Irgun intelligence officer, who left Israel in 1951 to serve as a rabbi in Sweden and is now a rabbi in Houston, Texas. "He taught his sons about the spiritual strength of the Jews, as well as about their physical prowess with stories from the Bible." Charles also taught them about the Old Testament's "eye for an eye" vengeance.

Indeed, young Kahane was enraptured by Jewish Biblical history—especially the life of King David, who composed the Psalms and led his people to war. When Meir turned fifteen, his father urged him to join Betar. The fusion of right-wing political Zionism, Biblical nationalism, and Meir's own inborn sense of Messianic destiny, combined with a street-smart curiosity about the outside world, would later grow into a darker vision.

Charles had himself joined the right-wing Revisionist Movement in the early 1920s. New York was then like a giant intellectual hothouse, where competing ideologies struggled for the souls of young Jews. The Communist and Socialist revolutions had captured the allegiance of many with promises of justice for the oppressed, especially for the Jewish minority in Russia. At the same time, the Zionist dream fermented and split into the rival visions of Jabotinsky and Ben-Gurion. Many newly arrived Jewish immigrants, lured by the glamour of America, chose the path of least resistance—assimilation.

Many of these currents competed and clashed at Yeshiva Rabbeinu Yitzchok Elchanan, the New York seminary affiliated with Yeshiva University that Charles entered after arriving in the United States. Though strictly Orthodox, the yeshiva provided forums for students to debate rival religious and political ideologies. Charles became the head of the yeshiva's Revisionist chapter, which was second in size only to the Mizrachis—the Religious Zionist Party.

"My father was an unusual man," Nachman recalled. "On the outside he was a model of scholarly decorum, lovely and quiet. On the inside he was an extremist. Maybe there was some kind of, I don't know, a genetic division, but people say my brother and I each sort of inherited one aspect of my father."

By the mid-1930s, Charles had become one of the Irgun's key U.S. operatives, raising money to purchase weapons, which he helped smuggle to Palestine. "Our father had a great connection to the underground in Palestine that dominated the spirit of our house," said Nachman. It is not surprising, then, that many right-wing Zionist luminaries found their way to Charles's Friday evening Sabbath dinner table. Yosef Burg, who later became head of the powerful National Religious Party in Israel was a frequent guest. And so too was a smallish, unprepossessing man who was to direct the Irgun's terrorist war against the British and the Palestinian Arabs—Menachem Begin. "Charles and [Bernard] Bergman formed the Israel Club in Brooklyn," Sonia recalled, "and whenever Begin was in town they would organize a big reception."

When Meir was about four, the most controversial and possibly the most charismatic figure in Zionism, Ze'ev Vladimir Jabotinsky, appeared in his life for the first time. In March 1940, he visited the Kahane house the day after delivering a spectacular marathon speech to an overflow crowd at the Manhattan Center, where he called for the founding of a Jewish army in Palestine that would fight alongside the Allies. "The next day, Jabotinsky showed up at our house," Sonia recalled. "He walked over to my husband and they conversed quietly. Then I heard my husband say, 'Don't worry, I'll take care of the money.' " Jabotinsky stayed on for a brief time as a guest in the Kahane home.

Although he was a highly cultivated, liberal-bourgeois intellectual, Jabotinsky was denounced by many Jews as a fascist; Ben-Gurion dubbed him "Vladimir Hitler." As early as 1906, Jabotinsky had established a Jewish self-defense corps in Odessa. During the Arab riots of 1920, he organized a Jewish self-defense brigade in Jerusalem. In 1923, in Riga, Latvia, he established Betar, an international paramilitary youth movement. He even founded a Jewish naval academy in southern Italy. Jabotinsky enjoyed tremendous support among Eastern Europe's pogrom-plagued Jews, who rallied to his call to form local Jewish military and police units for self-defense. Unavoidably, perhaps, his militaristic movement attracted a fair number of trigger-happy zealots, some of whom were drawn to Mussolini, and most of whom were opposed to the spirit of liberal democracy, which they felt had castrated Zionism.

While many of the Labor Zionists were Socialist utopians who believed that physical labor on Jewish soil could revitalize and even elevate the Jewish spirit on the road to a kind of secular Messianic redemption, Jabotinsky's followers, who came from the ranks of small shopkeepers, believed that political power and military might alone could cure the ills born of the diaspora.

While the Labor Zionists drained the swamps, built the settlements, and created the institutions of the state, the Revisionists built nothing more than an ideology based on the principle of "conquer or die."

Nevertheless, Jabotinsky saw more clearly than any Zionist leader of his time the likelihood of the impending Holocaust. "We are facing an elemental calamity," he declared in an address to the House of Lords in London on February 11, 1937, arguing that only the immediate establishment of a Jewish state in Palestine could save the imperiled Jewish people. Opposed to Palestine's Socialist-dominated Jewish Agency on a host of issues—ranging from immigration policies to relations with local Arabs—and intensely displeased with their go-slow, "acre after acre, goat after goat" diplomatic approach to securing a Jewish homeland, Jabotinsky broke away from the main international Zionist body and formed an independent Zionist organization, the Revisionist movement, in April 1935.

Although he was adored by his tens of thousands of disciples, his movement was chronically short of funds and Jabotinsky himself lived in third-rate hotels and always had to scrounge for money. Much of his financial support came from the Jewish communities in Poland and New York. Even though he was opposed to the anti-democratic spirit of Orthodox Judaism, Jabotinsky introduced what one historian called a "quasi-religious plank" into the Revisionist constitution in 1935 in order to raise money from the Orthodox community. According to Sonia, Charles raised $3,000 for Jabotinsky during his March 1940 visit. "He didn't have fifteen cents to buy a pack of cigarettes when he came to our house, but I remember he smoked Murad, the most expensive brand," Sonia said. Although he was a gifted linguist who spoke twelve languages, his Polish was rusty. "He sat for hours and hours in our library studying Polish," said Sonia. "I recall him saying, 'If I'm going to Poland, I must speak flawless Polish.'" Sonia remembers that Meir was in awe of their famous guest. "He followed him from room to room. One day Meir was literally sitting at his feet and Jabotinsky said, 'Meir, follow my footsteps.' I'm telling you, he hypnotized that child!"

Meir's rarefied home life, where Zionist legends abounded and family members from Palestine passed through as a matter of course, kept him in touch with the major developments in Jewish life—the Holocaust and the creation of the State of Israel.

His encounter with Jabotinsky gave him a militant hero to emulate. His knowledge of the massacre of his relatives by Palestinian Arabs and his father's covert contacts with the Jewish terrorist underground taught him that the use of incredible feats of arms and daring in defense of the Jewish people was not only necessary but holy as well. But most of all, the call to fulfill the ancient promise to settle and build the land of Israel dominated his early thinking. "You see, for us Eretz Yisrael was no abstraction," Nachman told me in his small, austere synagogue, tucked away in the Muslim quarter of Jerusalem's old walled city. "We had the most natural ties to Palestine. We always knew we would go back. It was just a question of when."

Like a lot of Jewish boys who grew up during the war years, Meir was obsessed with the Holocaust. "*I* knew about the Holocaust when *I* was a boy of ten," Kahane told *The Washington Post* in 1984. "So when Jewish leaders said, 'We didn't know,' that's all baloney. *I* remember hearing about it." Indeed, as word of the Nazi death camps began to rumble through New York's Jewish community, young Meir could be seen leading high-stepping Jewish youths wearing Boy Scout uniforms in mock military drills up and down quiet, tree-lined streets in Flatbush. "Marty always talked about the Holocaust—that it would not happen again—that American Jews were going to be different!" said a childhood friend.

Marcia Greenwald, who sat behind Meir for three years at Flatbush Yeshiva Elementary School, recalls the day before Passover 1943, when Meir, then ten years old, was sketching a map of the railway lines to Auschwitz on the blackboard, crying, "Why doesn't Roosevelt give the order to bomb the tracks? Doesn't he understand there are gas chambers there? If the Allies bomb the tracks, they can't gas the Jews!"

If Roosevelt was going to ignore the plight of defenseless Jews, young Kahane would create a fictional character who would save his people from the horrors of genocide. In the seventh grade, Greenwald remembers that Meir invented a comic strip called "The Adventures of Bagelman," which was about a bagel in a Superman cape who saved Jews from Nazi Germany. "Look, up in the sky, it's a matzoh, it's a roll, no it's Bagelman," he wrote, parodying the famous introduction to *Superman*. "Meir was a passionate kid," said Greenwald. "Whether he was singing solo at assembly or doodling, it was with tremendous intensity."

Kahane took his role as a defender of the Jewish people seriously, at least as far as his family was concerned. Not long after creating Bagelman, Kahane imitated his comic strip hero by rescuing his twelve-year-old kid brother from neighborhood bullies. Nachman, a pudgy, timid boy, was playing basketball in the park with a friend when they were surrounded by twenty Italian kids who started beating them. "My friend escaped, but they smashed my head and I was bleeding all over," Nachman recalled. "I thought I was going to die. I closed my eyes, counted to three, and with what I thought might be my last breath, I ran to the park attendant's shack and locked myself inside." Nachman's assailants encircled the shack screaming, "Open up, we want to kill the Yid." Just then, Meir came charging through the park on his bike. But unlike Bagelman, who could crush foes with a single blow, Kahane was accompanied by two police cars. Nachman spent three weeks in bed following the incident, recovering from a severe concussion.

In September 1945, Kahane entered the Brooklyn Talmudical Academy to begin the ninth grade. He was in trouble the second he walked through the door. It seems that he was not the "vanderkind" his parents bragged about. BTA's curriculum was heavily weighted in favor of Talmud study, and Kahane—who was later to base his political party's violently anti-Arab platform on *Halacha*, Jewish religious law—was a poor Talmud student.

"There were a number of students, including Meir Kahane, who had difficulty in adjusting to the intensive Talmud study," recalled BTA's former principal, Rabbi Abraham Zuroff, a stocky, precisely mannered man now living in Israel. "But in his case there was an additional factor. In Yiddish there is an expression *kein sitzfleish*, which means the inability to sit. He was an extremely nervous child and couldn't sit still. I think it was in his genes. In any case, he was unable to study the Talmud three hours a day. He was capable, but because of his nervousness he couldn't measure up; there was a gap between his performance and what he actually achieved. His grades were barely average."

In class, Kahane was a high-wire act of gags and mischief. Motivated by a constant desire to seek the limelight and propelled by seemingly unlimited pent-up energy, he was difficult to discipline. "He was constantly talking, chattering away," recalled Zuroff. "He never kept quiet. He was a source of annoyance to many of his teachers." He was also an annoyance to his father, who was routinely summoned to BTA to discuss his son's poor performance. "You could see the tension between father and son," Zuroff said. "Charles wanted the childish pranks to stop."

Charles Kahane was equally upset that his son could not catch up with the other students in Talmud studies, however much he was tutored at home. "His father was a rabbi from Safed so he knew what intensive Talmud learning was," said Zuroff.

Meir Kahane was more inclined to talk about going to Palestine to fight Arabs than to study, though he himself never volunteered. At the same time, he gathered around him a cadre of followers—working-class, non-observant Jewish youngsters from Betar, who, like him, believed that he was destined to play a decisive role in the struggle for Jewish survival. "We used to rib Marty that he would end up being premier of the Jewish state," said Allan Mallenbaum, a friend from Betar, who later became the JDL's first executive director. "Underneath the jest, all of us thought that's where he was headed. He felt he had divine gifts, and I guess we did too."

Those feelings were not shared by his fellow classmates at BTA. For all their religious study, like the boys in Bernard Malamud's "The Chosen" they seemed more attuned to baseball than Begin. They were also ambivalent towards Zionism, a common attitude among Orthodox Jews prior to the founding of the State of Israel. "It wasn't fashionable among us kids who were playing ball all day to be concerned with Zionism," said Norman Dachs who went to BTA with Kahane. "He would talk about Jabotinsky and (Joseph) Trumpeldor.* I didn't even know who they were. I thought they played first base and right field for the Chicago Cubs. That was true for most of us. We were interested in Israel's fate, but not as violently or as deeply as Kahane."

Irving "Yitz" Greenberg,* Kahane's classmate for four years at BTA, said that "the combination of fantasy and megalomania" were emblematic of Kahane's personality. "In general, Kahane found daily life very frustrating," said Greenberg. "He couldn't follow through on daily tasks like doing his homework, but he could fantasize, he could dream, and he always loved fairy

---

* Joseph Trumpeldor was a legendary Zionist pioneer who was killed in 1920 defending Tel-Hai against Arab attackers.

* Greenberg is currently president of CLAL, the National Jewish Center for Learning and Leadership, a religious organization in New York that is dedicated to building bridges between Judaism's major branches.

tales in which he was the hero." Greenberg said Kahane talked incessantly about patterning himself after his idol, Ze'ev Jabotinsky. "Jabotinsky was his knight errant—the visionary nobody appreciated who went around the world warning Jews of the impending Holocaust. What appealed to him was the dramatic, violent gesture that with one stroke could destroy the enemy. He loved it every time he read that the Irgun had planted a bomb in an Arab marketplace. He didn't have the interest or the patience to talk about how to build the Jewish state—it was lash out at the people you don't like, lash out at the people who cross you or disagree with you."

It was in high school that Kahane became renowned for his derisive brand of sarcasm. Unlike the self-deprecating humor Jews are traditionally known for, Kahane sounded like an Old Testament prophet reincarnated as a Borscht Belt insult comic. All of his observations ended with: "What a schmuck!" "He had total contempt for other Jews," said Irwin Fleminger, a New York artist, who befriended Kahane in high school. "He used to stand on the steps of his father's synagogue on Saturday morning sneering at the rather ordinary, lower-middle-class Jews who were dressed in their best clothes for temple. 'Look at those middle-class Jews, in their middle-class clothes, with their middle-class minds. They are totally ignorant of Judaism,' he mocked. 'What schmucks!' "

On the one hand, the introverted Fleminger admired Kahane's glibness. A teenager taking on grownups was daring. Still, to Fleminger, the sarcastic barbs that Kahane aimed at his father's congregants were a total perversion of Judaism. "I remember reading about a Talmudic injunction that says a Jew should never put down another in terms of his religious beliefs," said Fleminger, still frowning. "Marty trampled on that one!"

Kahane's inflated ego sometimes trampled on reality itself. One day when Kahane was about sixteen, he ran over to the Mallenbaums' house proudly cradling an essay that he had written. Allan Mallenbaum's younger brother, Victor, recalls Kahane pacing around his bedroom as he read the paper, often stopping to boast about its brilliance. "It was well written," said Victor Mallenbaum. "The only problem was the theme—it was why Kahane thought he was the Jewish Messiah. At that point, I thought the guy was definitely nuts!"

While Kahane harbored delusions of grandeur, he also honed his ability to stir a crowd. Despite a pronounced stuttering problem, he was a good debater. "He never had the patience to do careful preparation," said "Yitz" Greenberg who was on BTA's debating team with him. "He always wanted quick solutions and quick answers. That was his pattern all the way through school. He had this terrific instinct for thinking on his feet—responding quickly to an audience's reaction. Even when he was just kidding around in class, he had that ability. He used to come up with these spontaneous skits in English lit class that were very entertaining. I would say his greatest strength was his quickness combined with his ability to size up a crowd to see what would arouse them."

At the start of his senior year, Kahane decided that he would have a more receptive audience among the secular, working-class Jews who attended public school. He had had enough of Talmud studies, Orthodox Judaism, and doctrinaire rabbis. He already secretly listened to the radio on the Sabbath, and there were a lot more forbidden pleasures he hoped to enjoy. In September 1949, he entered Brooklyn's Abraham Lincoln High School. His parents were terrified about what was going to become of him. Although Kahane later claimed that his father encouraged him to encounter the world beyond the yeshiva academies, Charles was enraged when he left BTA. But Meir had no intention of becoming a small-time neighborhood rabbi like his father. "He told me that his father was not respected in the community," said a friend. "That he wasn't a respected scholar."

Some of the myths surrounding Kahane were born during his interlude at Abraham Lincoln. He would later claim to worshipful members of the JDL that he had been a 10,000-meter track star there, that he had perfected a deadly, right-handed hook shot for its basketball team, and had palled around with the baseball team's star pitcher, Sandy Koufax, who went on to become a celebrated major league player for the Los Angeles Dodgers. In truth, though he was quick and wiry, none of Kahane's high school friends remembers him going out for anything more physically demanding than the school choir. And if Kahane enjoyed breaking away from the narrow confines of yeshiva life, he was also confused and struggling with his identity. "He was going through a crisis," said one of several Betarniks who also attended

Abraham Lincoln. "He was unpopular at BTA and his stuttering problem was getting worse. He was thinking of leaving Orthodox Judaism, but it was causing him a lot of pain."

The competition within Kahane between the pleasures of the secular world and the rigid strictures of Orthodoxy forced him to make elaborate, sometimes absurd, rationalizations for his behavior. Because he no longer wore a *yarmulke* (skullcap), he would sit under a tree in the school yard to eat his lunch. That way, he told friends, he was not breaking kosher dietary laws because the tree branches kept his head covered. When Kahane realized how far he had strayed, he returned to BTA to finish the last semester of his senior year. "He was anguished by his fall from Orthodoxy," said a friend. "Those were his words."

His graduating class yearbook, "The Elchanite," which was published in 1949, not only reveals how he was viewed by his classmates, but illuminates his own obsessive ambition to become the savior of his people as well. In a poll taken of his twenty-three-man class, Kahane was not chosen as the most brilliant, most dependable, most dignified, most likely to succeed—or even as the class Zionist! Instead, he was chosen the class journalist. "Martin Kahane is good looking (so he says), intelligent, and possessing a grand personality. (If you don't believe it, ask the man who knows—Martin Kahane.)" said his class profile. "This baby is packed for delivery in Israel. In the meantime, he's becoming a journalist to wile the time away. He joined the Herut movement to get out of school."

Kahane did not make the school honor society, which was chosen by the faculty based on academic excellence and participation in extra-curricular activities. According to the yearbook, he participated in the school's debating team, sang in the choir, and was secretary of the Hebrew club. Although the school had a basketball team, Kahane was not on it. However, as associate literary editor of the class yearbook, Kahane filled "The Elchanite" with his odes to Zionism, revealing, observes his principal Rabbi Zuroff, "the seeds of what he was to become."

In one poem entitled, "Land," Kahane writes that it is good to die in the struggle for Israel:

Land of present, land of past, land of future consecration,
Land, though we die,
Land still we'll cry,
'Tis good to die for our great nation . . .

Land chosen for rule, land chosen for pain,
Land, when may I call you mine again?
O land, the road is long,
And the enemy strong,
But still we'll conquer this son of Cain.

In a five-page short story that he wrote for "The Elchanite" called "The Judgment," Kahane staged a heavenly courtroom scene between Lord Moyne, the British colonial secretary who was assassinated in Cairo in November 1944 by the Stern Gang, and Josef Hein, one of his young Jewish assassins, who was subsequently tried and hung by the British. In the story, Kahane argued that Jews must free themselves from moral constraints if they are ever to free themselves from their tormentors. Still, Hein is convicted by the heavenly tribunal and sentenced to Hell, only to win a last minute reprieve from none other than God, who booms down on the assemblage that even though Hein sinned, he is forgiven because he acted in defense of the Torah and the land of Israel:

> The bombs they throw, the blood they shed are measures of the desperateness of their exile. Therefore have I seen their tears and have forgiven them. Soon shall I return them to their sacred homeland, Israel, and my dwelling place, Jerusalem. From the wilderness and this Lebanon, even unto the great river, the river Euphrates, all the land of the Hittites and unto the great sea, encompassing both sides of the Jordan, shall be their boundary. And this child standing trial before me is my dearest dream. For two thousand years have I waited for such a generation to arrive. . . .

In the last scene, the chorus swells and the great gates swing open. As his hero walks through mist and clouds into the arms of the angels, one can imagine Kahane himself entering Heaven to a hero's welcome. So strongly did Kahane identify with Hein that some years later, in the name of Israel and the Torah, he would build his own terrorist underground.

Kahane may have brought tears to his own eyes, but his classmates found in his maudlin Zionism rich comic material. In a wickedly prescient, *Mad Magazine*—type lampoon, "The Elchanite" depicted a fictional newspaper named *The Star Gazer*, whose front-page headline screamed: "KAHANE DEMANDS

ASIA!'' ''Martin Kahane, candidate for (Israel's) president . . .
today closed his campaign with a reaffirmation of his party's slogan, 'Reannexation of Asia and Reoccupation of Europe,' the
story began. ''He again stated his party's platform,'' which
included, ''a Jewish state on both sides of the Pacific . . . . As
candidate of the 'mildly' expansionist Herut (Freedom) Party . . .
Mr. Kahane reaffirmed his determination to buy Patagonia for
$7,200,000, though some critics have labeled it 'Begin's Folly.' ''

CHAPTER THREE
Betar
Path to Militancy

Meir Kahane's militancy eventually found an outlet in Betar, the youth wing of the Revisionist Movement, which he joined shortly after his Bar Mitzvah in 1946. With its emphasis on violent street demonstrations, paramilitary training camps, torchlight parades, and myths of Old Testament heroes, Betar would be the model for the JDL.

Ze'ev Jabotinsky had organized Betar in Riga, Latvia in 1923, in response to the spread of virulently anti-Semitic European nationalist movements. Its twofold purpose was to train Jewish youth in self-defense and to prepare them for the fire-and-blood struggle that would transform Palestine into a Jewish state.

The Betar youth movement in America was incorporated on June 10, 1940, in New York City. That same year it opened a paramilitary training camp in the Catskill Mountains near Hunter, New York in a run-down hotel that was donated by a supporter. Jabotinsky died on August 3rd during a visit to the camp shortly after it opened. By the early 1940s, Betar claimed several hundred members in the New York area. One of its first U.S. leaders was Moshe Arens, who in the 1980s became Israel's ambassador to America and Israel's foreign minister.

Betar's most urgent activity was smuggling weapons to the Irgun. In the 1940s, Irgun's leader Menachem Begin sent several deputies to America to procure arms. Eli Tavin, Irgun's overseas intelligence chief, supervised the operation, using his position as educational director of the World Zionist Organization as a cover. In all, Tavin set up weapons procurement networks in twenty-three countries, as well as a number of self-defense units, including one in Shanghai to protect Jews still in Chinese displaced persons' camps following the Second World War. Tavin also masterminded Irgun's terrorist campaign against the British in Europe. On October 31, 1946, for example, he engineered the bombing of the British Embassy in Rome.

Tavin obtained weapons in the United States from Jewish GIs returning from the Second World War as well as from the Mafia. "Jewish veterans would come in with packages wrapped in newspapers and say: 'I heard I could give this to you for Israel,' " said Sylvia Zweibon, the owner, along with her husband, of a floor-covering store in East New York, then a predominantly Jewish neighborhood in Brooklyn, where they stored arms. "At one point we had so many weapons we had to rent another store," added Zweibon, who was a member in Poland before coming to America.

Israeli operatives trucked the weapons to docks in New York and New Jersey run by Mob boss Charles "Lucky" Luciano, a close associate of Meir Lansky—an impassioned right-wing Zionist, who, with other Jewish gangsters like Mickey Cohen in Los Angeles, contributed large sums of money to the Irgun. The Mob-dominated Longshoreman's Union helped the Revisionists sabotage weapons shipments en route from U.S. ports to Arab states as well.

Charles Kahane, himself deeply involved in the arms smuggling ring, encouraged his sons to join Betar. "Betar was my father's kind of ideology and I naturally gravitated toward it," said Meir Kahane, who made midnight trips to the Hoboken docks to crate arms destined for the Irgun in Israel. It was not without risk. In 1947, two of Meir's comrades were arrested in a Manhattan fur loft with 144 machine guns, 203 rifles, and 268 pistols. The young men were acquitted one month later thanks to their lawyer, Paul O'Dwyer. Despite this setback, between February and March 1948 alone, Tavin smuggled forty-three shipments of weapons from New York to Tel Aviv.

Meir and Nachman also raised money for the underground. The brothers rode up and down Brooklyn's Pitkin Avenue in a Betar sound truck that blared patriotic Hebrew songs and speeches by Jabotinsky, soliciting donations. "Ten big Jews would get out of the truck and put an Israeli flag down in the street," Nachman said. "People just pulled huge fistfuls of cash from their pockets and threw it on the flag. They were fighting with each other to throw the *gelt* [money]. You won't see something like that again until the Messiah comes!

"And I can remember dark moments, too, like when a cache of arms for the Irgun was discovered by the police on the roof of the Habad Synagogue [in Brooklyn]. At our house it was like Tisha B'Av [the commemoration of the destruction of the Second Temple] when that happened. My father's own Sha'arei Tefila congregation also raised money for an ambulance that people say went down on the Altalena [an Irgun arms ship that was sunk by the Haganah], although I haven't actually confirmed that."

(During the 1940s, the Haganah operated a separate, competing arms smuggling operation in America. Run by Teddy Kollek from Manhattan's McAlpin Hotel near Macy's department store in Herald Square, its key operatives included Hank Greenspun, the late publisher of *The Las Vegas Sun*, and Al Schwimmer, an Israeli arms merchant who would become involved in the Iran-contra arms-for-hostage negotiations.)

After Israel's creation on May 15, 1948, the Betar movement in America evolved into a right-wing, pro-Israel activist youth group, often holding noisy protest demonstrations at Arab UN missions in Manhattan. According to a high-ranking Justice Department official, these activities were coordinated by Moshe Rivlin, then Israel's vice-consul in New York. When contacted for comment, Rivlin said that he could not recall being involved in these demonstrations.

Kahane was usually at the forefront of Betar's militant actions. "He was a heck of a lot more radical in Betar than I was," said Allan's brother, Victor Mallenbaum, now a clinical psychologist in North Carolina who was part of Kahane's inner circle of childhood friends. "He was always ready to go and do some militant activity. He wanted to bomb a book store in Manhattan that sold pro-Nazi material."

In 1947, Kahane gained the notoriety he sought with his attack on the anti-Zionist British Foreign Minister Ernest Bevin. "Allan and Victor Mallenbaum had run over to the market and bought a crate of vegetables,'' recalls Irwin Fleminger. ''I remember the look on Bevin's face when we pelted him. He was absolutely shocked!''

After his arrest, Kahane was charged with assault. But Judge Morris Rothenberg gave him a suspended sentence. It was the first of what would be a long, unbroken string of light or suspended sentences that Kahane would receive from sympathetic Jewish judges in the United States and Israel. ''The judge was very anti-British and sympathetic to Betar,'' Kahane later told me. It did not hurt that Kahane's father was then the politically well-connected president of the Flatbush Board of Rabbis, nor that Judge Rothenberg was the president of the Jewish National Fund in America, had an agricultural settlement in Palestine named in his honor, and had himself assailed Bevin in 1947— the same year that Kahane was brought before him—in a speech to a national Zionist conference.

Kahane, however, chose his confrontations carefully, displaying considerably more daring when he was in a group. One summer day in 1949, Kahane and his fifteen-year-old Israeli cousin, Abraham Kahane, were hassled by a couple of teenagers as they entered the subway station near Prospect Park in Brooklyn. ''We were walking down the subway steps when some goys in back of us started laughing at our yarmulkes,'' said Abraham Kahane. ''I spoke to Martin in Hebrew, 'You have a fist, let's turn around and let them have it.' I was from Jerusalem. I told Meir if an Arab was starting up I'd turn around and smash him. You know I was a kid. It was my Israeli arrogance. Anyway, Meir said: 'Ah, ah, ah, in America you don't do that.' Even though he was in Betar he wouldn't fight goys who were laughing at us.''

Abraham Kahane's anecdote runs counter to Meir's carefully cultivated image of the fearless Jewish freedom fighter. In 1984, Meir Kahane told *The Washington Post* that as a youth, ''I had fights [with non-Jews] regularly over my yarmulke, and then afterwards I'd drink beer with them.'' The reporter, whose admiring portrait of the rabbi appeared in the paper's popular ''Style'' section, asked Kahane if the fights were traumatic. ''Nah, it wasn't every single day,'' Kahane replied. ''Once you did it two, three, four times, and you got bloodied, if you bloody back, then you're okay. Just, God help the guy that lets himself get pushed around. Then there's no end to it.''

From the moment he joined Betar, Kahane schemed to take over the organization. He gathered around him a band of young followers from working-class homes who were inspired by his single-minded devotion to Israel. Several of these young men would later help him establish the JDL. Irwin Fleminger, a secular Jew who was recruited into Betar by Kahane in 1947, recalls the strong first impression the ambitious Kahane made on him. "We talked at his father's synagogue about Betar and it sounded terrific," said Fleminger. "Kahane said they practiced judo and riflery on the Lower East Side. I was deeply impressed by his militancy. I was ready to join from day one."

Fleminger was initially drawn to Betar out of a sense of help-lessness and rage. "I think that Jewish kids of that time were struck by the victimization of European Jewry and were looking for some way to strike back." Kahane, he said, offered instant expression of that anger. "Kahane was a doorway to understanding something that I felt very ambivalent about—my Jewishness. I grew up in an assimilated, artistic, liberal Jewish home. Knowing Kahane was a way of looking into a militant, Orthodox Jewish world that I had stayed away from and was somewhat repelled by."

After a few months, however, Fleminger decided that joining Betar had been a big mistake. "I chafed at the discipline," he recalled. "Playing soldier was all right, but they made us wear these uniforms with blue pants and brown shirts. It was weird walking around in brown-shirted uniforms right after World War II. There was this guy from national headquarters—a German Jew named Zvi Rentel—who some of us used to jokingly call the Nazi. He used to walk around in his uniform with his thumb in his belt, with this tremendous, overbearing manner. At meetings he used to launch into hysterical diatribes against Labor Zionists, particularly Ben-Gurion."

Although Rentel was the head of their *ken* (chapter), Fleminger said that Kahane conducted many of the meetings. "Marty had a very good voice and he taught the songs," said Fleminger. "But while Rentel gave the political lectures, Kahane talked about religion. I sensed a conflict between the secular-minded leaders like Rentel and Marty, who was trying to make Betar more of a religious organization."

At one meeting, Kahane stood at the lectern in his brown-shirted uniform, contemptuous, angry, power hungry, strutting. "I remember him getting up at this meeting with one leg on a chair, leaning on his knee with his head on his hands," said Fleminger. "He would lean into whatever he was discussing. He started to rant about turning Israel into a theocracy, and that only he could save the Jewish people. I got the feeling I was at a fascist rally.''

But Kahane also had a less strident side. Betarnicks regularly congregated at Charles's shul on the Sabbath, where Meir would lead them in patriotic Zionist songs. ''He had a magnificent voice,'' said Morton Dolinsky, then Betar's Manhattan chapter president. ''He used to write these wonderful anti-British lyrics like, 'There'll be Jews all over the White Cliffs of Dover tomorrow, just you wait and see.' It drove the girls in our group crazy. He had those bushy eyebrows and long lashes some women loved.''

Kahane was acutely aware of his effect on women. ''Women followed him,'' said Fleminger. ''All that charisma wasn't just wasted on males. It was wonderful for me because I picked up the crumbs.'' Kahane was already infamous for his vanity. He spent hours preening in front of the mirror, combing his tangle of black hair. ''He had thick wavy hair that he wore piled high up front,'' recalled Norman Dachs who attended BTA with Kahane. ''The *rebbes* [rabbis] used to get mad at him because they thought his hair interfered with him putting on his *tefillin*,'' the black box that Orthodox Jews strap on to their foreheads before praying.

Although Kahane was already beginning to exhibit flashes of the sexual intolerance that is the hallmark of his movement in Israel today, his teenage years were filled with poker games, dances, and his first fumbling experiences with the opposite sex. ''In the '40s and '50s, you'd go out with a girl and try to go to bed with her,'' recalled Dr. Victor Mallenbaum. ''They knew you were going to try, and they knew they weren't going to let you. It was very amicable.'' Childhood friend Bernard Beiber remembers one double date when Kahane was in the back seat of the car frantically trying to remove his date's bra. All he got for his effort, however, was the girl's taunts. '' 'I'll tell you what, if you can get me hot you can have me.' '' Beiber recalled her saying. ''Martin started working away on her breasts, but he wasn't getting anywhere. She just made fun of him.''

Like many youth groups, Betar had a girl who helped ease young men into manhood, and Kahane tried to take advantage of the opportunity. ''There was this rabbi's daughter who slept with everybody in Betar,'' said Dr. Mallenbaum. ''One day in

Camp Betar, Marty, who was then seventeen, decided that he was going to have her. I was his best buddy so I waited outside the cabin door for him to finish. About five minutes after he entered the cabin, he came out and said: 'I couldn't do anything—I got her undressed, but it was just disgusting!' As far as I know Marty didn't lose his virginity until he got married— at least that's what he told me.''

Although Kahane had a succession of girl friends in high school and college, ''he talked about women with such contempt, it was incredible!'' said Fleminger, who later married one of Kahane's college flames. ''The contempt was a dominant part of his personality. Women who had relationships with him were increasingly frustrated, unless they were totally masochistic. He treated women like they didn't exist as people, like they were just a collection of body parts—not all of which he liked.''

In the end, Kahane was more adept at placing bets on baseball and basketball games with the seedy neighborhood bookie than at figuring out women. At Betar's weekly poker games, Kahane earned a reputation as an ungracious winner and a rotten loser. ''We played for peanuts,'' said Beiber. ''But Kahane took the games very seriously. He hated to lose. Winners were supposed to treat everyone else to something to eat after the game. He didn't care for that. He always wanted to keep the money, but we wouldn't let him get away with it.''

During the poker games, Beiber says, Kahane ''always tried to be the center of attention. He talked incessantly. He could be nice to people who had more status and power, and contemptuous of those who had less than he. He was very condescending and sarcastic.''

Kahane's sarcasm did not help the time that he and Allan Mallenbaum were mugged after dropping their dates off at about three o'clock one morning in Manhattan. Mallenbaum had stopped his father's car at a light on East 15th Street, ''when two guys came up to the window and stuffed a gun in my face,'' Mallenbaum recalled. The gunmen took about $100 from the youths, forced Kahane into the back seat, and made Mallenbaum drive around the city for several hours at gunpoint. Finally, the gunmen stole their ID's and warned them, ''We know where to get you if you go to the cops.'' Mallenbaum said that there was no way he could convince the ''future fearless leader'' of the JDL to go to the precinct and look at mug shots. ''He was absolutely convinced there would be retribution if we tried to ID these fellows.''

But what Kahane lacked in fearlessness, he more than made up for in cunning. When he was about seventeen, a leadership position opened in Betar's New York chapter. Kahane moved to grab it. The general consensus of the national leadership, however, was that he was too young and lacked maturity. ''When we turned him down, he turned against us,'' said Dolinsky.

Meir walked out of the movement in a huff, announcing that he was going to start his own religious Zionist party that would merge Jewish nationalism with Torah ideology. ''He said his goal was to turn Israel into a theocracy,'' said his younger brother, Nachman. ''He printed leaflets and flyers, which he ran off on my father's shul's mimeograph machine.''

Shortly after Kahane abandoned Betar, Dolinsky noticed that the youth movement's $100-a-month subsidy check from the World Zionist Organization stopped coming. ''After three months of not receiving the subsidy, I went over to the WZO office in Manhattan to find out what was wrong. They said that Martin Kahane had come in and told them that he was the new head of Betar and should receive the funds.'' Meanwhile, Kahane had managed to obtain Betar's mailing list. ''All of a sudden, parents who sent their children to Camp Betar got a letter saying: 'Sign up your kids now for Betar summer camp headed by Meir Kahane.' '' recalled Dolinsky. ''We warned him: 'Meir, cut it out! If you want to start a camp, start a camp, but don't bother us.' ''

When he continued to send out his camp flyers, Betar's national directorate decided it was time to teach young Kahane a lesson. Late one Saturday night in 1950, as Kahane walked out of a party in Brooklyn, he was yanked off the street, blindfolded, bound, gagged, and dumped into the back seat of a Plymouth filled with five of his former friends from Betar. ''I was quite apprehensive that he would start to fight because he was a very powerful boy,'' said the driver, Israel Herman, who was then Betar's national secretary. ''But he didn't resist.''

''He was in a state of terror,'' added Dolinsky who helped mastermind the abduction. ''He was white as a ghost. He thought we were going to kill him.''

They drove Kahane over the George Washington Bridge and threatened to dangle him over the river by his heels. ''He got so scared he actually vomited in the car,'' grimaced Herman. ''It was my mother's new car and I got hell from her the next day. She never forgot it until the day she died." The Betarniks then drove Kahane to a desolate wooded area in New Jersey. They told him that this was the spot where the Irgun murdered traitors. Then they drove into Manhattan, where Herman was stopped by a cop near the Brooklyn Bridge for driving the wrong way on a one-way street.

"Meir, one word and you're dead," hissed Dolinsky, who stripped off Kahane's gag and blindfold, but left his hands bound.

"I'm not going to do anything," Kahane whimpered.

Herman walked over to the police car and explained that he was from Queens and was unfamiliar with Manhattan. The officer warned him to be more careful and drove away without looking inside the car.

Next, they drove Kahane to Dolinsky's home in Washington Heights in upper Manhattan. His parents were in Florida on vacation. The Betarniks tied the terrified Kahane to a kitchen chair and tried him as a traitor. "He had nothing to say in his own defense," said Dolinsky.

"We told him the Torah authorized us to give him forty lashes," said Herman. But instead, the boys gave him a dime for the subway and told him to go home. "That's the last time I ever saw him," added Herman, who today is an aeronautical engineer in Israel.

The next night, Brooklyn District Attorney Eddie Silver, himself a passionate Zionist and a close friend of Charles Kahane, had the entire national leadership of Betar arrested and brought to his office. "Do you know what the fuck you did?" he screamed. "You're fucking kidnappers. Don't you know the fucking penalty for kidnapping? It's the death penalty. It's fucking mandatory. I have no choice. Didn't you ever hear of the Lindbergh Law? You fucking kids are going to fry! If you boys want action, why don't you go to a border settlement in Israel and fight Arabs?"

Charles ultimately dropped the charges against the Betarniks, and Meir dropped his plan to subvert Betar. Instead, he joined B'nai Akiva, an Orthodox Jewish youth group. He nearly ran that organization into the ground after staging an unsuccessful coup d'état.

Few American Betarniks ever took up Silver's call to go to Israel and fight Arabs. As for Kahane, he was usually too busy battling his fellow Jews. "In Betar, we always talked about going to Israel to fight with the Irgun," recalled Fleminger. "I can't remember Kahane ever saying he was going to go. I think it's important that though Kahane fantasized as a teenager about actually running Israel, he never fantasized about fighting for the Jewish state. He stayed in America and went to college and law school. It's ironic that the people he attacks in Israel today are the people who created the state, fought for the state, defended the state. He claims he is the embodiment of Israel, yet he has never done anything positive for it."

CHAPTER FOUR
The Battle of
Howard Beach

^^^^^^^^^^^^^^^^^^^^^^^^^^^^^^^^^^^^^

After Meir Kahane left Betar, the anti-Semitism that he feared but had seldom experienced struck close to home. In 1952, vandals smeared swastikas on a number of synagogues in his neighborhood. His father, who was then president of the Rabbinical Board in Flatbush, met with city officials about increasing police patrols in Jewish areas. Charles returned home from one meeting particularly dejected. "Unwittingly, I said it would be a good idea if Jews would organize an underground," he told a reporter many years after the incident. "Meir took it seriously. 'That's the only thing we can do,' he told me."

Though the seeds for the Jewish Defense League may have been sown by Charles's offhand remark, it would be more than fifteen years before his son would establish the militant, semi-underground movement. During the interim, he tirelessly cast about for a group or a cause that could propel him into the national spotlight. In 1955, the FBI opened the first of many investigations into his radical Zionist activities. The classified report identified Kahane as having "domestic, subversive tendencies."

Before blossoming into a subversive so disruptive that Richard Nixon and Henry Kissinger would accuse him of attempting to sabotage détente, Kahane finished his education. He graduated with a B.A. in political science from Brooklyn College in 1954 and with a law degree from New York Law School in 1957, the same year that he also received an M.A. in international affairs from New York University and rabbinical ordination from the Orthodox Yeshiva Mirrer in Brooklyn.

Of all the schools he attended, Yeshiva Mirrer seems to have had the most lasting impact on his religious and political thinking. It had been established in Mirrer, Poland in 1817. Its teachers and students moved en masse to Shanghai at the outbreak of the Second World War, before coming to Brooklyn. Like rabbis at many ultra-Orthodox yeshivas, Mirrer's rabbis had mixed feelings about Zionism. They believed that Jews would return to the land of Israel as a prelude to redemption. But they had trouble accepting David Ben-Gurion as the "anointed one."

Kahane was among the first group of American Jewish students to enter Yeshiva Mirrer. His Talmud skills were no better developed than when he was at BTA. "He knew nothing of the Talmud when he came to Mirrer," said Rabbi Marcel Blitz, who went to Mirrer with Kahane, and who today lives in Baltimore where he is a fervent Kach supporter. "The teachers used to scream at him, curse him, and insult him in Yiddish. They called him a dummy!"

Kahane was castigated for his ignorance of Judaism, but he eagerly absorbed Mirrer's ultra-Orthodox dogma, using it as a bulwark against what he perceived to be the corrupting influence of the secular world, which nevertheless continued to entice him. At the same time, he changed his name from Martin to Meir, and, outwardly at least, began to adhere to an increasingly strict Orthodox code of behavior.

Kahane was no better at studying law than the Talmud. After he graduated from law school in 1957, he flunked his only attempt to pass the New York State bar exam; he would later claim that he had never taken the exam because his interest in law was peripheral to his goal of becoming a full-time Jewish activist and scholar.

Nor did Kahane make a very favorable impression at NYU. "He was not intellectually impressive," said Jerry Goodman, who took a course with Kahane called "Africa South of the Sahara," and is the former executive director of the National Conference on Soviet Jewry. "He seemed to sincerely care about the Jewish community, and he had a fierce family pride, but his sincerity was mixed with demagoguery. He told me he'd be the first American Jewish prime minister of Israel. He was sincerely committed to his ideals, but he was bizarre."

What Kahane lacked in academic aptitude, he more than made up for in determination. His undergraduate schedule was rigorous. Sonia picked him up at 4:30 P.M. at Yeshiva Mirrer and drove him to Brooklyn College, where she would return after midnight to drive him home. "He never had any time to do homework," she said. "He was all day in the yeshiva and at night he went to college."

Intense and driven like his mother, Kahane, who was very skinny and nervous, could survive a fifteen-hour school day on a couple of sandwiches. "Every day for seven years I had to make him two sandwiches," said Sonia. "One was cream cheese and jam and one was salmon and tomatoes. I was sick to my stomach from salmon after seven years!"

Sonia was not the only one who admired Meir's frenetic energy. Libby Blum was a seventeen-year-old religious high school student in Brooklyn when she met Meir, who was five years older. "I was her leader in [B'nai Akiva] a Zionist youth movement," Kahane said. "She was a very smart girl and a very, very sweet girl." She was also young and naive. They were married in 1956, one year after they met. Charles Kahane and the dean of Yeshiva Mirrer presided at the ceremony. Sonia warned Libby that she was marrying a revolutionary and advised her to steer Meir away from a life of Jewish militancy. But there was little Libby could do. From the outset, relatives predicted that there would be trouble between the highly-strung, self-centered Kahane and the painfully shy and passive Libby. "Meir treated Libby like Charles treated Sonia," Isaac Trainin says today. "He walked all over her. Libby is a nice little weakling." Within a few years, Kahane's marital infidelities would create a deep and lasting rift between the Kahane family and Libby's father, Jacob Blum, a former investigator for the New York State Department of Welfare. (Blum recently retired and moved to Jerusalem, where he lives in a predominantly Orthodox neighborhood barely a block away from Sonia Kahane. "I have nothing to do with him," Sonia told me. "He's a very peculiar person." For his part, Blum told me that "heart problems" prevent him from talking about his "notorious son-in-law.")

In 1958, Kahane began serving as the rabbi of the Howard Beach Jewish Center in a working-class section of Queens. He had spent his first year out of school living off his wife's dowry,* unsure about which way to take his career. He had failed the bar, and although the rabbinate really did not interest him, he had a one-year-old child and Libby was pregnant again. "One doesn't necessarily study for the rabbinate to practice as a rabbi," Kahane said many years later. "Every Jewish person should have the knowledge of a rabbi. If you ask, 'When did I decide to be a scholar?' Always. If you ask, 'When did I decide to be a rabbi?' Never. I sort of fell into it. I never got too much pleasure out of it."

The Howard Beach Jewish Community Center was a small synagogue in a mixed-Jewish-Italian neighborhood that was rapidly becoming home to poor Blacks and Hispanics. The synagogue itself was located in a run-down, two-storied frame house. The temple was upstairs, and the offices and classrooms were on the ground floor. The congregation was part of the Conservative Jewish movement, which is less strictly observant than Orthodox Judaism.*

The synagogue president liked Kahane, although he worried that the young rabbi would try to impose his more Orthodox views on the congregation. But Kahane, desperate for a job, promised to conform to the congregation's existing values. Kahane was hired, and the synagogue board provided him with a small salary and a rent-free apartment.

Kahane suppressed his zealous Orthodoxy while he built a base of support inside the congregation. His energetic fundraising and membership drives won him enthusiastic approval. "He would send out five or six couples every Sunday morning to knock on the doors of Jewish neighbors, inviting them to become members of our congregation," said Bob Falk, the synagogue's treasurer. "No rabbi we had ever did that before."

---

* Yeshiva scholars traditionally receive dowries and stipends so they can continue their studies.

* In 1986, Howard Beach became the focus of international attention when a gang of white teenagers brutally attacked three Black men after they walked out of a pizza shop. One Black man was struck and killed by a car as he fled his attackers.

More importantly, however, it was at the synagogue in Howard Beach that Kahane discovered what is undoubtedly his greatest gift—his ability to entrance children. If he initially trod carefully on the adults' religious sensibilities, he pushed his Orthodox ideas on their children with stunning success. "My kids were crazy about him," said Falk. "My daughter, who was then about eight years old, used to walk about a mile every Saturday to the Shabbos Club that Kahane began. It was a long walk for a little girl. She started bringing her gentile neighbor and she loved him too. There was something about him. He had these leadership qualities. He had people do a lot of things that they wouldn't have done for anyone else."

Attendance at the synagogue's Hebrew school soared. His fire-and-brimstone sermons ridiculed the Reform and Conservative movements for destroying the very foundations of Judaism itself. Kahane declared that Orthodox Judaism was a special, separate, demanding life that was at odds with Jews who strove to mix, climb the ladder, enjoy life without painful rules, worship God at the altar of chopped liver temples—the very symbol of the assimilated American Jew's Bar Mitzvah. Orthodoxy may not be the preferred path for American Jews on the way up, Kahane would say, but Orthodoxy was the *authentic* path for Jews!

"If you were a fourteen-year-old boy in 1957 from an assimilated Jewish home and you heard Kahane, it was like sailing with Christopher Columbus and discovering a new world," says David Cohen, who was that age when he entered Kahane's Hebrew school class. "Religion was very real to him and it became very real to us. He had a clear idea of right and wrong—a strict Orthodox line," Cohen, now a New York City school teacher, continued. "Either you did everything by the book or you did nothing. He gave us a choice. Some of us opted for nothing."

However, others embraced Orthodoxy, in some cases driving their parents crazy. More than one of Kahane's students came home donning yarmulkes, refusing to eat on their parents' non-kosher dishes, and prowling around their homes on the Sabbath turning off lights and electrical appliances. "My son Avi even turned off the light in the refrigerator on Shabbos," moaned his mother Belle Kirschenbaum, still annoyed some thirty years later. Some of Kahane's students also started spouting nationalist Jewish slogans. "He taught us that we should stand up for our people," said Cohen. "He talked about Jewish unity and of his deep distrust of non-Jews. He seemed to live the Holocaust and its shame."

One Saturday morning worshipers walked into the temple and found a screen, or *mehitza*, running down the middle of the sanctuary from the floor to the ceiling. The *mehitza* was the barrier that Kahane could never get his father to erect in his own synagogue a decade earlier. Now Kahane declared that he would no longer be their rabbi if men and women sat together during prayers. Though dissatisfaction with Kahane had been growing among the adults, he had finally crossed the line. Shocked congregants called a general meeting to decide their rebellious rabbi's future. On a March night in 1960, in the middle of a freak blizzard that made the streets nearly impassable, more than 150 people, about 95 percent of the congregation, traveled to the synagogue.

The most serious charge leveled at Kahane was that he was trying to brainwash the children. "He was taken aback and was very upset," Falk recalled. "He said he never taught the children to be disrespectful to their parents, and if they'd become more Jewish, what's the shame in it?" But parents of the "born-again" Jewish children were on the verge of hysteria. "I called him a Hitler!" said Belle Kirschenbaum, whose son Avi had become a strictly observant Orthodox Jew. After several hours of heated debate, which was tape-recorded in anticipation of a possible lawsuit by Kahane, the besieged rabbi was asked to go home so that the members could cast their ballots. "A rabbi should bend to the needs and wishes of the congregation, and Kahane insisted that he was the law," said Jonathan Berkowitz, a congregant who attended the meeting. "It was like running into a stone wall! We were a Conservative congregation and he turned it into an Orthodox synagogue." Finally, at two o'clock in the morning, a large majority voted to oust him.

"I called him at home to tell him he was fired," said Esther Falk, who voted for Kahane, although her husband voted to remove him. "Meir was very upset," she said. "I loved him. I used to keep special foods for him when he came to visit. He had increased our membership from 40 families to 125, and this is how we repaid him! It was a black day in Howard Beach," she added bitterly.

The next day, Charles Kahane called several board members to plead for his son's job, promising that Meir would be more flexible. But it was too late. The congregation was so badly polarized that many members were no longer on speaking terms with each other. After Kahane left, nearly half the congregants resigned from the synagogue. "The synagogue never recovered," said Mrs. Kirschenbaum.

Details of the civil war at the Howard Beach synagogue spread through the local Jewish community. *The Brooklyn Daily*, a secular newspaper owned by an Orthodox rabbi, invited Kahane to come to the paper and describe his experience. Kahane told the editors that he was fired because he had "turned the synagogue president's son into an observant Jew." But he really did not mind being fired, he told them, because he did not like being a traditional rabbi, and he hated the nouveaux riche Jews in his congregation "who lived in $100,000 homes without furniture." Impressed with the feisty, articulate rabbi, the publisher asked him to write a first person account of his travails. The article, called the "Miracle of Howard Beach"—about how a young rabbi brought religion to ignorant assimilated Jews—turned Kahane into something of a minor folk hero in New York's large, Orthodox Jewish community. At the same time, Kahane used the opportunity to develop a father-son relationship with Rabbi Sholom Klass, the *Daily's* publisher. In the coming years, Kahane would help transform the paper, which had consisted largely of legal advertisements, into a powerful Orthodox Jewish weekly, renamed *The Jewish Press*. With a circulation of nearly 200,000, the paper became a political powerhouse in New York City and beyond. It also became a platform for Kahane to build the JDL and later the Kach movement.

But Kahane's stardom at *The Jewish Press* was several years away when he first walked into *The Brooklyn Daily's* dilapidated offices on Surf Avenue in Coney Island. After describing the injustices he had suffered at Howard Beach, he said: "By the way I'm looking for a job—do you have anything for me? I know how to write. I could write about sports. I just need something to tide me over until I can get a pulpit."

The *Daily* needed a sports writer. Klass agreed to pay Kahane a nominal stipend, and got him a press pass for Yankee Stadium. "He covered the Yankees for us for a whole season writing under the pen name of Martin King," said Arnold Fine, Kahane's editor. "His reporting was superlative." So much so in fact that he won the Grantland Rice Newspaper Sportswriting Award.

Kahane once told me that the year he covered the Yankees was the happiest in his life. But in 1962 the budding sports writer suddenly moved to Israel, temporarily leaving his wife and four children behind in Queens. It was an impulsive, inexplicable act that Kahane does not like to talk about even to this day. At the time, Kahane told relatives that he was going to Israel to become a member of the Israeli cabinet. "He thought Ben-Gurion was going to meet him at the docks," his uncle, Rabbi Isaac Trainin, snorted sarcastically.

But there was no brass band playing "Hatikva," Israel's national anthem, when Kahane walked off the gangplank of a small, cramped Israeli cargo ship at Haifa harbor. For a man who grew up with visions of one day saving Israel, the Jewish state seemed to be getting by perfectly well without him. And though Kahane may have thought that he was a hero for showering Bevin with tomatoes, his antics in Betar paled in a country where heroism was commonplace.

Kahane traveled to Yeshiva Kafr Ha'roa, situated in a small Yemenite Jewish village near Hadera, to study Talmud. He stuttered so badly in Hebrew that he quickly became an object of scorn. As a teenager, Kahane's parents had sent him to an expensive private speech therapy school in New England where he learned to control his stuttering, but he could not transfer the techniques to spoken Hebrew. He next moved to Sa'ad, a religious kibbutz in the Negev near the Egyptian border, where he worked as an assistant rabbi. But he was ridiculed by the kibbutzniks for his arrogance. After three months, he moved in with cousins in Tel Aviv in a state of culture shock. "He wouldn't talk to anyone about his feelings or his plans," said his cousin Moshe Kahane, in whose apartment Meir stayed. "Then one day he said he was leaving and would come back to Israel when he was somebody."

Before leaving Israel, however, Kahane wrote to his parents, boasting that he had "met with the chief rabbis of Jerusalem and that he was the first rabbi who was an American and so young, to be admitted among them," said Sonia. He also told his parents that he had been invited to set up a law department at Bar Ilan University, and that he had privately studied Talmud with Israeli Chief Rabbi Isaac Herzog.

After returning to his wife and children in Queens, broke and unemployed, he went into seclusion until his battered ego was repaired. He never told his parents the truth about his traumatic failure in Israel, though it was clearly the lowest point in his life. When pressed to explain why he returned to America, Kahane said it was because he was upset that Israel was "riven with warring political factions" and "squabbling Sephardim."

Rabbi Marcel Blitz, who had attended Brooklyn College and Yeshiva Mirrer with Kahane, remembers how Kahane bragged before leaving for Israel that he "wasn't coming back until he was prime minister." About a year later, Blitz says he attended a wedding party in Brooklyn where he ran into one of Kahane's cousins. "I asked, 'How's Meir doing in Israel?' His cousin said he was back in the States incognito—that he was in hiding because he was ashamed that he had lost his job in Israel because of his stuttering."

CHAPTER FIVE
The Underground Years

After recovering from his sojourn in Israel, Meir Kahane was desperate to find a job. He was living with his wife and four children in Laurelton, Queens, a working-class neighborhood of Archie Bunker-style, clapboard row houses. Though he was writing articles for *The Jewish Press* and even had a column called "A Small Voice," he needed a more substantial income. He asked *Jewish Press* editor Arnold Fine to help him find work. Fine put him in touch with a man in the Laurelton area who had a newspaper route to sell. Kahane bought the route for a few thousand dollars with money he borrowed from friends and family.

Rabbi Kahane became a familiar sight to early risers in Laurelton. "I used to see him up at dawn pitching newspapers from his little red Austin," said Fred Horowitz, a Queens businessman who fled Nazi Germany for Palestine in 1937, was a flight sergeant in the RAF during the Second World War, and later provided financial backing for several of Kahane's ventures. To Horowitz and many others in Laurelton, Kahane inspired sympathy more than anything else. One rainy night Kahane came to Horowitz's house soaked to the bone and with torn shoes. "His broken-down Austin had stalled in the rain again," said Horowitz.

Kahane diligently built up the route, handing out samples, making contacts. Despite his diligence, "his paper route wasn't

looked upon as the most prestigious work,'' said Elyahu Rominek, the rabbi of the Young Israel Synagogue in Laurelton where
the Kahanes worshipped. ''The community generally felt sorry
for him. He had a family. How much money could he be making? Not much. And a man of such ability.''

Charles Kahane too was troubled that his pride and joy, an
ordained rabbi with a law degree and an M.A. in international
affairs, was a mere newspaper delivery boy. Charles told friends
that Meir took the job because he could finish work by 6 A.M.
and study Torah for the rest of the day. Meanwhile, Kahane's
family and friends worried that delivering papers around the
periphery of poor Black neighborhoods early in the morning was
dangerous. ''He always replied, 'God is with me, and he won't
hurt me because he knows my real mission,' '' recalled Fine.

Despite his low-status job, many people in Laurelton were fond
of the soft-spoken Kahane. ''He had this facade of piety,'' said
Rabbi Rominek. ''That's why people liked him.'' And he still had
a magical charm with children. ''Kahane always stopped to play
ball with the kids, *tzitzes* [the fringed garment worn by observant Jews] trailing in the wind,'' said Horowitz. On Simchus
Torah, ''Meir would jump to the sky with the Torah,'' Rabbi
Rominek recalled. ''The kids were crazy about it. He leaped up
and down, up and down, dancing with such frenzy.'' He danced
with every child in the synagogue, except his own children who
stood quietly on the sidelines, with a look of rejection much like
their mother's.

On Saturdays Kahane conducted a special children's service
in the synagogue. He lectured on the Bible and Zionism, while
Rabbi Rominek officiated downstairs. Kahane also encouraged
his young students to come to his home for Hebrew and Talmud lessons, or simply for comradeship.

''It was an honor for a child to be invited to his Shabbos table,''
said Edith Horowitz. Libby, however, resented the attention that
her husband showed other children. ''Once when my son Elliot
was in high school I came to Kahane's house with a problem,''
said Fred Horowitz, ''and I could see her say with her eyes: 'Why
the fuck don't you get out of here! Why do you have to come
to us with your problems? What is he, the savior?' But everybody came to him in Laurelton. You'd come to him so often that
he'd get all your IOU's, so later when he came to us for money—
it was hard to say no.''

It was not long before the pious newspaper delivery man found a profession that better suited his aspirations. Sometime in 1963, Kahane removed his *yarmulke* and *tallis* and stepped into the world of covert action. Using the name Michael King, he began a research and intelligence gathering business with Joseph Churba, a childhood friend and fellow Betarnick.

Before long, Kahane, the self-proclaimed descendant of twenty-eight generations of rabbis, was cruising for shiksas in East Side singles bars, ordering martinis, and infiltrating domestic extremist groups for the FBI. "There was some bit of nastiness in the secular world that he liked," said a source familiar with Kahane's early career. And there were parts of that world that nearly destroyed him.

Isaac Trainin speculates that if he had been able to get his nephew a job when he returned from Israel, he may have saved Kahane from his destructive impulses. "I got him an interview at the Hawthorne School for emotionally disturbed children," Trainin recalled. "They loved him. He was so good with children. But they were non-Orthodox and they turned him down. Who knows how his life would have turned out if Hawthorne had hired him?"

And who knows what might have become of Kahane if he had not teamed up with the lanky, dark-haired Churba. In 1963, Churba, then working on his doctorate at Columbia University, had already forged links with the CIA and Israeli intelligence, giving Kahane an entrée to the shadowy world of spooks and prominent cold warriors. Although Churba went on to become a Middle East specialist for Air Force Intelligence, a foreign affairs adviser to Ronald Reagan during the 1980 presidential campaign, and senior policy adviser to the Arms Control and Disarmament Agency, little is known about his early years. And Churba has assiduously worked to keep it that way.

One of twelve children, Churba was born on May 23, 1933, in Flatbush, Brooklyn, and was raised in a small, two-storey house on Ocean Parkway in an area that was inhabited by Jews from Aleppo, Syria. Today the Syrian Jews make up one of the wealthiest and least-known Jewish communities in the world. Many of them journeyed to America at the turn of the century, when events at home made it prudent to leave. Ill at ease with the Yiddish speaking, bagel-and-lox-eating Eastern European Jews of the Lower East Side, where they first settled, the Arabic speaking Syrian Jews traveled to Williamsburg, then Bensonhurst, and finally to Flatbush. There they bought the neat two-family houses along Kings Highway and Ocean Parkway. They were as close knit and intolerant of outsiders as the most Orthodox European Jews. In 1935, the Aleppo Jews' religious court even banned marriage to converts to Judaism.

The Churbas were desperately poor. Joseph's mother, a short, stooped woman who always looked ragged, died after a prolonged bout with cancer when he was a child. His father, Rahamim, a sexton in a local synagogue, was excommunicated in the 1950s after a religious dispute with the community elders whom he had accused of compromising traditional values. Having challenged their authority and lost, Rahamim never again set foot in a synagogue. Nor would he ever again hold a job. He spent his remaining years shut in his study, a mystic devoutly consuming esoteric religious doctrine—leaving the mundane matters of making money to his children, whom he sent out to work.

Joseph Churba grew up an outsider—with a powerful disdain for those who had cast aside his father. In a tribute written to Rahamim in a local newspaper after his death in November 1987, Churba lashed out at New York's Syrian Jewish community, which, he declared, never offered his father more than "a silent internment in an anonymous grave." He revealed as much about his own fundamentalist fervor and feelings of alienation as he did about his affection for his father. "He was *from* but not *of* the Aleppo community," Churba wrote. "He would stand alone: the lonely man of faith. For he believed that no generation, however abominable, could abrogate the Divine promise or abort the Jewish destiny. That promise is not conditional, but absolute. In time, the Sephardim would return to their heritage. If not this generation then the next. An awesome process, the struggle is of cosmic proportions."

As a child, Churba found a safe haven in the Kahane home, where he often ate dinner and spent the night. The Kahanes also helped the Churbas financially. "One day I went to the drugstore for some rubbing alcohol," Sonia recalled, "and the druggist said, 'Mrs. Kahane, do you know you owe me $165?' " Sonia, who never bought anything on credit, learned that Meir had told the druggist that he had permission to charge his family for Mrs. Churba's medication. Later, when questioned about the bill, Sonia said Meir replied, "Mamma, we are Jews and we have to help Jews. If somebody's sick and they haven't got a penny, we've got to help them.''

Joseph Churba and Meir Kahane went to the same schools, joined Betar, attended its summer camp in the Catskills, and later studied together at Yeshiva Mirrer. Churba, however, eventually obtained his rabbinical ordination from a Sephardic yeshiva in Jerusalem. Although his top-secret U.S. military file describes him as a brilliant Middle East analyst, Churba's Betar buddies nicknamed their gawky, six-foot-two friend "the dumb Arab." "We had to write all his high school papers," Dr. Victor Mallenbaum says today. "He was considered a dope. We were shocked when we heard he got a Ph.D. in political science from Columbia."

Like Kahane, Churba continued his ultra-right-wing Zionist activities into adulthood. In 1956, for example, Churba organized a number of demonstrations protesting Western arms sales to the Arab world, according to information obtained from Churba's secret FBI file. In February 1956, Churba led a pro-Israel rally in front of the British Mission in New York. Two months later, he led Betar picketers in a demonstration in front of the Egyptian Consulate.

That same year, during the Suez War, Churba turned up at Mevo Betar, a settlement 22 kilometers southwest of Jerusalem, and about 300 meters from the Jordanian border. The Israelis handed him a machine gun and put him in a trench. On the first evening, with tensions mounting along the border after Israeli armored columns attacked Egyptian positions in the Sinai, Churba left his post "to take a leak and never came back," said Morton Dolinsky, his trench mate. "We figured Churba had chickened out," said Israel Herman, who was also in the trench.

Churba currently heads the Center for International Security, an ultra-right-wing think tank in Washington funded by Reverend Sun Myung Moon's political arm, the Confederation of Associations for the Unity of the Societies of America (CAUSA).*

---

* CAUSA was founded in 1980 by Bo Hi Pak, a former Korean CIA agent, and Kim San In, the former Korean CIA station chief in Mexico City. CAUSA's first executive director was Warren Richardson, formerly general counsel to the anti-Semitic Liberty Lobby. CAUSA's advisory board includes General George Keegan and Daniel Graham, former deputy director of the CIA.

In 1985, Moon was imprisoned for thirteen months in the United States for income tax evasion. His felony conviction has not stopped him from having influence in the nation's capital through his newspaper, *The Washington Times*, and other organizations. Even though he is a strong supporter of Israel, Moon has been criticized by some Jewish leaders for attracting numerous young Jews to his cult-like Unification Church, which preaches a strange brew of Christianity, Confucianism, and anticommunism.

Churba has refused repeated requests to speak either about Kahane or himself. His silence is not surprising given his close relationship with the Reagan and Bush Administrations. In any case, while Kahane was still tossing newspapers from his Austin two-seater in Laurelton, Churba was already in Washington lobbying on behalf of the CIA-installed South Vietnamese puppet Ngo Dinh Diem, according to U.S. government sources.

In early 1963, Churba introduced Kahane to Washington night life, front groups, and covert action. The possibility of infiltrating domestic extremist groups as well as the growing anti-war movement—perhaps even secretly aiding Israel—excited the failed rabbi.

Kahane and Churba struck an odd pose together. There was Churba: the tall, elegantly dressed bachelor who took young women on buggy rides through Central Park and dined in glittery restaurants where he knew the maître d's by name. And there was Kahane: dark, intense, furtive, indifferent to fine food—and married. "In a way they became stuck together," said Fred Horowitz. "Churba couldn't write well and he needed someone who could popularize his views. But if anybody led the excursions through the intelligence and diplomatic worlds, it was Churba leading Kahane. Churba could play all kinds of roles. He could play an ambassador, a diplomat. He had class. Kahane looked like a typical yeshiva boy from Flatbush—like a Woody Allen movie character."

But Kahane, whose skills at improvisation were already evident in high school, soon became adept at playing any number of roles. By his own account, he would spend much of the next four years leading a double life. He would leave his house in Laurelton on Monday for Washington or Manhattan and return for the Sabbath on Friday. He posed variously as a foreign correspondent, a college professor, and a well-to-do-bachelor. He spent one summer in the Hamptons at Churba's house. A New York public relations woman told *The New York Times* in 1971 that she remembered running into Kahane at a party on Long Island. "I knew him only as Michael King," she told the *Times*. "He told me he had been a correspondent for a wire service in Africa, and I recall at one point he volunteered that he was a Presbyterian."

The closest Kahane ever came to being a foreign correspondent was delivering *The New York Times* in Laurelton. However, family and friends marvelled at how well the former newspaper delivery boy seemed to be doing in his new life. "We knew Kahane was doing some projects for the government in Washington, but nobody knew what," said Rabbi Rominek. "He sold his paper route and suddenly he was in Washington. There was this mystique about his work."

Kahane and Churba worked hard to enhance their reputations. The more they postured, the more they boasted about the important people they knew in Washington, the easier it was for them to raise money by selling limited partnerships in their newly created Washington-based think tank, which they called the Institute for Research in Foreign Affairs. But the huge return on investments they promised was as illusory as the institute itself. They claimed the think tank was in Georgetown, but it was never listed in the Washington, D.C. phone book, nor in other directories of Washington organizations or institutes.

One of their first projects was the publication of a short-lived weekly gossip sheet called *The Night Owl*, ostensibly about embassy night life in Washington. Fred Horowitz gave the men $10,000 to start up the paper, which folded after two issues. Like many of their projects, the paper was a scam. The two hoped to get money from various embassies for planting stories and information, according to Horowitz, who himself wanted to become an influential Washington publisher. "I thought I'd get a press card, and be able to go to gala affairs," Horowitz says today. "Don't laugh. Look, I trusted them. I would have trusted them with my life."

Churba and Kahane next tried their hand at ghostwriting reports for congressional committees. "Once we did a position paper on the Greek view of the Cyprus situation for [New York] Senator [Jacob] Javits's office," Kahane told me. "In the late '50s and early '60s, doing research for the government was the greatest avenue to make money."

Sometime in 1963, said Kahane, the FBI asked if he and Churba would infiltrate the then little-known John Birch Society to find out the source of its funds. This secretive society of right-wing extremists was founded in 1958 by Robert Welch, a successful confectionery manufacturer. "One day the FBI came to us and complained that since they had such a bad public image from only investigating leftists, would we investigate the Birchers for them?" Kahane told me. "They said they didn't have the right people, so they wanted to contract it out to us, which they do sometimes. But we really couldn't do a decent job . . . using conventional research methods. I could clip articles and go to meetings and write reports . . . but that's not what the FBI really wanted. So I said, 'I'll tell you what. Why don't I join the Birchers?' They thought that was phenomenal. 'That's exactly what we want you to do,' they told us. I got deeper and deeper into it.''

Kahane claims that he went underground using the name Michael King because, he told me, "naturally, Meir Kahane with a yarmulke wouldn't have gotten very far. I constantly had to make up reasons why I couldn't attend meetings on Friday nights.'' For many months between 1963 and 1965 he says that he traveled through Southern California and the Southwest. It was in this bastion of right-wing conservatism, he says, that he was first exposed to virulent anti-Semitism. He met middle- and upper-middle-class Birchers who theorized that America's social ills, from drug abuse to racial tension, were orchestrated by an international Jewish conspiracy to destroy the nation from within so it would fall to communism.

After he tracked down leading Birchers, he said, the F.B.I. would move in and threaten to reveal their identities—which, Kahane claims, usually cooled their ardor, because they did not want to risk public embarrassment. "It was a very dangerous job,'' Kahane recalled. "I rooted out the monied Birchers, then the FBI went in and leaned on them. . . . I must say that the FBI should be given credit. I'm no fan of the FBI, but they did a job on these wealthy people.''

An FBI spokesman in New York said that Kahane never worked for the Bureau. Kahane said: "If the FBI says it isn't so, then they have their reasons.'' But a senior Justice Department official admitted that Kahane and the Bureau were well acquainted. The official, who reviewed Kahane's classified FBI file before our meeting in November 1987, told me that Kahane provided "useful information on domestic security matters'' to the Bureau during the 1960s, although he stopped short of confirming Kahane's claim that he and Churba were contracted by the FBI to infiltrate the Birchers. "Kahane provided some information on the Birchers, but wasn't paid,'' said the official, who requested anonymity. "He was a cooperative citizen, not a regular informant. Even then it was believed he had his own axe to grind. We thought it served his purpose to provide information on his competition. Kahane was a Zionist and the Birchers were anti-Catholic, anti-Black, anti-liberal, and anti-Jewish. Anyone who is really working for the FBI [in deep cover] doesn't boast. . . . He can't prove it, and you can't expect me to document it.''

David Ryan, the former head of the FBI's notorious Domestic Intelligence Division, or Division Five, which spearheaded Bureau Director J. Edgar Hoover's campaign to undermine the civil rights and anti-war movements in the 1960s and 1970s, told me that he did not believe that Kahane was involved with the Bureau "to the extent where he could make enough money to make a living. He was a good citizen. He would call to express his concern. I know our current President Ronald Reagan did that.'' Indeed, in the late 1940s Hollywood actor Ronald Reagan served as both an informant for the FBI about the alleged Communist infiltration of the film industry and a friendly witness for the House Un-American Activities Committee (HUAC).

No less so than in the 1940s and 1950s, the Sixties was a ripe time to work as a professional informant-infiltrator for the government. It was a time when paranoia ran deep. So much so, in fact, that hundreds of organizations and political gatherings were infiltrated and disrupted by government agents. At the same time, a number of right-wing "think tanks" provided the CIA and the FBI with information about "subversives" that the government might otherwise be prevented from obtaining because of constitutional and legislative restrictions. One student of the era estimates that there were as many as ten thousand political informants then working for the government. Informants, writes Victor S. Navasky in his 1980 book, *Naming Names*, had become "fixtures on the landscape. . . . The espionage exposers, the kept witnesses, and the confidential informants had in common that they were ultimately volunteers, enthusiasts of betrayal.''

Kahane's and Churba's enthusiasm was apparently limited only by the amount of money they could make. Sometime in early 1965, they set up yet another front group called Consultant Research Associates (CRA). CRA's primary aim was to promote the Vietnam War inside the American Jewish community. They also continued to spy for the government, mostly on left-wing student groups opposed to the war. Again they turned to Horowitz for funding. "They wanted to do various kinds of projects,'' Horowitz said. "Churba wanted to make a film about the importance of Vietnam. He used to go to Vietnam and had an 'in' with the Vietnamese ambassador in Washington.'' Horowitz put up $20,000 and became CRA's president. The Queens businessman wanted a lawyer to draw up a partnership contract, but Churba protested, claiming falsely that he was an international lawyer and would write the contract himself. Horowitz later regretted caving in to Churba's request.

In May 1965, Churba and Kahane rented a mail drop and a phone number under the name of Consultant Research Associates, 509 Fifth Avenue in Manhattan. They also rented an apartment at 351 East 85th Street on New York's Upper East Side under the name of Michael King. Both men stayed there at times. The aspiring spooks never told Horowitz about the apartment, nor did Kahane tell his family. "What we wanted was an East Side address that could impress prospective clients," Kahane later explained.

Kahane almost certainly never used the East Side pad to entertain prospective investors from New York's Orthodox Jewish community. Instead, he made the rounds of Orthodox synagogues, mining his contacts for funding. "They were collecting money all over Laurelton, constantly boasting about what an important job they were doing for the government," Rabbi Rominek recalled. "Churba cashed in on Kahane's goodwill. Nobody had ever heard of Churba. But Kahane had a wonderful name in the community because he was so good with kids."

During this period, Kahane also began to write more frequently for *The Jewish Press*. On March 19, 1965, the Orthodox weekly ran a gushing profile of Churba that portrayed him as an up-and-coming political star who would one day be as big as the Dulles brothers who headed the CIA and the State Department. The article said that Churba was an ordained Orthodox rabbi, a professor of government at Adelphi University, and a top-level consultant for the Pentagon and the State Department, who was often whisked away at a moment's notice to huddle with government big shots. Churba boasted about his personal relationships with Third World leaders such as Alex Quasson Sackey of Ghana, then president of the UN General Assembly, Tom Mboya of Kenya, and Joseph Kasavubu, president of the Congo. "In my talks with these people, while apparently a disinterested party to the Arab-Israeli dispute," he told the paper, "I will say that

I have more than a little desire to sway them towards understanding the Israeli position.''

At the end of the interview, the *Jewish Press* reporter breath-
lessly summed up his impressions: "Churba was at home in two
worlds—the world of the Torah and the intricate world of foreign affairs and intrigue. In my mind I came back once again to
his desk loaded with international papers of all kinds, on top
of which rested a Baba Kama [one of the tractates of the
Talmud].'' The article was written by Hayim Yerushalmi, one
of Kahane's growing list of pen names. Kahane undoubtedly
wrote the laudatory article to impress potential investors.

The underground men had become consummate con men. In
1965, they even cooked up a scheme for Churba to marry a girl
from a wealthy Long Island family so that they could get their
hands on her father's money. Lois Upbin, a gullible, nineteen-
year-old coed at Stern College, an Orthodox university for
women in Manhattan, was the intended victim. Her father owned
an army-navy store, a laundromat, and a check-cashing business
in Bedford-Stuyvesant, a poor Black neighborhood in Brooklyn
where he also had an interest in a night club called Town Hall,
which then featured great Black entertainers like Chubby Checker
and Lena Horne.

"Churba swept me off my feet,'' recalled Lois, adding that it
was a friend of Kahane's who introduced Churba to her family.
"I liked the whole idea of older men. I liked the idea of successful men. I liked the idea of power. In those days women were
going to get power and prestige through their husbands. And
Churba exuded power and Washington connections. He took
me out in chauffeur-driven limos to expensive restaurants. He
was very gallant. He spent money like it was no object.''

Churba and Lois became engaged after several dates, although
it was becoming increasingly obvious that he was more interested
in her parents than in her. "He used to walk through the door
and throw his arms around my mother and father and completely
ignore me,'' she said, still pouting from the memory.

The engagement party was held in the ramshackle Churba
family home on Ocean Parkway. Churba's nine brothers
attended. So did his two sisters, who waited on the guests and
ate alone in the kitchen "like servants,'' Lois recalled. The affair
was presided over by Churba's father, who forbade dancing. "Joe

gave me an engagement ring at the party," said Lois. "I remember thinking, what a tiny, cloudy ring for someone who claims he's such an important person."

A few days later, Lois and Churba spent the afternoon together in a hotel on 8th Avenue and 34th Street in Manhattan. "I was scared to death," said Lois. "He was very sloppy. That's all I can say."

The following day Churba laid down the law. "First, he told me he was going to be away a lot on government business, which he ordered me never to question him about," Lois recalled. "Second, he told me he wanted $60,000 from my father for his business with Kahane."

Lois's father liked Churba, but the request took him aback. "He said, 'You can have our daughter, but not the money', " she recalled. Soon after, Churba invited Lois to dinner at Longchamps in midtown Manhattan. After dessert, Churba abruptly ended the engagement. "He put me in a cab and I never saw him again," Lois said. "I was just an addendum to the whole situation. He was really interested in marrying a bank account."

Churba later told Edith Horowitz that he broke off the engagement because Lois did not want a large family. "Edie, she's a white girl [Ashkenazi Jewess]. Maybe I should go to Turkey and get a black girl [a Sephardic Jewess] who can't read or write.' He didn't believe a woman should have any say about anything."

In the spring of 1965, Churba and Kahane set up the July Fourth Movement. According to Kahane, the organization tried to create cells on American college campuses to support the Vietnam War and to block the spread of the radical student Left. Kahane later told me that their pro-Vietnam venture received "seed money" from the government "and certain groups within the labor movement," including the AFL-CIO under the leadership of George Meany. Churba and Kahane also received support from legendary cold warriors Jay Lovestone and Irving Brown, who had been top officials of the American Communist Party in the 1920s before undergoing a "Damascus Road" conversion and who subsequently ran the AFL-CIO's powerful International Affairs Department under the tutelage of the CIA.

It was under the CIA's direction that Lovestone and Brown—using Corsican and Italian mafiosos—set up right-wing death squads in Marseilles and other European cities after the Second World War to break the burgeoning left-wing labor movement.

In an article entitled "I'm Glad the CIA's 'Immoral,' " which appeared in the *Saturday Evening Post* in May 1967, Thomas Braden, who headed the CIA's clandestine services in Western Europe in the early 1950s, wrote that it was his idea "to give . . . $15,000 to Irving Brown . . . to pay off his strong-arm squads in Mediterranean ports so that American supplies could be unloaded against the opposition of Communist dock workers."* Brown's success in France led to similar CIA-funded campaigns of subversion against trade union movements elsewhere in Europe and the Third World. "When they [the AFL-CIO] ran out of money, they appealed to the CIA," wrote Braden, until recently the co-host of Cable News Network's "Crossfire." "Thus began the secret subsidy of free trade unions."

By the mid-1960s, the AFL-CIO was busy propping up South Vietnam's trade union movement as part of the war effort.* "I visited South Vietnam to work with trade unionists quite often," Irving Brown told me shortly before he died in Paris in February 1989. Brown said that he and Lovestone "supported the July Fourth Movement" because "we liked their position on Vietnam." According to Irving Brown's son, Robert, who worked with the movement, his father introduced Kahane and Churba to wealthy conservatives, as well as to the heads of individual labor unions—like Mike Sampson, president of the Con Ed Local in New York, who contributed $5,000 to the July Fourth Movement from the union's political slush fund.

Robert Brown was twenty-three when he first met Churba and Kahane in 1965 at his father's office, where the two spelled out

---

* Thanks to Brown, by 1953 his key contact in the Marseilles underworld, Pierre Ferri-Pisain, had control of the city's port, where he built an international heroin trafficking empire. This was not the first time that American intelligence purchased the services of the Mafia. Prior to the Allied invasion of Sicily in the Second World War, the OSS established contacts with the Sicilian Mafia through the same Lucky Lucianio who allowed Betar to smuggle weapons from Hoboken to the Irgun in Palestine. The Sicilian Mafia provided intelligence on the Germans, and after the war assassinated hundreds of Italian left-wing political activists. CIA agent Miles Copeland later boasted: "Had it not been for the Mafia, the Communists would by now be in control of Italy." If the covert backing of wholesale political assassinations and tolerance for heroin dealers bothered Irving Brown, he never let on. "Why shouldn't covert action be acceptable in peace time to try and prevent the possibility of war?" Brown said in a 1977 speech.

* The operation was run by the CIA through Brown, then director of the International Confederation of Trade Unions (ICFTU), an international trade union movement dominated by the AFL-CIO. According to former CIA agent Philip Agee, the ICFTU was "set up and controlled by the CIA," and the "principal CIA agent for control of the ICFTU" was Brown.

the goals of their group. He recalls that Kahane, who went by the name of Michael King, "appeared to be the more forceful of the two—a little too glib, a little too slick." Nevertheless, like his father, Robert was impressed with their plan to build a student movement on college campuses that would support the Vietnam War. "Their presentation was fantastic," said Robert Brown. "There was a screaming need for a student organization that would support the war. Remember this was the spring of 1965. The first U.S. Marine unit had arrived in Danang and President Johnson had raised the draft. King generated a certain sense of urgency and a desire for action, which was very appealing to us. Finally somebody on the Right wanted to do something."

Churba and Kahane were certainly fortunate to meet Irving Brown and Jay Lovestone. The pair dominated the government's postwar policies toward the international labor movement. The men themselves were part of a vast network of former Communists turned hard-right CIA assets who were dedicated to waging a no-holds-barred war against Soviet aggression. "My father saved Western Europe," said Robert Brown. "Every time I drink good French wine I thank my father. Imagine what it meant for Churba and King to meet my father. They thought they were going to have it made."

The July Fourth Movement rented an office near Union Square in Manhattan. On June 29, 1965, a quarter-page ad appeared in *The New York Herald Tribune* announcing the formation of the organization. It was signed by "Joseph Churba, chairman and Michael King, director." Robert Brown and his childhood friend Roy Godson, then a graduate student in political science at Columbia University, became the group's student directors. Godson's father, Joseph, a close friend of both Irving Brown and Jay Lovestone, had been a labor attaché in the U.S. Embassy in London during the 1950s.*

Some twenty years after meeting Kahane, Roy Godson, by then a National Security Council consultant and a close friend of the late CIA chief William Casey, drew the attention of congressional committees investigating The Iran-contra scandal for his role as

---

* Joseph Godson owed his job to Lovestone, who as head of the International Labor Division of the AFL-CIO hand-picked virtually every major labor attaché post at U.S. embassies. After Joseph Godson retired from U.S. government service, he set up the London offices of the Labor Committee for Transatlantic Understanding and Georgetown University's Center for Strategic and International Studies.

middleman in a complex series of financial transactions to provide funds to Nicaraguan opposition groups at the behest of the Reagan White House. As early as 1983, the late Senator Edward Zorinsky of Nebraska had called for an investigation of Godson for allegedly using youth organizations and international youth exchanges for covert intelligence gathering.*

Roy Godson's hard-line, anti-Communist views and his penchant for using front groups was already evident when he teamed up with Kahane and Churba. Godson told me that he joined the July Fourth Movement to help "counteract the Communist-dominated student movements then prevalent on college campuses."

On July 4, 1965, *The New York Journal-American* published a story about the July Fourth Movement under a picture of the two leaders. The caption identified Rabbi Kahane as Michael King. "It [The July Fourth Movement] will try to fill the void in the colleges and among the young people of our cities where there seems to be no voice to answer back the Communist-inspired appeasement drives and the 'Let's get out of Viet Nam' crusades," said King. Kahane later explained that he went through some anxiety before allowing his picture to be taken. "But the man writing the story convinced me that Jews don't read *The Journal-American*," he said.

The movement never attracted the groundswell of student support that Kahane and Churba had expected. "What we had at NYU was me," Robert Brown recalled. "I was able to recruit a few people. Roy recruited a few people at Columbia." Kahane later claimed that he also established outposts at Fordham and the University of Wisconsin.

One of the movement's few activities other than recruiting students was to award a posthumous medal at a sparsely attended press conference to the parents of a Green Beret killed in Viet-

---

* A self-styled expert on Soviet front groups and disinformation techniques, Godson apparently has become involved in the funding of right-wing organizations in Europe and America. According to a U.S. government memo released during the Iran-contra hearings: "Roy Godson reported that he met earlier this week with a group of private donors that Charlie Wick brought to the sitroom two months ago. The group made their first commitment of $400,000, which includes support to Freedom House, a pro-INF group in Holland, Accuracy in Media [an ultra-right-wing media "watchdog" group in the United States], and a European-based labor program [possibly the Labor Committee for Transatlantic Understanding, whose London office his late father headed.]"

nam. "I remember giving the father the award," said Brown. "He was visibly shaken by what had happened to his son. Very little was said. He stood very erect. I still remember his eyes. They became small and very frightened and sad when I handed him the award. *The Journal-American* took some pictures and that was that.

"We did little worthwhile things like that, but then we ran out of money," Brown went on. "I remember calling individuals, trying to raise money because we couldn't pay the rent. Roy and I tried to get support by going to the various unions using our fathers' connections."

Meanwhile, Godson and Brown clashed with Kahane and Churba over how to spend the movement's dwindling bankroll. "The dispute centered on whether to spend funds on newspaper advertising or for actual organizing on campus," said Roy Godson, adding that Kahane and Churba were more interested in buying newspaper ads. Finally, after less than three months, Godson and Brown quit the movement. Churba, who was staying in the Hamptons for the summer, phoned Brown begging him not to desert. But by then, Brown says that he was thoroughly disenchanted with both men.

Although the July Fourth Movement never had enough money to pay its modest bills, Kahane and Churba always seemed to have plenty of cash for restaurants, booze, and women. In fact, much of the money that the two men raised during their partnership apparently went to support their lavish lifestyles. "They were uninhibited in bars," said Brown, who accompanied them on many of their cruising expeditions through the singles bars that then proliferated on Manhattan's Upper East Side. "They liked to drink. They loved beautiful women. Kahane lusted after them. We'd get drunk in bars and pick up girls. We were all interested in getting laid. Churba acted a little stiff around women, but Kahane was on fire. He had no problem going to bed with any woman as long as she was good-looking."

Brown recalls that Kahane was on good terms with the landlady of an East Side high-rise, who tipped him off when new women moved into the building. On one of his frequent visits, the landlady told Kahane that two stewardesses had just moved into a fourth floor apartment. Kahane and Brown dashed upstairs and rang the buzzer. "The door opened," said Brown, "and King just came crashing through. He was very funny. He began to joke about being a city health inspector. Before I knew it, he had dates with both girls. He had great moves on girls he didn't know.''

On nights that Kahane spent in Manhattan, he told Libby that he was in Washington on secret government business. If the deceit bothered him he never showed it. He was having too much fun. Sexual charisma was a power that he discovered somewhat late in life—and he was making up for lost time.

The merry prankster side of Kahane's personality also emerged, especially at the expense of his more up-tight partner. One story that Kahane often told over a drink in his favorite East Side bar, said Robert Brown, was about the ice goddess from Sweden that both he and Churba had desperately pursued, showering her with flowers and candy. The woman, who lived in their building, finally decided to reciprocate. One night, she knocked on their door with a plate of Swedish meatballs. Thinking it was Churba who had just stepped out to pick up a newspaper, the rabbi dropped his pants and opened the door waving his penis. It took weeks to scrape the meatballs off the ceiling, Kahane joked.

In June 1966, while living as Michael King, Rabbi Kahane met a twenty-one-year-old woman named Gloria Jean D'Argenio in a Second Avenue bar. The woman, who worked as a model under the name of Estelle Donna Evans, was more than just another one-night stand. Kahane fell in love with her.

Estelle had moved to New York when she was eighteen years old, in search of a modeling and acting career. The adopted daughter of a solid, working-class couple from Bridgeport, Connecticut, Estelle was like many single women who flock to New York in search of a glamorous career, yet never quite make it. Still, to all who knew her at that time, she was stunning, with smooth olive skin, long black hair, and a full figure. Kahane, captivated by her looks, played on her frailties.

Not long after they met, Kahane proposed marriage. He set the date for August 1, 1966—his birthday. He never told her his real name, nor that he was a rabbi with a wife and four children in Queens. He even visited her house in Bridgeport several times, telling her parents that he worked in a top-secret government job.

Two days before their wedding, Kahane ended the affair with a "Dear Jane" letter. He confessed that he was married, though he never admitted his true identity.

At about 4:30 A.M. on Saturday, July 30, a distraught Estelle Donna Evans walked along the lower level of the Queensboro Bridge near the Manhattan side with her roommate, Laura

Warner. Sobbing convulsively, Estelle asked her roommate how she could have been such a fool. Afraid that she was going to commit suicide, Laura broke away from her friend and ran toward a passing car and called out: "Help! Help! She wants to jump!" A motorist sped to the foot of the bridge and alerted the police, but not before Estelle bolted for the rail and plunged 135 feet into the East River. Incredibly, she survived. Severely injured, she was rescued by two policemen, who dived into the water from the Manhattan side of the river.

The suicide attempt made the front-page of the Sunday *New York Daily News*, complete with a photo of the officers straining to hold Estelle's head above water. The story said, "Miss Evans told police she had become despondent after receiving a letter from her boy friend breaking off their romance." The police found $183 in her handbag and a check drawn to her order for $137. They also reportedly found a letter from Michael King in which he ended their affair.

Estelle Donna Evans was rushed to Lenox Hill Hospital, where she underwent a two-hour operation for internal injuries. At 6:40 A.M. on August 1, she died. It was Meir Kahane's thirty-fourth birthday. Deeply depressed, Kahane attended her funeral where he dropped to his knees and cried out: "Oh my darling, please forgive me." In the years after her death, he would sometimes place roses on her grave.

Kahane told a few friends who knew about the affair that Estelle committed suicide after learning that she was dying from terminal cancer. According to a JDL source who was then close to Kahane, however, Estelle did not have cancer. But she was pregnant, possibly with Kahane's child.

Kahane later set up a charitable, tax-exempt foundation in the name of Estelle Donna Evans. By his own admission, the foundation raised more than $200,000. Fred and Edith Horowitz were the president and vice-president. Kahane claimed the money was given to Israel's poor, although he has no records and cannot document how the funds were spent. Kahane even advertised in Jewish publications that the foundation adopted orphans in Israel.* "The schtick was he would give you a picture of an

---

* "Throughout the land of Israel there are children who need help," began one ad. "Some are orphans, others from broken homes. . . . All these children need two things very much. One is money to better their own and their families' lives. The other is love and the knowledge that others care about them."

orphan kid and you'd adopt him,'' says former JDL official Irving Calderon. In reality, Kahane used the money to help finance the JDL, which he created in 1968.

In 1971, *New York Times* reporter Michael Kaufman was assigned to do a story about Kahane, by then the controversial leader of the JDL, which was waging a campaign of violent harassment against Soviet officials and their families in New York. Kaufman noticed that JDL publications carried ads for the Estelle Donna Evans Foundation. When asked about the fund, Kahane explained that she had worked as a secretary for one of his think tanks and had died tragically. He said her wealthy parents from Connecticut established the fund as a memorial.

Teamed up with fellow *Times* reporter Richard Severo, Kaufman soon exposed Kahane's lie. Severo first located Evans's parents, who recognized Kahane's photo as Michael King, their daughter's fiancé. Kaufman found Laura Warner at her apartment on the West Side of Manhattan. The ex-roommate confirmed that the ''Dear Jane'' letter was written by Kahane. Then the reporters flew to the United States Air University at Maxwell Air Force Base in Montgomery, Alabama where Churba was teaching Middle Eastern studies. ''It was a hot day and Churba started sweating,'' recalled Kaufman, who is now the assistant foreign editor of the *Times*. ''The half-circle sweat stains under his armpits began to grow. He confirmed that Kahane had had a physical relationship with Evans.''

Kaufman and Severo presented Kahane with their evidence at a New York television studio, where the JDL leader had just finished taping ''The David Susskind Show.'' ''The three of us went upstairs to a little office and I said to Kahane: 'Tell me about Donna,' '' Kaufman recalled. ''He reached over and put his hand on my knee and he said, 'I loved her.' '' Kahane completely unburdened himself to the startled reporters. He admitted that he had ''stumbled'' into Estelle in a Second Avenue bar where he often went to pick up women under a variety of pseudonyms. He confessed that with Estelle he had never known such passion, that they had lived together in an East Side apartment, that she was in the process of converting to Judaism, and that he knew that breaking off the affair had driven her to suicide. He also said that his relationship with Libby was ''unsatisfactory'' and that he felt his sex life was confined by the strictures of Orthodoxy.

"During the course of the conversation, Kahane appealed to Mike as a Jew not to hurt another Jew by including details of the affair in the *Times*," Severo recalled. "We were so repulsed by what we had collected, and it was such volatile stuff, that we drove to Arthur Gelb's house." Gelb was then the *Times* Metropolitan page editor. When Gelb heard what his reporters had learned, he phoned Abe Rosenthal, the *Times* managing editor, who joined them. Kaufman had composed a lead for the story that described a distraught Kahane placing roses on his dead lover's grave. Gelb and Rosenthal told Kaufman to rewrite the lead, deleting references to the rabbi's adulterous relationship. They argued that emphasizing the affair "would generate anti-Semitism," said Severo. Kaufman has a different recollection. He said that the editors decided that leading with the graveside scene would violate the *Times*'s standards of fairness.

Several days later, while Kaufman was polishing his story, Kahane turned up at the *Times*. Kaufman recalled:

> He told me a parable about the old rabbi and the young rabbi. The young rabbi says he wants to save all the Jews in the world. And as he grows older he says he wants to save all the Jews in Poland, and then when he grows much older he says he wants to save himself. And I said, you are that old Jew, and he said yes. Then he tried to make a deal. He promised he would disappear from public life if I didn't write what I knew about his dead lover. I said that's not my role. I'm not here to chastise you, but you have this Damocles sword hanging over your head. You're the one who put the ad in the JDL paper for the Estelle Donna Evans Foundation. He said, 'Yes, I know, but my mother has cancer; my wife is innocent; I have four children.' And then ensued a lot of soulsearching on my part, and a lot of conversations with my editors.

Although the *Times* would expose many sensational aspects of Kahane's career in a January 24, 1971, front-page story, only an elliptical reference was made to Evans. The *Times* reported that Kahane considered her "an unusual person," and that he was so shaken after her suicide that he attended her funeral, and in the year after she died he would sometimes place roses on her grave. There was no mention of the fact that they were lovers. "I wrote it in such a way that I knew he could manipulate the truth and explain to his wife and children that there was no truth to the rumors about him and Evans," Kaufman confessed.

Arthur Gelb, who in 1990 retired as the managing editor of the *Times*, told me that the paper knew a lot about the peccadilloes of powerful men in the 1960s, but it was a more innocent time "when a lot of sexual gossip was floating around that didn't make it into the paper," said Gelb. "Should papers have reported that President Kennedy was having sexual liaisons? There were reporters who knew, but it was never reported. I guess in those days a person's sexual life was his own business."

If the paper of record had published all it knew about Kahane, a self-righteous, Orthodox rabbi who constantly moralized about personal relationships, then perhaps both he and the JDL would have been destroyed. The *Times*'s skittishness, however, let Kahane dodge what almost certainly would have been a barrage of criticism. "We could have changed the history of Israel" had we publicized the affair, Richard Severo says today. "I wonder how many of his Orthodox supporters would have continued to follow him . . . if they knew the man was a charlatan?"

Perhaps Kahane unconsciously wanted to be exposed for the fraud that he was. He certainly invited discovery. Naming a JDL charity after his dead lover opened him up to pointed questions about the woman's true identity. Kahane was in the public eye, and he must have wondered what he would do if an enterprising reporter got hold of the story. His feelings of guilt over Estelle's suicide may have led him to risk his career and family as an act of atonement, but his narcissism and delusions of grandeur undoubtedly protected him from too much painful self-examination. In any case, this would not be the last time that Kahane would set himself up for humiliating failure.

Shortly after Evans's death, Fred Horowitz, who had given Kahane and Churba $20,000 for CRA, asked to see an accounting. Horowitz discovered that he had been swindled. Nearly all of CRA's checks had been made out to Churba or Kahane for cash to cover personal expenses. "I called both of them to my house," said Horowitz. "I grabbed them by the shirts and told them to pay me back or I'd break their heads. They did not refute what they had done. They did not apologize." Churba eventually settled with Horowitz for $5,000. "With Kahane it was much more difficult. He paid me about $2,000." Horowitz later sued

Kahane, winning a judgment, but when he could not collect, he let the matter drop.

Undeterred by the threat of scandal or by lawsuits, Churba and Kahane continued to promote the Vietnam War in the Orthodox Jewish community. President Lyndon Johnson had criticized American Jews for their broad-based opposition to his policies in Vietnam. Privately, he complained that most of the leaders of the burgeoning anti-war movement were Jewish. The American Jewish community's leadership tried to take a neutral stand on the war, not wanting to hurt Israel, which was dependent on U.S. aid. Not surprisingly, the most prominent Jewish leader to support Johnson's war effort was Israeli Prime Minister Golda Meir, who declared that she could not afford to betray the Jewish state's patron.

Kahane claims that the CIA covertly funded his lobbying efforts for the government's position on the Vietnam War among America's 400,000-strong Orthodox Jewish community. This is a credible claim, given that the CIA has long used religious organizations and clergy for both intelligence collection and covert operations. The Senate Select Committee on Intelligence revealed in 1976 that the CIA penetrated numerous domestic institutions during the Vietnam era, especially the National Student Association. Because Orthodox Jews traditionally took right-wing stands on most social and political issues, they appeared to offer fertile ground for the government's gung-ho views on Vietnam.

Kahane and Churba traveled around the United States and Canada promoting the Administration's views on college campuses, synagogues, and at parlor meetings. In 1967, the Association of Orthodox Jewish Scientists invited Kahane to speak at a gathering in the home of a professor of mathematics at Harvard. He struggled to convince his audience that Israel's fate was somehow linked to Vietnam, but found no takers, according to the professor who requested anonymity.

Kahane apparently had more success winning over the less sophisticated readers of *The Jewish Press*. By then an assistant editor of the paper, Kahane wrote a series called the "Jewish Stake in Vietnam." Vietnam might seem like an arcane subject for an Orthodox publication concerned primarily with Israel and religious law, but Kahane had already used the paper to publish densely written, multiple-part series on Chinese Communism and on Soviet Communism. In Kahane's roundabout view, communism was always linked to Arab resistance to Israel—a besieged country that would be placed in even greater jeopardy if the United States deserted Vietnam. "The marriage between the Arabs and the Chinese seems to have been consummated," Kahane wrote in *The Jewish Press* on February 17, 1967. "For Israel, the union is a foreboding sign of the future. As the power and the prestige of the Chinese Communists and their allies grows, the danger to Israel increases. Let the opponents of the U.S. efforts in Vietnam take note."

The first of Kahane's articles about the Jewish stake in Vietnam appeared in *The Jewish Press* in the winter of 1967. "All Americans have a stake in this grim war, but Jews have a very special interest in the successful outcome of this struggle," Kahane wrote in the introduction to the series, which appeared in boldface on the front page of the tabloid. "For whenever the Communist machine achieves power, not only are political, social, and economic rights swept away, but spiritual persecution is inevitable and mercilessly practiced. Because of this, it is vital that Jews realize the danger to their very survival as free human beings should Communism ever achieve victory."

Kahane also used his forum in *The Jewish Press* to blast liberal Jews for not supporting the Vietnam War. His reason was simple: liberal Jews who opposed the war would also sell out Israel. Kahane's undisguised hatred of liberals, particularly Jewish liberals, was by then a standard part of his repertoire. "I remember one discussion we had about liberals where he said they were basically self-hating masochists filled with guilt about the racial thing," Robert Brown recalled. But if the Jewish liberal was wracked by guilt, for Kahane, the Orthodox Jew was the standard-bearer of authentic Judaism, and as such could be counted on to defend Israel, support the war, and oppose communism. "It is the Orthodox Jewish community which has vocalized true American Jewish sentiment," Kahane wrote in May 1976. "Many Orthodox Jewish groups and individuals have spoken loudly and clearly in support of U.S. efforts in the war and why we are there."

Kahane even lobbied his Sunday School students in Laurelton, declaring that it was their obligation from a Torah point of view to join the army and fight in Vietnam. He called the Vietnam

War a *Milchemet Shel Mitzvah*—a holy war like the war of liberation that the Maccabees had waged against the Greeks, commemorated in the Jewish holiday Chanukah.

When several of Kahane's students announced that they were joining the army, Rabbi Rominek, who received calls from the children's outraged parents, warned Kahane that the community would turn on him if he did not dissuade the youths from enlisting. "What disturbed me," said Rabbi Rominek, "is that here he was writing in *The Jewish Press* as an idealist, concealing the fact that he and Churba actually had a financial stake in Vietnam. He was a rabbi using *The Jewish Press* like a pulpit to justify the Vietnam War. If some government agency was paying me to propagandize my congregants from the pulpit, what would that make me?"

In 1968, Kahane and Churba wrote a book, *The Jewish Stake in Vietnam*, which argued that if the United States reneged on its commitment to South Vietnam it would do the same to Israel. It was therefore vital for American Jews to support the war, though Kahane and Churba themselves never volunteered for military service. *The Jewish Stake* was published by Crossroads Publishing at 2 West Twenty-third Street in New York. Kahane told me that Crossroads Publishing had been funded by "the government" solely to distribute its pro-Vietnam polemic. *The Jewish Stake* listed Churba, Kahane, and Kahane's alter ego, Michael King, as its authors. They dedicated the book "to the enslaved Jews of Russia, with the fervent prayer for redemption." Kahane said that the book sold three thousand copies, though his claim is now impossible to verify.* "I didn't give a damn about Vietnam," Kahane later told me, adding that he wanted to keep America strong so that it would be able to protect Israel.

After the book came out, Churba drew Kahane, as Michael King, into another publishing venture, according to *The New York Times*. This book, another pro-Vietnam War polemic, was

---

* How likely is it that the CIA published *The Jewish Stake*? According to the Church Committee's comprehensive investigations of the CIA's covert operations, the CIA has sponsored or subsidized thousands of books and magazine and newspaper articles to spread disinformation at home and abroad. In 1967 alone, the CIA published two hundred books whose topics ranged from African safaris and wildlife to a translation of Machiavelli's *Prince* into Swahili. The FBI has refused my Freedom of Information Act request for its files on Crossroads Publishing on the grounds that disclosure would constitute an "unwarranted invasion of personal privacy," and would "disclose the identity of a confidential source."

to be financed by friends of Jay Lovestone and Irving Brown. The proposed backers included David Aldrich, whose father was a former U.S. diplomat. Aldrich told the *Times* in 1971 that he believed Churba was in the U.S. intelligence establishment, and that he had excellent sources and contacts. He also said that Churba introduced King to him "as an expert on infiltration and front groups." The book was dropped after Churba failed to get promised endorsements from top government officials.

At this point Churba and Kahane seemed to part company. Kahane became more involved with his editing job at *The Jewish Press* while Churba went on to pursue a stormy career in U.S. intelligence. Soon after Churba was hired as a special adviser on the Middle East by Air Force Intelligence in December 1972, an anonymous letter sent to the Justice Department accused him of being a security risk. The FBI launched an investigation, but could neither prove nor disprove the allegations, according to a U.S. government official who requested anonymity. At the time, Churba was considered the top U.S. contact with Israeli intelligence in the United States, the official said.

In October 1976, Churba told a *New York Times* reporter that there was a "tilt against Israel in the Defense Department" after General George S. Brown, then U.S. chairman of the Joint Chiefs of Staff, called Israel a "burden" to America. Churba also leaked to *The New York Times* an unpublished research paper that he had written called "What are America's Fundamental Interests in the Middle East?", which posited that Israel is a strategic asset to the United States. That concept, which guided U.S. foreign policy in the Middle East under the Reagan Administration, was novel in its day. Churba told *The Times* that his research paper's publication had been blocked by "anti-Semites in the Pentagon," and he characterized General Brown's remarks about Israel as "dangerously irresponsible." Churba lost his special security clearance and resigned.

Yet he was not banished from politics. In 1977, Churba assembled a list of "pro-Arab" bureaucrats in the Pentagon and the National Security Council who he believed should be removed from their jobs because they did not "understand" Israel's special security needs, according to former government officials. He allegedly gave the list to the late Senator Richard Stone of Florida, then a member of the Senate Foreign Relations Committee and chairman of the Subcommittee on Near Eastern and

South Asian Affairs, which had jurisdiction over the Middle East. Stone summoned several high-ranking officials to his office and interrogated them about their views on Israel. Later, Stone, who was Jewish, presented the list to then National Security Advisor Zbigniew Brzezinski. A spokesman for Brzezinski told *The Washington Post* that his boss found the meeting with Stone "interesting" and "helpful," although no one that Stone allegedly had targeted was fired. Nevertheless, according to one official who was grilled by Stone, the witch-hunt had a chilling effect on government officials whose views ran counter to the powerful pro-Israel lobby.

In 1980, Churba became an adviser to the transition team of President-elect Ronald Reagan, writing position papers on the Middle East and on defense policy.* But he lost the post after he declared in a speech in Johannesburg that the United States should support the apartheid regime. Subsequently, he was appointed senior policy advisor to the U.S. Arms Control and Disarmament Agency, where he remained until 1982. He then founded the Unification Church–funded Center for International Security—an organization of former military and intelligence officers dedicated to promoting their hard-line positions. In a 1984 book, *The American Retreat*, Churba accused Reagan of failing to build up America's defense despite record military budgets, of cheating on campaign pledges of unqualified support for Israel by making Saudi Arabia the keystone of his Middle East policies, and of underassessing the Marxist thrust in Latin America. More recently, in October 1986, Churba's think tank held a conference in Tel Aviv on the subject of terrorism. The panelists included Peter Goldman, then the director of the far-right, pro-Israel lobby group Americans for a Safe Israel, who

---

* The Brookings Institution's Middle East expert William Quandt notes that an article by Reagan called "Recognizing the Israeli Asset," which appeared in *The Washington Post* in August 1979, "suggests the influence of Joseph Churba . . . who may have well been the ghostwriter . . . ." The similarity in the rhetorical flourishes, the line of argument, and the key passage in Reagan's article and a passage in Churba's 1977 book, *The Politics of Defeat: America's Decline in the Middle East*, "suggests either a single author for both or plagiarism," wrote Quandt in *The Middle East, Ten Years After Camp David*. Reagan's article says: "The Carter administration has yet to grasp that in this region conflict and tension are endemic, a condition traceable largely to the fragmented sectarian nature of Middle Eastern society." In his book, Churba wrote about "the conflict and tension endemic to the [Middle East] region. This condition is traceable largely to the sectarian and fragmented nature of Middle East society."

subsequently became a leader of Kahane's Kach Party in America, and Rafi Eytan, Mossad's former chief of operations who was then running Israeli spy Jonathan Jay Pollard—a U.S. naval intelligence officer who received a life sentence in 1987 for passing U.S. military secrets, including top-secret codes, to Israel.

Churba's role as the conscience of the fire-eating far Right has brought him the kind of wealth and power that he could only dream about when he was a youngster sharing a pot of beans and rice with his twelve brothers and sisters, his chronically ill mother, and his austere and demanding father. From his luxury penthouse at the top of the Crystal Gateway in Washington, the flamboyant fifty-five-year-old bachelor holds court with some of the most notorious right-wing characters in the world. That is, with all but his boyhood chum, Meir Kahane. Or so he says.

Churba claims that he has had nothing to do with Kahane since 1968. "He is a danger to Israel and the Jewish people," he told me in a brief 1984 telephone interview. But according to several former top JDL officials, Churba was instrumental in helping Kahane set up the JDL—an organization that initially was not unlike other front groups that the two men had concocted. Moreover, according to Sonia Kahane and several well-connected Kach sympathizers in Israel, Churba still visits Meir in Jerusalem.

I asked retired General George Keegan, former head of Air Force Intelligence, why he hired Churba for such a sensitive job after his less than distinguished years with Kahane. Keegan dismissed Churba's earlier escapades with Kahane as youthful exuberance. Almost as an afterthought, he linked Churba to the JDL—an association that Churba categorically denies. "I was aware . . . Joe was involved with the JDL," Keegan told me. "It was a phase he went through, which I considered very carefully before I had him come to work with me."

Despite running what he calls an exhaustive background check on Churba ("I knew every day of his life," claimed Keegan), the General said that he knew nothing about Churba's and Kahane's July Fourth Movement, their alleged penetration of the Birch Society, their book about Vietnam, or even the 1971 *New York Times* exposé. "I hired him because he was the finest scholar on the Middle East I could find in the country. . . . I consider him to be one of the most extraordinary and perceptive defenders of the faith of the Republican society! He just took a while to grow up. He's a very emotional fellow—or was."

Kahane is also driven by his passions. When asked to explain why he worked as an informant and propagandist for the government during the 1960s, he declared that he did it for the sake of his fellow Jews. "My concern with the Birchers and with the left-wing student movement was always a Jewish one," he told me in 1984. "I saw a growing sense of isolation on the part of Americans from world affairs. To keep our noses out of world affairs is not good for Jews. After Vietnam, I knew the days of American Jewry were numbered. America was a paper tiger. It would never fight for Israel."

Kahane still likes to boast about his underground years. He uses tales of his exploits as a covert agent to impress his youthful followers. Yet there remains one aspect of that period that he chooses to bury—his affair with Estelle Donna Evans. In 1984, he told the *Long Island Jewish World* that "there is no truth to the allegations" that he and the woman were lovers. "I make it a rule never to debase myself by responding to these kinds of charges." In 1988, he told *Newsday* that Evans was his secretary and that together they had infiltrated the Birchers for the FBI. "They gave us new identities," he said.

Although Kahane has deliberately obscured his past, one thing is certain: by the time he created the JDL in 1968, his modus operandi was set. An Orthodox rabbi who hides behind a facade of piety, he would never completely abandon the world of illicit sex, easy money, and covert action. Perhaps if Kahane had passed the New York State bar exam, or had successfully made his conservative synagogue at Howard Beach more Orthodox, or had been embraced by the religious establishment in Israel during his unhappy visit there, his destructive sexual encounter with Evans, his cloak-and-dagger escapades, and his eventual founding of the violence-prone JDL and the anti-Arab Kach Party would not have followed with the inexorable logic of Greek tragedy.

CHAPTER SIX
Every Jew a .22

It was no accident that Meir Kahane founded the JDL in 1968—the pivotal year of a tortured decade. It was the year when Black Americans rioted in 168 cities, when college campuses were hotbeds of radical protest, when high school students staged more than 2,000 classroom rebellions, when Bobby Kennedy and Martin Luther King were assassinated, and when FBI boss J. Edgar Hoover cranked up a massive domestic spy operation, fearing that America was on the verge of revolution.

Kahane realized that the time was ripe to cast about for a new cause that he could transform into a movement important enough to satisfy his rampant ego. The thirty-seven-year-old rabbi had taken his career as Michael King, such as it was, about as far as it could go. It did not take a genius to recognize that racial tension in New York was escalating, especially in the Orthodox and white ethnic working-class neighborhoods, which were becoming home to growing numbers of poor Blacks and Hispanics. Combined with minority demands for jobs, open housing, and open admission to city universities, the polarization in New York over race was on the verge of exploding into violence.

Out of this racial turmoil, Kahane built the JDL. Its mission ostensibly was to preserve Jewish political power and to protect Jews too old or too poor to leave America's decaying inner cities where, Kahane claims, they were victims of Black street crime, which had skyrocketed in the 1960s.

If nothing else, the JDL demonstrated Kahane's enormous talent for marketing. Preaching Jewish pride and Jewish power, he captured the imagination of thousands of Jews, particularly from the lower-middle-class sections of Brooklyn and Queens that were near Black ghettos. His slogans were "Never Again" and "Every Jew a .22." With a Torah in one hand and a gun in the other, Kahane set up a weapons and martial arts training camp in the Catskill Mountains in New York State, just a shotgun blast away from Grossingers, the famed Jewish-owned hotel. A handful of his elite bodyguards, known as "*Chayas*" (Hebrew for animals), were trained in munitions and sharpshooting in Israel by former officers of the Irgun and the Stern Gang. Soon the JDL graduated from confronting Black militants to bombing Russian and Arab embassies and beating and harassing Russian and Arab diplomats in Europe and the United States. It seemed that post-Holocaust Jews had found a firebrand who would speak and fight for their interests.

Ultimately, however, the JDL would become little more than a fundraising vehicle for Kahane. Far from defending anyone, he would use the organization to soak thousands of anxiety-ridden Jews for millions of dollars.

"Confrontation made headlines, and headlines brought in dollars and power," said Rabbi Elyahu Rominek. "Therefore, confrontation served Kahane's ends. Whether the issue was the Negro or Russian Jews, he sought out confrontation to advance his career. He said he was the fire extinguisher, but he actually fanned the flames of hatred and destruction. He said he was coming to the Jewish community's rescue, but he actually created its problems."

* * *

The Jewish Defense League was conceived one overcast Saturday afternoon in May 1968, following morning services at Laurelton's Young Israel Synagogue. The group's three founders resembled anything but freedom fighters. Joining Kahane in the synagogue were Bertram Zweibon, a pudgy, pugnacious probate lawyer whose father had been a colleague of Jay Lovestone's in the Communist Party and whose uncle had been a cofounder of Betar in America, and Morton Dolinsky, a loud, loopy PR man who ironically had masterminded Betar's kidnapping of Kahane some two decades earlier. The trio had one thing in common besides their allegiance to right-wing Zionism—an intense hostility to Blacks. The growing militancy among American Blacks and their demands for affirmative action and community control, frightened the men. More than that, they did not want to watch helplessly as their neat, tree-lined, predominantly Jewish neighborhood was inundated with Blacks from surrounding, less affluent areas. "Laurelton homeowners didn't want Blacks in!" says Dolinsky emphatically. "We knew what would happen to property values." Of course, Dolinsky's fears about integration were widely shared by whites across America.

The prophetic tradition of Judaism teaches Jews to fight social injustice. As far as the three men were concerned, it was Jews who were being mistreated by Blacks who were moving into their neighborhoods, taking over their schools, and turning their streets into battle zones of drugs and crime. It was Jewish civil rights, they asserted, that needed to be defended!

By the late 1960s, Kahane had begun to write in *The Jewish Press* about the likelihood of an impending holocaust, skillfully juxtaposing images of strutting Black militants with goose-stepping Nazis. He told me that the newsroom of *The Jewish Press*, where he worked as an associate editor in 1967 and 1968, was flooded with disturbing items about anti-Semitic acts all over the country—including, Kahane said, numerous, brutal acts of violence by Blacks and Puerto Ricans against Jews. Behind every outbreak of urban disorder, he wrote in *The Jewish Press*, was the hand of militant Blacks who were trying to "control our cities and establish a Black Klanism."

To be sure, a fiery generation of radical Black leaders had singled out the Jewish community for criticism, ignoring the decades-long, Jewish-Black alliance in the struggle for civil rights. "In every major ghetto, Jews own the major businesses," charged Black Muslim leader Malcolm X. "Every night, the owners of those businesses go home with that Black community's money, which helps the ghetto stay poor." Stokely Carmichael denounced Zionism, equating it with racism and vowing to liquidate it "wherever it exists, be it in the ghettos of the United States or in the Middle East." Black poet Leroi Jones called Judaism a "dangerous, germ culture."

Kahane claims that when he expressed concern about growing Black anti-Semitism to leaders of major Jewish organizations, they told him to suppress the news to avoid aggravating the situation. "The blindness and negligence of the Jewish Establishment is criminal," he wrote. The apparent indifference to the fate of Jews trapped in transitional neighborhoods created a vacuum that Kahane and his friends decided to fill.

Unsure about what form a militant Jewish self-defense organization should take, the men sat in the Laurelton synagogue arguing about what to name it. Dolinsky proposed calling it "The Protocols of the Elders of Zion," after the fraudulent tract first printed in Russia in 1905 by the Czarist secret police that purported to be a Jewish plan for world domination. "Every anti-Semite was sure of its existence," said Dolinsky, who now lives in Jerusalem where he briefly served as head of the Israeli Government Press Office during the Begin Administration. "It had name recognition. And if the Jewish establishment didn't like it, too fucking bad! We had spent our whole youth in Betar fighting the organized Jewish community— so going up against the establishment was perfectly natural." In the end, Kahane opted for a less incendiary title—the Jewish Defense Corps, which later became the Jewish Defense League.

On May 24, 1968, Kahane took out a small advertisement in *The Jewish Press* seeking Jews interested in "Jewish Pride"— the first step in organizing the JDL. In the weeks leading up to the JDL's inaugural meeting in June, Kahane churned out a steady stream of noxious stories in *The Jewish Press*—many splashed across the tabloid's front page—about Black anti-Semitism in New York. He did this with the blessing of the paper's top editors and its publisher, Sholom Klass. Managing editor Yehuda Schwartz, the publisher's son-in-law, and senior editor Chaim Lipshitz, a politically well-connected rabbi who sometimes opened Congress with a Jewish prayer, signed the JDL's incorporation papers.

Even before Kahane became the dominant editorial voice of the paper, *The Jewish Press* treated its readers to outlandish stories about gentile men's insatiable lust for Jewish women and Syrian poison gas attacks on Israel that never took place. "The paper was a cartoon," said Dolinsky. "It was written in an awkward English that read like it was translated from Yiddish. Still, it was a powerful platform that made Kahane."

The support that the Klass clan provided Kahane was more than just a street-corner soapbox. *The Jewish Press* gave him entrée into tens of thousands of Jewish living rooms every week, where he played on the fears that Jews have carried with them for two thousand years. Klass stuck with Kahane no matter how outrageous his conduct, no matter how many world-renowned Orthodox Jewish leaders told him to dump the militant rabbi. That is, until the day Klass had to choose between the principal cause that he advocated and his pocketbook.

The JDL's first meeting was held on Tuesday June 18, 1968, at 8:30 P.M. at the West Side Jewish Center on West 34th Street in Manhattan. The synagogue is still run by Rabbi Shlomo Kahane, Meir's first cousin. Meir Kahane had just returned from a week-long trip to Israel where he successfully sought support for his nascent movement from Menachem Begin and other high-ranking Revisionist leaders. During his brief stay, Kahane traveled around the newly conquered Arab territories and was swept up in the post-Six Day War euphoria that gripped Israel.

Zweibon remembers the first meeting as "a rather balanced affair. Kahane had not yet warmed up to his oratorical peak. . . . It was a studied, concerned meeting that didn't draw the usual crowd of kooks we later became accustomed to." Most of the thirty-five people in attendance were professional men. One, Jerome Hornblass, now an acting New York State Supreme Court justice, helped Kahane launch the movement.

The main topic of discussion that night was the May 8th reassignment of nineteen teachers by a Black-run district school board in Ocean Hill-Brownsville, formerly a predominantly Jewish neighborhood in Brooklyn that had become a Black slum. The New York City Board of Education had begun experimenting with a plan for school decentralization designed to give communities, especially minority communities, greater control over their children's education. Kahane cried racism when the white teachers, most of whom were Jewish, were summarily reassigned. To Kahane, decentralization signaled the death knell of the government-administered merit system, which had allowed Jews who entered the civil service to progress so far in New York.

Dressed casually in gray slacks and a white shirt open at the neck, Kahane circled the small but attentive audience as he issued stinging denunciations of mainstream Jewish organizations for failing to discern "what the dullest cretin could understand"—

that "Black-Jew hatred" was rampant in the land. He ridiculed the Jewish establishment for supporting Black civil rights at a time when the hard-won political power of Jews in New York was being eroded. He accused the "liberal do-nothing" mayor of New York, John Lindsay, of pandering to Blacks, rather than cracking down on Black street crime. It was time, Kahane declared, to form a militant group that would not only put Jewish socioeconomic interests first, but would also instill Jewish pride—especially in Jewish youth, who, in his view, were drifting to the Left and away from Israel. "I was very upset that young Jews didn't give a damn about being Jewish anymore," Kahane later told me. "They were fighting for Blacks, for the Vietcong, for Cubans, for lettuce, but not for themselves."

Typically, Kahane's sales pitch ended with a plea for money, equating the survival of the JDL with that of the Jewish people. "We are talking of Jewish survival," he declared. "To turn the other cheek is not a Jewish concept. Do not listen to the soothing anesthesia of the establishment. They walk in the paths of those whose timidity helped to bury our brothers and sisters less than thirty years ago."

The day after the meeting in his cousin's West Side synagogue, Kahane opened the JDL's first office at 156 Fifth Avenue in Manhattan. The rent was $200 a month. His mother, Sonia, was ensconced as the JDL secretary. Mother and son were ready for battle. They did not have to wait long. That same day, Kahane traveled to Washington to testify in front of the House Committee on Un-American Activities (HUAC)—the redbaiting committee that hunted down Americans whose political views had strayed beyond the narrow bounds set during the McCarthy era. It was Kahane's first official act as head of the JDL.

Kahane's testimony was arranged by Herbert Romerstein, HUAC's investigator in New York. Like Irving Brown and Jay Lovestone, Romerstein had been an official of the American Communist Party before undergoing a conversion to militant anti-communism. [While Romerstein worked at the United States Information Agency as an expert on Soviet disinformation in the 1980s, the agency set up the International Youth Year Commission, which it used as a conduit for funding the contras. A leader of the commission was none other than Roy Godson.]

Romerstein was a frequent visitor to *The Jewish Press*, where he was friendly with the paper's editors and publisher. Long impressed with Kahane's writing, Romerstein remembers "schlepping" Kahane down to Washington on the day of his testimony. "He forgot his *tefillin* and he had to go all the way back home to get it." On the train ride to the nation's capital, Kahane talked about the JDL. "His attitude was he wouldn't use violence, but rather he thought he could intimidate people by threatening violence," Romerstein told me. "This was before the Weathermen bombings started and before the SDS* Days of Rage in Chicago. All the radical groups were talking violence and revolution. But revolutionaries have to make revolutions, and Kahane's idea was he could simply talk about it. . . . I think at the time he actually believed that he was not going to do anything bad."

Not surprisingly, the former FBI informant came prepared to name names. And just as predictably, the objects of Kahane's scorn were fellow Jews whose views he found pernicious. According to his published testimony, Kahane introduced himself to HUAC as a founder of "a group called the Jewish Defense League, which is currently being organized to defend Jewish people against anti-Semitism and to defend this country against various extremist groups, such as the Communists and the Black nationalists, functioning at the present time." Kahane spoke for more than an hour about a fifteen-year study of communism and Soviet anti-Semitism that he claimed to have made. Following a lunch break, Congressman Albert W. Watson of South Carolina asked Kahane to enlighten the committee about the activities of the American Council of Judaism (ACJ)—a small, maverick group that opposed Zionism. "Ordinarily, I hesitate to comment on other Jewish organizations," Kahane disingenuously replied. "However, in this case since you have asked me, I thank you for asking me." Kahane called the ACJ and its president, Richard Korn, agents of a Soviet-Arab plot to destroy Israel. He offered no proof for his allegations. "It is an anti-Zionist and, in a sense, truly anti-Semitic group," he concluded.

Kahane's testimony impressed the committee. "It was well documented and scholarly in the sense that he showed a thorough knowledge of the study of basic Soviet doctrine and actions," Francis J. McNamara, HUAC's director from 1962 to 1969, told me.

* Students for a Democratic Society was a left-wing student organization that staged numerous protests against the Vietnam War.

HUAC was so impressed with Kahane that its operatives began to work closely with the JDL. According to Zweibon and Allan Mallenbaum, the JDL's first administrative director, Romerstein and another HUAC agent were constantly traipsing in and out of the JDL's Fifth Avenue office, trading information on militant Blacks and other so-called subversives, usually on the Left. "Kahane regularly closeted himself with the government men," said Zweibon, who added that the HUAC men had an office at JDL headquarters that was off limits to the rest of the JDL members.

Of course, the JDL was not alone in this regard. According to Victor Navasky, two mainstream Jewish defense organizations, the American Jewish Committee and the Anti-Defamation League of the B'nai B'rith, worked closely with HUAC, sharing investigative files on prospective witnesses. "In their attempt to protect the reputation of the organized Jewish community, these Jewish organizations with the best motives accepted the premise of the internal security establishment with whom they were collaborating behind the scenes," wrote Navasky in *Naming Names*. "Such conduct gave HUAC a more respectable frame of reference, thus dignifying a committee whose conduct deserved to be denounced, and making it acceptable to ordinary people."

In addition to HUAC, Kahane also pulled in financing and support from Churba's hawkish friends in the intelligence community—an invisible government that operates in the shadows, cloaked behind the veil of national security that allows it to hide from the public and Congress. Churba himself was instrumental in helping the JDL get off the ground. Certainly, the JDL was not unlike other front groups that Churba and Kahane had set up to promote issues dear to the government. "Unlike the July Fourth Movement, however, the JDL took hold," said Zweibon. "The JDL had an impact on campus. It turned many left-wing Jewish students to the Right, and it helped to counteract the Left and Blacks. The government's cause was served." For a time, that is. By 1970, the JDL was running amok like Frankenstein's monster, nearly wrecking détente. "We picked the wrong man" to head the JDL, Churba later told a former JDL official—another indication that the militant Jewish group initially may have been sanctioned by an arm of the government.

At noon on August 5, 1968, the JDL staged its first demonstration. It was held at New York University to protest against the hiring of John F. Hatchett, who had been selected to head the Martin Luther King, Jr. Afro-American Student Center. Several months before his appointment, Hatchett had earned the enmity of some Jews for writing an article in the *African-American Teachers Forum*, in which he claimed that Jews "dominate and control" New York schools, "where Black children were mentally poisoned. . . . This spells death for the minds and souls of our Black children."

Kahane and twelve followers picketed NYU for about an hour, chanting "no Nazis at NYU, Jewish rights are precious too." The following day, the demonstration made the morning papers, including *The New York Times*, which over the next few years eagerly covered the JDL's adventures, giving visibility to the movement.

The JDL staged several other highly publicized demonstrations to protest against "Black anti-Semitism" following its march on NYU. But just as the JDL began gaining momentum, Kahane was forced to devote more time to supporting his family. He became the rabbi of the Rochdale Village Traditional Synagogue, which was in a low-income, predominantly white Queens housing complex surrounded by Black slums. He also started teaching Jewish philosophy at Yeshiva-Central Queens, a private day school. Several of Kahane's associates speculated that he had become less active in the JDL because he had had second thoughts about where his militant fervor would lead him. Maybe the impatient rabbi viewed the JDL as a slow boat to stardom. He certainly had a history of starting groups only to abandon them. Perhaps he even got lonely driving around Black ghettos in a JDL sound truck by himself at night warning "the *Schvartzes*" (the word in Yiddish for Black, which has taken on a pejorative connotation) to keep their hands off Jews. Kahane kept up his drumbeat of hatred in *The Jewish Press*, letting others direct the day-to-day activities of the nascent movement. But by January 1969, with enough cash coming into the JDL to pay Kahane a decent salary, he reemerged to lead the militant group into the world of vigilante violence and terrorism. There would be no turning back.

Two issues consumed Kahane in 1969—combating Black militancy and unseating Mayor John Lindsay, who was up for reelection. The issues coalesced around the September 1968 teachers' strike, which had shut down the New York City school system. One aim of the striking teachers' union, which was 90 percent white and 60 percent Jewish, was to remove the flamboyant, pipe-smoking Ocean Hill-Brownsville district school board chief, Rhody McCoy, a Black man who had recently reassigned nineteen white teachers without any form of due process. The strike was accompanied by racial violence and extremism on both sides. Albert Shanker, the president of the United Federation of Teachers, made sure that every verbal attack on the union by radical Black groups, no matter how obscure, was given massive publicity. White parents rushed to send their children to private schools. Housing prices in the suburbs leapt by 15 percent. Mayor Lindsay tried to steer a middle course between the Black community and the Jewish-dominated teachers' union. In response, the union took out a full-page ad in *The New York Times*, accusing the mayor of "vacillation, indecision, permissiveness, and backtracking." Jewish schoolteachers, meanwhile, flocked to the JDL.

Suddenly, JDL goon squads seemed to be everywhere, brawling at school board meetings, heckling and beating up anti-war protestors, phoning death threats in the middle of the night to Black leaders and Jewish liberals. The JDL's first demonstration in 1969 was staged in January in Brownsville against Leslie Campbell, a Black teacher who had criticized Jews for controlling the teachers' union. A few weeks later, Kahane led several dozen club-wielding JDL members on a raid against WBAI, a left-wing radio station in Manhattan where Campbell had read an anti-Semitic poem on the air dedicated to Albert Shanker:

Hey, Jew boy, with that yarmulke on your head,
You pale-faced Jew boy, I wish you were dead.
I can see you Jew boy—no, you cannot hide,
I got a gun scope on you—yeh, you gonna die. . . .

You came to America, the land of the free,
And took over the school system to perpetuate
                    white supremacy.
Guess you know, Jew boy, there's only one reason you
                    made it—
You had a clean white face, colorless and faded. . . .

Twelve JDL members were arrested at WBAI for trespassing and assault. Over the next few weeks, the JDL precipitated melee after melee. On February 24, the JDL was involved in a brawl at PS 261 in Brooklyn after it was called in by Jewish teachers to oppose a militant Black parents group; on February 25, burly JDLers took over a board of education meeting; on March 10, the JDL escorted Gideon Goldberg, dean of students of Eastern District High School, past crowds of jeering Blacks into his own school. On March 16, JDL picketers jostled Mayor Lindsay as he entered a board of education meeting.

Kahane basked in the publicity, reveling in the comparisons made in the media between his tactics and those of Black militants, whose techniques for manipulating the media he carefully studied. "The Talmud says, 'Who is wise? He who learns from all people,' " Kahane boasted. "We are happy when people call us Panthers, because we know a Panther doesn't mess with a Panther."

One of Kahane's most ingenious media events was his public feud with Black militant leader James Forman, who announced in May 1969 that he was going to lead a march on the prestigious Temple Emanuel on Manhattan's Upper East Side to demand reparations from the Jewish community. Kahane responded by surrounding the temple with armed JDL youth. On June 24th, Kahane took out a full-page ad in *The New York Times* that pictured a group of young JDL toughs in combat fatigues and berets, brandishing lead pipes and baseball bats, defying Forman to make good his threat. Forman never showed. But the ad, which appeared under the title, "Is this any way for a nice Jewish boy to behave?" undoubtedly shocked the staid American Jewish establishment more than Black militants like the Panthers, whose urban macho pose the JDL self-consciously imitated. The ad certainly helped the JDL inch its way up the chart of 1960s radical respectability. "I hate your politics, but I love your tactics," Yippie leader Abbie Hoffman teased Kahane on a New York radio talk show.

The FBI watched the deepening conflict between New York City's Black and Jewish communities with growing pleasure. These guardians of the public order had been working behind the scenes for years to crush Black nationalism and the civil rights movement, which the Bureau believed were controlled by Communist subversives agitating normally docile Blacks into protesting segregation.

In 1956, the FBI had begun a massive campaign to disrupt organizations that Bureau officials disliked. The campaign, known as COINTELPRO (counterintelligence program), grew out of J. Edgar Hoover's frustration with Supreme Court rulings limiting the government's power to neutralize so-called dissident groups. Hoover's first target was the American Communist Party. The program was later expanded to include mainstream civil rights groups and activists like Martin Luther King and anti-war groups and protesters like Dr. Benjamin Spock, as well as white hate groups like the Ku Klux Klan.

In the summer of 1967, with urban disorder spreading like a firestorm, the FBI set up a new, top-secret counterintelligence program directed against Black nationalist groups like the Black Panthers. Not surprisingly, the FBI took advantage of the New York City teachers' strike to whip up a white backlash against the Black community, according to FBI memorandums detailing the Bureau's campaign, which I obtained. The Bureau's arsenal of dirty tricks included mailing racist letters purportedly written by Black extremists to white school teachers and union officials.

Hoover and the men around him were primitive racists who, according to declassified FBI documents, talked about prominent Black leaders as though they were worthless subhumans. Pulitzer Prize-winning author David Garrow observes in *The FBI and Martin Luther King, Jr.* that "the Bureau set out to destroy Black leaders simply because they were Black leaders." Hoover's vendetta against King was so extreme that the Bureau tape-recorded evidence of King's extra-marital affairs, and then sent the civil rights leader letters that urged him to commit suicide. Similarly, in the 1950s and 1960s, Garrow says, the FBI "spared no effort to uncover Communist infiltration of the NAACP" in order to discredit the organization. (Hoover's illegal conduct has been exhaustively examined by two congressional committees investigating FBI abuses.)

The FBI's plan to use Kahane and the JDL in its counterintelligence program to disrupt Black nationalist groups was first mentioned in a September 5, 1969 memo from the Bureau's New York Office (NYO) to FBI Director J. Edgar Hoover. Under a section entitled "Operations Under Consideration," it states: "The NYO is presently considering an attempt to contact and establish some rapport with the Jewish Defense League in order to be in a position to furnish it with information the Bureau wishes to see utilized in a counter-intelligence technique. . . ."

In what appears to be a follow-up memo dated September 10, 1969, the director of the Bureau's New York Office wrote to Hoover, recommending that the FBI establish contact specifically with Kahane for "counter-intelligence purposes." "The individual with JEDEL [the FBI's early acronym for the JDL] who would most suitably serve the above stated purpose would be Rabbi Meir Kahane, a Director of JEDEL," says the internal FBI memorandum. "It is noted that Rabbi Kahane's background as a writer for the NY newspaper *The Jewish Press* would enable him to give widespread coverage of anti-Semitic statements made by the BPP [Black Panther Party] and other Black Nationalist hate groups."

A September 22, 1969 memo from G.C. Moore, head of Division Five, the FBI's "racial intelligence section," to the Bureau's number-two man, W.C. Sullivan, requested that the New York office be permitted to use the JDL against the Panthers:

Attached is a letter authorizing the New York Office to mail an anonymous communication, purportedly from the father of a Black extremist, to a leader of a Jewish group called the Jewish Defense League. This communication seeks to establish a relationship between the sender and JEDEL for the purpose of furnishing JEDEL with instances of anti-Semitism by the Black Panther Party and other extremist groups.

JEDEL is a Jewish vigilante-type organization formed and operated in New York City. Its aims and purposes are to protect Jewish people from all sorts of anti-Semitism. At this time its aims and purposes are not of an illegal nature and apparently not political. The Black Panther Party, as well as other extremist groups, are anti-Semitic in nature. Many instances of anti-Semitism by the BPP have been noted. This information, when placed in the hands of JEDEL, could easily operate against the best interest of the BPP with resultant disruption.

JEDEL is apparently financially well-off and has access to newspaper coverage. It is our intent to create a fictitious source of information who will furnish public source data to Rabbi Meir Kahane. . . . It is expected that the information will ultimately be published and cause embarrassment to the BPP and other extremist groups.

New York has proposed the mailing of an anonymous letter from a pro-Jewish Negro father of a BPP member. The
letter is addressed to Rabbi Kahane and professes sympathy and friendship for the Jews and criticism of the BPP.
It leaves the way open for additional communications.

RECOMMENDATION: that attached letter granting New
York authority to mail the suggested communication be
approved and forwarded. This letter insures that strict security be maintained and the communication be prepared on
commercially purchased paper and envelope.

Pitting extremist groups against each other like gladiators in
ancient Rome was a tried and true FBI tactic. Hoover must have
loved the idea of using Kahane to attack the Panthers, whom
he once called the "greatest threat to the internal security of
the country." Soon the FBI began to send the JDL leader
"reports" about the Panthers' alleged anti-Semitic and anti-
Zionist activities. Kahane promptly regurgitated the FBI's "facts"
in his *Jewish Press* column, "Spotlight on Extremism," which
became a clearing house for the fecund minds at Division Five.
Ironically, at the same time as Kahane was dutifully publishing
"exposés" on extremist groups, he began to receive threatening letters ostensibly from Black extremists, but actually written by federal agents. One such letter sent to Kahane declared:
"We will get you one by one. Israel will have to be destroyed.
Too much Jewish Political Power now. In the future it will be
Black power. (signed) The New Era Black Boys."

The FBI was playing a dangerous game. The JDL was no match
for the street-tough Panthers. Nevertheless, on May 5, 1970,
Kahane announced at a press conference that the JDL was going
to stage an armed demonstration against the New York Black
Panther Party on its own turf in Harlem. Founded in Oakland
in 1966, the Black Panther Party was composed of slum-bred,
self-styled revolutionaries who called for the overthrow of "the
racist white power structure in America." Unlike white student
radicals, the Panthers not only carried guns, but also used them,
sometimes with deadly effect. "The Panthers called me about
a reported JDL demonstration," recalled Jerry Lefcourt, a prominent New York attorney who represented the Panthers, "and
I just begged them to let it go. The Panthers wanted to rip them
apart. I had all I could do to protect the JDL."

The Bureau's Black-baiting nearly turned into tragedy when on an overcast spring morning on May 7, 1970, a rented Hertz truck loaded with chains, sticks, and numchucks pulled up in front of the Black Panther headquarters on 123rd Street and Lenox Avenue. About thirty-five uniformed and bereted young JDL members piled out of the vehicle unfurling a five-foot banner bearing the League's logo—a clenched fist thrust through a Star of David. "We jumped out of the truck and stood facing Panther headquarters, arms folded, with a grim look on our faces," recalled former JDL member Arnie Beiber, who added that Kahane had pumped them up by constantly comparing the Panthers to Nazis.

Dozens of Panthers poured out of their store-front office swinging clubs, chains, and baseball bats. "The police got there fairly quickly and tried to separate us," said Beiber. "I got a broomstick broken over my head." As the fracas began, Kahane scrambled on top of the Hertz truck with a bullhorn, yelling various JDL slogans and slinging crude slurs at the Panthers. "When it looked like it was getting really hairy, Kahane ordered us back into the truck and we drove off," said Beiber. "I don't remember Kahane being involved in any fighting."

Filmed reports of the JDL's tangle with the Panthers led the local evening TV news programs. An elated Kahane later boasted to reporters that because the Black Panthers now properly feared the JDL, "then Black hoodlums everywhere would think twice about acting against Jews. And that was precisely our purpose."

The FBI, too, was pleased. Kahane was the perfect stooge. Whether or not he participated unwittingly in the FBI's plot, his racist sentiments were perfectly in tune with those of the men who ran the Bureau. In a May 21, 1970 congratulatory memo to Hoover, under the heading, "Tangible Results," the FBI's New York Bureau chief reported: "On 5/7/70 . . . approximately 35 members of the JDL picketed the Harlem Branch of the BPP in NYC. The purpose of this demonstration was to show that the JDL feels the BPP is anti-Semitic in its acts and words. In view of the above action by the JDL, it is felt that some of the counter-intelligence measures of the NYO have produced tangible results."

While the FBI stoked the JDL's fires, the New York Police Department, the State Department, and assorted other government agencies were frantically trying to stamp them out. In the summer of 1969, while Hoover used the JDL to toy with Black militants, Kahane set up a paramilitary training camp in the Catskills, paying two Queens doctors $35,000 for the Joy-Del Bungalow Colony near Grossinger's in the heart of "the Borscht Belt." Some fifty young JDL members spent the summer at the newly christened Camp JEDEL receiving karate instruction from two black belts, and drilling with an ex-marine who taught them how to shoot pistols and automatic rifles. A more elite unit called the *Chayas* was taught how to make Molotov cocktails and pipe bombs. Kahane had the camp's pool drained so that it could be used to practice throwing firebombs.

Kahane told the *Chayas* that they were training to become Jewish fighters in the tradition of the Irgun and the Stern Gang. The enemy, he declared, was everywhere: ex-Nazis, neo-Nazis, Arabs, Soviets, Blacks, do-nothing politicans, leftists of all sorts. Even Jews who chose the wrong side of an issue were fair game as far as the rabbi was concerned.

Arnie Beiber joined the *Chaya* squad as a way to gain the approval of his father, a concentration camp survivor who became one of Kahane's bodyguards. Beiber said that initially he was also attracted to Kahane's "cool, rabbi image." "He came off as someone you could approach with your problems," Beiber recalled. "But I noticed that when you did approach him there was a real wall up. Even in private he was more like a public figure."

Kahane's own children were cut off by that same wall. "Neither Libby nor the children existed if he had something to do," said Gloria Zweibon, whose husband Bertram was the JDL's cofounder. "I remember at the camp, Libby would sometimes sit for hours with her four babies screaming and crying, while she pleaded with Meir that it was time to go home. He had no concept of the needs of his children."

As Kahane's career in extremist politics took off, Libby went back to Brooklyn College to obtain her Master of Arts degree in Library Science. "She was not a career woman," said Edith Horowitz. "She was content to stay at home. But she realized she had to start living her own life. She had strong opinions and a strong intellect, but she always lowered herself to him. It's ironic, because in public Meir talked about her with reverence. He told everybody she had a better mind than he. But in public you never saw them talking to each other. He gave orders. It was do this, do that, come, go.''

Although Libby's parents begged her to divorce Meir, she endured the humiliations and the cold neglect for the sake of her children. ''Her kids went to yeshiva,'' said Edith. ''The JDL kids went to jail. Libby sheltered her children,'' keeping them away from their father's organization.

Camp JEDEL's 1969 summer session was barely a week old when TWA flight 840 bound from Los Angeles to Tel Aviv was hijacked by a team of Palestinian terrorists led by Leila Khaled. In retaliation, three armed JDL men broke into the PLO office on Manhattan's East Side, and rifled the organization's files. They reportedly discovered the names of Arab students in the United States who were involved in pro-PLO causes, as well as the names of Americans who contributed to the organization. According to Kahane's version, which is supported by several ex-JDL officials, the rabbi handed over the file to an Israeli official at Israel's UN Mission.

Thus began a long, fruitful relationship between the JDL and various Israeli intelligence organizations. The conduit for the JDL's intelligence gathering was usually a member or sympathizer of Menachem Begin's Gahal Party, the large right-wing opposition block in Israel. Though Begin did not publicly support the JDL's violent activities in the United States, privately he professed great admiration for the fiery American rabbi. Begin's affinity with the JDL was quite logical. Many adults in the JDL had been Betarnicks, and some JDL members were very prominent in the Revisionist movement, which Begin, as Jabotinsky's heir, headed. Indeed, the JDL was little more than a pale imitation of the Irgun, with American Blacks replacing the Nazis and the British as the group's enemies. The JDL's philosophy, as spelled out in the official JDL handbook, was a simplistic reformulation of Jabotinsky's ideology. So when Begin had occasion to meet Kahane in New York shortly after the JDL's raid on the PLO's New York office, the former underground commander praised the operation.

''Begin felt the JDL was needed in the United States to protect Jews,'' said Irving Calderon, a Queens trucking company executive, who, as Kahane's operations chief in the early 1970s, planned and carried out many of the JDL's violent missions. ''Begin wanted us to keep tabs and provide intelligence on the

PLO and its supporters in the United States,'' Calderon continued. ''We gave the intelligence to the Gahal Party, and they passed it on to Israeli intelligence. We would do things that might be too risky for a foreign government to do: put wiretaps on phones, ransack offices, take photographs, and conduct surveillance. Begin never asked us specific questions about our activities. Presumably, he didn't want to know the answers. But he never said tell Kahane not to do this or that. He admired Kahane.''

Following the JDL's raid on the PLO, the New York Police Department's Bureau of Special Investigation (BOSI) infiltrated the group using a young Jewish cop who had been in Air Force Intelligence. The officer, Richard Rosenthal, was fluent in Russian and a half-a-dozen other languages and had a photographic memory. ''He could spit out a couple of hundred pages of his handwritten notes verbatim without looking at them,'' former Assistant U.S. Attorney Joseph Jaffe told me. Rosenthal picked up some JDL literature at an anti-Lindsay rally, mailed in a $10 application fee, and joined the chapter nearest his home in Midwood, Brooklyn. At his very first meeting, Rosenthal was appointed head of security by Rabbi Aron Leider, the Midwood chapter president.

Kahane, meanwhile, kept devising schemes for continued media coverage. At the time, the JDL was getting a lot of attention for patrolling neighborhoods where Jews were subject to attack by Blacks. But the patrols were more often than not just hype. ''JDL patrols were only out there if there was press coverage,'' said Allan Mallenbaum, the JDL's former administrative director. ''There was no apparatus for defense. The perception we created was far more important than the fact.'' Mallenbaum recalled one time when two yeshiva boys, trapped by a gang of Blacks in an elevated subway station in Brooklyn, called the office frantically pleading for help. ''There was nothing we could do,'' said Mallenbaum. ''I had a couple of guys sitting in the Manhattan office. It would have taken them an hour to get down there. I called the local chapter in Brooklyn. They said they didn't have the manpower.'' In desperation, Mallenbaum called the cops for help, but they said they were too busy. ''So I called the cops back and told them a truckload of armed JDL men were racing to the scene. They immediately dispatched a squad car. There was a perception in New York that the JDL had scores of armed men. Usually, there were never more than five or six *Chayas* around.''

But the JDL sometimes did patrol Jewish neighborhoods in high crime areas, often earning it good will and grass-roots support. When a carnival held by the Young Israel Synagogues of Wavecrest and Bayswater was disrupted by Black street gangs, the Rockaways Jewish Community Council of Brooklyn summoned the JDL to keep the peace. ''The unselfish response of your members, who came from different parts of the city and gave up evenings to see that nothing interfered with the carnival proceedings, was most commendable,'' wrote Joel Phillips, Rockaways Council vice-president, in a thank-you note to the JDL. ''Whenever there was the possibility of disturbance, some JDL members sauntered over, dispersed the crowd, and did it so unobtrusively that few knew anything had been amiss.''

Kahane may have feared and despised Blacks. But he loathed John V. Lindsay, the tall, blond Waspish mayor who had dubbed New York ''Fun City.'' Lindsay had restored New York's sense of glamour and style, but as far as Kahane was concerned, he had turned the city over to Blacks and Hispanics. Under Lindsay, city government was opened up to minorities. Anti-poverty programs received large budgets; welfare rolls bulged. Lindsay won national acclaim for venturing into Harlem on the night of Martin Luther King, Jr.'s assassination. His act may have saved New York from riots that seared other American cities.

Though liberal Jews applauded Lindsay's politics of compassion, Kahane complained that the mayor was threatening to destroy hard-won Jewish gains. Having compassion for Blacks, Kahane stated, was easy for white liberals who lived safely in the suburbs. But who cared about poor Jews living in New York's deteriorating, crime-infested neighborhoods? The rabbi's divisive rhetoric touched a raw nerve in New York's Jewish community. Long before Lindsay took office, newly prosperous Jews had begun to leave New York City for the suburbs. One-time Jewish enclaves like the Lower East Side were a pale shadow of what they had been by the time Lindsay succeeded Robert Wagner. ''Lindsay was the mayor at a time when Jews came to recognize that their day had passed in New York in terms of the heights they had reached,'' said Marvin Shick, Lindsay's liaison with the Jewish community.

In 1969, after losing the Republican Party's mayoral primary because of his pro-minority views, Lindsay ran for reelection on the Liberal Party ticket. Week after week, Kahane, who backed Republican candidate John Marchi, hammered away at Lindsay in *The Jewish Press*, accusing him of being a vicious anti-Semite. The JDL's well-financed anti-Lindsay crusade did not stop there. It took out several anti-Lindsay ads in *The New York Times*, distributed tens of thousands of anti-Lindsay flyers, and dispatched "truth squads" to attend the mayor's public speaking engagements where they mercilessly heckled him. "We are going to make it impossible for him [Lindsay] to be mayor of this city," Kahane vowed. Meanwhile, the FBI continued to send out thousands of pieces of hate mail to Black and white teachers in order to keep the pot boiling.

On October 15, 1969, 1,700 persons crammed into the East Midwood Jewish Center, where they jeered Lindsay as he tried to explain his reasons for supporting school decentralization. According to a front-page account in *The New York Times*, "The Mayor stood with facial muscles twitching, one white-knuckled hand gripping the podium, and shouted, while he pointed at a teachers' union officer: 'Our city will not survive if teachers are illegally transferred any more than it will if this gentleman here leads the teachers in an illegal strike. I say to you that there have been acts of vigilantism on both sides.' " The crowd, filled with rabidly anti-Lindsay JDLers, surged toward the stage, forcing the mayor to flee by a side door. "It was a very ugly situation," recalled Sid Davidoff, a top aide to Lindsay from 1966 to 1973. "We had to use a decoy car to get Lindsay out of there. The JDL used this incident as a springboard to sabotage the mayor's appearances in other Jewish areas."

Kahane's polarizing tactics began to erode Lindsay's support even among more mainstream Jews—who represented the largest liberal voting bloc in the city. "The JDL was beating the hell out of us," Davidoff told me. "They were killing us in the polls."

Desperate to get Kahane off the mayor's back, at least until after the election, Lindsay aides cut a deal with *Jewish Press* publisher Sholom Klass. "I sold my soul for that," said Davidoff, now a prominent New York attorney. Marvin Shick arranged a private meeting between the mayor and Klass, who was chauffeured to Gracie Mansion in Lindsay's limousine. After taking the publisher on a tour of the mansion, Lindsay asked Klass for his political support.

According to Marvin Shick, "Klass, who was stuttering—he was a terrible stutterer—said, 'b-b-but M-m-ayor L-i-indsay, my readers think you're anti-Semitic.' "

"Rabbi Klass, what do you think?" asked Lindsay, the veins in his neck pulsing and turning deep red, according to Shick.

"M-my readers think that," replied Klass.

"But what do you think?" Lindsay asked, glaring sharply.

"W-well my r-readers . . ." Klass repeated.

"If that's what you think, I feel sorry for you," said Lindsay who stalked out of the room.

It looked like the meeting was a total fiasco. But as soon as Lindsay left, Klass announced that he was willing to fire Kahane if the city gave him a new building to house his newspaper. "We wanted Kahane off the paper," said Davidoff. "They wanted a new building for their paper. They were in Coney Island and their office had been condemned by Housing and Urban Development [HUD]. They wanted to move."

Klass was given a long-term lease on an old Transit Authority substation in Brooklyn for one dollar. In return, *The Jewish Press* publisher fired Kahane within hours of leaving Gracie Mansion. "To say we did a quid pro quo—that we gave them a free building to get Klass to muzzle Kahane until the elections were over, I'm never going to admit to that," said Davidoff. "The only thing I'm going to give you here—and you can draw any conclusion you want—the statute has run out on this one—is that people who witnessed the meeting certainly felt there was a deal made to drop Kahane for the building."

Kahane immediately orchestrated a letter-writing campaign to get himself reinstated at the paper. "We really did feel that Lindsay was taking Jewish power and just wrecking it," Kahane later told me. On October 24, 1969, Klass published an editorial explaining that Kahane was dismissed because he was unfairly criticizing Lindsay. "Honest dissent is the democratic way, but to use vilification is to use the very tactics the JDL has always condemned and which is contrary to our Torah," wrote Klass. "As a responsible newspaper we felt duty bound to present all sides in the mayoralty campaign. Accordingly, we visited Mr. Lindsay to learn his views so that we could present them to our readers. As a result we were accused of having 'sold out' to the Mayor—a libel as stupid as it is false."

Several weeks before the election, which the polls said was too close to call, Israeli Prime Minister Golda Meir contacted a top Lindsay aide offering to help the embattled mayor in his bid for reelection during her upcoming trip to New York. "Her timing was uncanny," Davidoff has recalled. "His [Lindsay's] polls showed he desperately needed more Jewish votes. If he could turn out the Black vote and the Hispanic vote, and if he could turn them out in numbers, all he needed was a couple of points to really turn the election around."

Lindsay's Deputy Mayor Richard Aurelio was also thrilled to have Golda Meir's support. "The biggest problem we had in the campaign was with a certain element in the Jewish population that felt Lindsay had gone overboard in favoring the Blacks," Aurelio, who today is president of Time-Warner's cable TV operations, told me. "The whole thesis of our campaign was to try to appeal to the Jewish consciousness in terms of the minorities. We had built a coalition of minorities and liberal Jews. We had to bring back some of the Jews who were not angry at Blacks."

On October 30, a jubilant, yarmulke-clad Lindsay hosted a state dinner for Prime Minister Meir in Brooklyn. They sang together and she toasted him with kosher wine. Combined with a defanged *Jewish Press*, Lindsay's prospects improved markedly.

A few nights before the election, Emanuel Rackman, the rabbi of the prestigious Fifth Avenue Synagogue in Manhattan, called Deputy Mayor Aurelio to say that Kahane was ready to make peace with Lindsay. Rackman, now dean of Bar Ilan University in Israel, was an early supporter and fundraiser for the JDL, permitting League members to speak at Yeshiva University where he was provost. Parlor meetings arranged by Rackman are said to have earned Kahane up to $50,000 for an afternoon's talk. Joseph Gruss, who heads his own investment firm in New York and is one of the wealthiest Jewish philanthropists in America, was among those introduced to Kahane by Rackman. "Gruss's contributions [to the JDL] were a kind of insurance money," Rackman has said. "He said that if his own grandchildren wouldn't be Jewish at least he would be causing others to have Jewish grandchildren." After one such meeting, where Kahane adroitly analyzed the decline of Jewish power, Zweibon recalled that Max Stern, the billionaire founder of the Hartz Mountain pet food company, turned to him and growled, "Yeah, but what's he going to do about the niggers!"

Now on election eve, Rackman was trying to smooth things over between Lindsay and Kahane. "It looks like Lindsay is going to be reelected," Rackman said to Aurelio. "You should come over to my study and meet with Rabbi Kahane. He's going to be important in the future."

Aurelio walked with Kahane from Rackman's study in the East 80s to Lindsay's campaign headquarters on Fifth Avenue. But rather than sitting down to the promised peace talks, Kahane declared war on the city of New York. Said Aurelio: "I remember crossing Fifth Avenue thinking, 'Wow, what a waste of time. This guy is from nutsville.' He wouldn't give me an inch on even the slightest little thing. I told him that he should renounce violent tactics. He said, 'Oh, I could never do that. That's our ultimate weapon. We must use violence.' I left thinking this guy can't possibly get anywhere. He can't become a major force. Eventually the JDL became a very significant factor in New York City politics and a major problem for law enforcement. Mayor Lindsay thought Kahane was an evil man—a man who was a little crazy. We all thought so."

* * *

If not for Israeli Prime Minister Yitzhak Shamir and ultranationalist Tehiya Party leader Geula Cohen, Kahane might never have risen above the ranks of a New York City rabble-rouser. Despite their vehement denunciations of Kahane in recent years, the two were part of a secret group that helped make the militant leader of the Jewish Defense League an international figure and a force to be reckoned with in Israel.

The secret relationship between Cohen, Shamir, and Kahane was forged one blustery cold morning in December 1969. Cohen, who had just been elected to the Knesset as a member of Menachem Begin's Herut Party, visited Kahane in his cramped JDL office on Manhattan's Fifth Avenue. At the time, Cohen thought that Kahane was frittering away his talents. "Why are you wasting time fighting the '*Schvartzes*'?" asked Cohen, who was in the United States on a speaking tour sponsored by the International League for the Repatriation of Russian Jews (ILRRJ), a group of Jewish businessmen and Orthodox rabbis who were lobbying Congress on behalf of Soviet Jews. Cohen, who in the 1940s had dropped out of Begin's Irgun underground to fight with the more extreme Stern Gang because she found Begin "too mild," told Kahane that "the vital issue for Jews is the plight of Soviet Jewry. The Russians are planning to liquidate our people." The meeting between them was arranged by Bernard Deutsch, a founding member of the ILRRJ, who says that Cohen was impressed by Kahane's militant credentials and obvious public relations talent.

Though the JDL was enjoying success as an anti-Black protest group, Kahane instinctively grasped that the predicament of Soviet Jews was an issue that could generate international headlines and turn the JDL into a more significant force. Now Cohen was offering him the chance to ride his brethren's concern for Soviet Jewry to stardom. "I really influenced him," Cohen told me in Jerusalem in October 1988. "He changed the JDL's program overnight."

During the next few months, Cohen said she helped lay the groundwork for a guerrilla war against the Soviet Union that would be waged by the JDL—and orchestrated by prominent right-wing Israelis, including several high-ranking members of Mossad. Cohen and Deutsch told me that the group's central player was the quiet, morose former Stern Gang commander Yitzhak Shamir. Shamir had been Mossad's chief of operations until 1965 and maintained close ties to the agency. "The JDL's decisions weren't made by Meir," said Deutsch, a key member of the covert group that oversaw the JDL's anti-Soviet operations. "If I were to tell you that Shamir was the head of our group and planned our activities, he would absolutely deny it. But I sat on his bed in his bedroom, which is where we had many of our meetings. I'm not looking to hurt Shamir, but that's a fact." When I asked Shamir in October 1988 to comment about his activities with the JDL, his spokesman said that the prime minister would not confirm or deny allegations about his involvement with the organization. Shamir's spokesman did say, however, that the prime minister was very sympathetic to the JDL's early work on behalf of Soviet Jews.

Besides Shamir, Cohen, and Deutsch, the group—which planned and funded many of the JDL's attacks on Soviet targets in the United States and Europe between December 1969 and August 1972—included Israeli attorney Pessach Mor, now a member of Tehiya Party's Central Council; several wealthy American and Israeli businessmen; three top Mossad officers; Herzl

Amicaham, a former Irgun operative who would often fly to the United States to confer with JDL officials; and several retired Israeli army officers who trained JDL youth in weapons and sabotage in Israel. Deutsch served as a courier, frequently meeting group members in Israel, England, and Switzerland. "I'd meet directly with the overall group and bring back money and instructions," he said. Although the exact workings of the operation are still partly shrouded in mystery, many of Deutsch's and Cohen's statements have been independently confirmed by sources in the United States and Israel, as well as by documents and letters that I obtained. "Our group planned how to fight the Soviet Union," said Cohen. "We wanted to pressure the Russian Embassy in the U.S., to warn them, to frighten them." She added that it was not their intention to use lethal violence.

Kahane's handlers calculated that the selective use of violence against Soviet targets in the United States and Europe would inevitably strain U.S.-Soviet relations, according to former JDL officials. They predicted that rather than risk détente, the Soviet Union would be forced to alleviate the crisis by freeing hundreds of thousands of Jews who would then be herded to the Jewish state. An influx of Soviet Jews could help redress the demographic imbalance caused when Israel swallowed the Occupied Territories with its large Arab population. Since the founding of the State of Israel, one of Mossad's prime directives has been to help bring Jews to Israel. It has operated underground networks in a number of countries, including Iraq and Ethiopia, to facilitate this task.

Golda Meir's Labor government apparently was kept in the dark about this covert cabal of right-wing zealots. "Golda Meir had favored using back-channel diplomacy to solve the Soviet Jewish problem," Deutsch said. "Many Revisionists felt it was exactly that kind of passive policy that led to the Holocaust. The Israeli government did nothing for Soviet Jews. Golda felt any kind of publicity endangered their lives. 'I make decisions that can send thousands of Israeli soldiers to their death, but I have no right to do that to Russian Jews,' she once told me. We thought militancy was the way to go."

Deutsch's involvement in this secret operation grew out of his long-standing ties to the leaders of the Revisionist Zionist movement. During the late 1960s and early 1970s, Deutsch was a prominent member of Brooklyn's Orthodox Jewish community. He was a confidant of Herut leader Menachem Begin, who slept in Deutsch's home whenever he was in New York on business, and was the chairman of the B'nai B'rith Anti-Defamation League's powerful Brooklyn chapter. His work on behalf of Soviet Jews was highly regarded. Malcolm Hoenlein, now executive director of the Conference of Presidents of Major American Jewish Organizations, said that Deutsch's ILRRJ "made an important contribution. They were activists when there weren't that many people involved." One of ILRRJ's key contacts was Richard Perle, Henry "Scoop" Jackson's Senate aide who went on to become a top Pentagon official in the Reagan Administration.

Deutsch's world collapsed in 1975, when he was convicted of stock fraud and conspiracy to evade taxes on more than $4 million in personal and corporate income made between 1968 and 1972, roughly the same period when he worked with the group overseeing Kahane. According to Zweibon, the JDL's cofounder and former chief counsel, proceeds from Deutsch's investments were used to help finance the group's secret operation. Since his release from prison, Deutsch has kept a low profile, but recently he and Geula Cohen have discussed writing a book that would tell the "real story" behind the movement to save Soviet Jewry. The project remains on hold because they are concerned that their revelations might hurt the political careers of some of their colleagues.

Soon after Deutsch introduced Cohen to Kahane in December 1969, the rabbi strolled into the JDL office and announced that henceforth the organization's primary focus would be Soviet Jewry. That Kahane had seldom mentioned Soviet Jews in the past did not bother the faithful.

The JDL's opening shot was a well-executed attack on four Soviet targets in New York. In one day—December 29, 1969—the JDL simultaneously took over the offices of Tass (the Soviet press agency), Intourist (the Soviet tourist agency), and Aeroflot (the Soviet airline), and boarded a Russian commercial passenger plane at Kennedy International Airport to spray-paint the cabin with Hebrew slogans like *"Am Yisrael Chai!"*—"The Jewish Nation Lives!"

The next day, more than one hundred JDL members rioted in front of the Soviet Mission in New York. In a press release, Kahane explained the JDL's actions:

Our attacks upon the institutions of Soviet tyranny in America represent the first step in our campaign to bring the issue of oppressed Soviet Jews and other religious groups to the attention of an apathetic public and indifferent news media. . . .

We have pleaded, implored, and tried the traditional methods of diplomacy. They have failed to open the gates. There is little remaining for us to do but to heed the requests of the Russian Jews themselves who have commanded us to shake the world.

On December 31, Russian Deputy Foreign Minister S.P. Kozyrev met with the U.S. ambassador to the Soviet Union to protest the JDL attacks, warning that if they did not cease, "The responsibility . . . will rest fully on the U.S. government." But the JDL intensified its campaign. A few days after an angry Kozyrev dressed down the U.S. official in Moscow, Kahane sent separate telegrams to U.S. Secretary of State William Rogers and Soviet Ambassador to the U.S. Anatoly Dobrynin, vowing that the JDL would disrupt all Soviet cultural appearances in the United States unless the Soviet Jews were freed.

Jewish impresario Sol Hurok, who was bringing Soviet performers to the United States, was singled out for particularly violent harassment. Kahane described him as a man "whose appetite for profits leads him to abandon his obligations as a human and his loyalties as a Jew," and dispatched a gang of thugs to occupy Hurok's Manhattan office in February 1970. One of the JDL men deliberately dropped a cigarette on Hurok's carpet, burning a small hole—a veiled threat of what could happen if Hurok failed to heed Kahane's demands to cease working with the Soviets. Soon Hurok's concerts, which featured the greatest names in Soviet classical music and dance, were disrupted by smoke bombs, stink bombs, and bags of frogs and mice that were released into the audience.

"The [JDL's] attacks on 'culture' brought down furious criticism," Kahane wrote in *The Story of the Jewish Defense League*—an account of the JDL that is more fantasy than fact. "The lovers of culture—who love art more than they love people—reacted with an indignation one never dreamed they were capable of. That which we had never heard on behalf of Jews in the USSR suddenly erupted with a mighty roar on behalf of 'culture'. . . ."

No one complained more vehemently than the Jewish establishment, which accused Kahane of fostering anti-Semitism. Because Kahane's attacks on the Soviets were provoking a crisis between the superpowers, many Jewish officials feared a backlash that could undermine both U.S. support for Israel and the security of the American Jewish community itself.

But for some American Jewish officials, Kahane commanded respect, even secret admiration—prompting them to consider whether quiet lobbying for Soviet Jews was antiquated and ineffectual. Jewish establishment organizations, which had relegated the Soviet Jewish question to the backburner, began to organize petitions and rallies in an attempt to steal Kahane's thunder. "Some of the JDL's outlandish activities, and the threat that they would undertake more extremist activities, caused some establishment people to view the JDL with alarm," said Jerry Goodman, the former executive director of the National Conference on Soviet Jewry (NCSJ)—an umbrella agency acting on behalf of Soviet Jews in the United States. "That was one of the reasons why there was support for the creation of the NCSJ. Now the NCSJ was an idea even before the JDL's anti-Soviet campaign started, but people . . . wavered about creating another bureaucracy in Jewish life. But when they saw the alternative was to leave the Soviet Jewish issue to 'crazies,' that encouraged them to support the creation of the National Conference."

Despite differences over tactics, the NCSJ and the JDL learned to work together. Malcolm Hoenlein, the NCSJ's director in New York City in the 1970s, shared information with Kahane about upcoming demonstrations and worked out a tacit understanding that allowed the JDL to participate in NCSJ's mass rallies, according to a number of ex-JDL officials, several of whom are now prominent establishment figures. Moreover, JDLers say that it seemed that Hoenlein occasionally encouraged them to stage some act of civil disobedience at the end of a NCSJ rally to grab additional media attention. "Hoenlein didn't say the JDL should stage a violent protest, but there was a wink and a nod," said Zweibon. "He knew how to get publicity, but was too much of a sissy to participate in violence." Hoenlein admitted to having contact with Kahane and other JDL leaders and acknowledged that the JDL was invited to participate in solidarity day rallies for Soviet Jews. "We didn't exclude the JDL," said Hoenlein. "We tried to be as inclusive as possible as long as they agreed to abide by the rules that bound everyone else." But Hoenlein insisted that it is a "complete mischaracterization" to say the NCSJ coordinated activities with the militant organization or that he encouraged violence. "Of course the NCSJ didn't coordinate activities with the JDL, Hoenlein did," said an ex-JDL official. Dov Hikind, assemblyman from New York's 48th District and a former JDL leader added: "We [the JDL] received a lot of support" from establishment leaders who "would swear today it's absolutely untrue. In fact, information was shared and help given in many, many different forms."

There is also no question that Hoenlein and other establishment Jewish leaders exploited the JDL's militancy. Like Kahane, Hoenlein had come to understand that the Soviet Jewish problem would not be resolved until enough Jews were sufficiently indignant to make it an international cause célèbre. Dov Hikind remembers the time when two prominent Jewish leaders urged him to stage a violent JDL demonstration to protest the arrival of the mayor of Moscow who was scheduled to speak at the UN. "They were nice respectable guys in suits and ties," said Hikind. "They didn't have the guts to do what they were telling me to do." Kahane himself urged establishment Jewish leaders to use the threat of JDL violence as a way to pressure the Soviets to lift restrictions on their Jews. Hoenlein said that Kahane once urged him to go to the Soviets and say: "If you don't deal with us you're going to have to deal with Kahane." Hoenlein said he never delivered the threat.

The JDL's Soviet Jewish campaign sparked enormous controversy in Israel. While much of the press and the public lauded it, the Labor government of Golda Meir denounced it as irresponsibly violent. "The JDL clearly embarrassed the Israeli government, which had always approached the question of Soviet Jewry with great discretion," said a confidential memo from the American Jewish Committee representative in Jerusalem to headquarters in New York. When Bernard Deutsch brought two prominent Soviet Jewish émigrés who were critical of Golda Meir's policies from Israel to America on a speaking tour in 1969, Yoram Dinstein, an Israeli official in New York, phoned Jewish leaders warning them not to invite the men to local functions, alleging they were KGB spys. Ironically, many years later, one of the émigrés, Yasha Kazakov, was appointed by the Israeli government to a diplomatic post in the Soviet Union.

For the many American Revisionists like Deutsch who supported the JDL, the Jewish establishment's quiescence on the Soviet Jewish issue was just the latest example of the Jews' complicity in their own destruction. "In 1942, when we learned about Auschwitz—we did nothing," began a full-page ad that appeared in the March 26, 1970 *New York Times*, which was written by Kahane and subsidized by Deutsch.

> Our leaders went to President Roosevelt and asked him to bomb the rail lines carrying the cars packed with Jews to the gas chambers. He refused. We did nothing. When the lives of hundreds of thousands of Jews were at stake, we did nothing more than hold rallies and mimeograph sheets of protests. And so—*OUR* HANDS HELPED TO SHED THAT BLOOD, OUR SILENCE HELPED TO SEAL THAT DOOM. . . .
>
> In 1970, when we know of the national and spiritual destruction of Soviet Jewry . . . where is the unceasing effort? Where are the huge crowds? Where are the huge protests? Where are all the demonstrators who bleed for every people, every cause, every group—except the Jew?
>
> We, by our silence, doom the Soviet Jew. We, by our apathy, shed his blood. We reject respectability. We will do what must be done. We wish to shake the world and spotlight the Soviet Jewish problem so that the U.S. government will be forced to demand justice for people if the Soviets want the West's friendship.
>
> Some day, your children or grandchildren will ask you: 'What did you do for Soviet Jews?' What will you say?

Kahane's chutzpah electrified the burgeoning Jewish activist movement in the Soviet Union, which was born in the wake of Israel's lightning victory in the Six Day War. The Israeli triumph over six Arab armies not only filled Jews around the world with a collective feeling of pride and glory, but in the Soviet Union, it also led to Jews beginning to extol their Jewishness and openly identify with Zionism. If tiny Israel could lick the combined Arab armies, perhaps the 2.1 million Jews of the Soviet Union could live with dignity and respect.

The specter of Jewish nationalism rocked the Politburo. A Soviet ethnic minority group had rarely defied the brute force of the Soviet state. The KGB cracked down on Soviet Jews, as part of an officially sanctioned anti-Jewish campaign reminiscent of the worst anti-Semitism practiced during the darkest days of the Czars.

Anti-Semitism has deep historical roots in the Soviet Union. Under the Czars, Jews were forced to live in the Pale of Settlement, the poorest areas of Western Russia and what is now Eastern Poland, where they were the victims of a series of violent pogroms, particularly in the late nineteenth and early twentieth centuries, which often took place with the connivance of the authorities. Although anti-Semitism subsided after the Communist Revolution in 1917, it grew again under Stalin, and exploded after the Six Day War.

Soon tens of thousands of Soviet Jews were clamoring to get out of the USSR, and Kahane, whose antics were widely reported in the Soviet press, became their hero. "Kahane became a symbol that Soviet Jews could hold on to," said Jacob Biernbaum, a founder of the Student Struggle for Soviet Jewry (SSSJ),* a small, non-violent activist group based in New York that predated the JDL by several years.

While Geula Cohen and Yitzhak Shamir directed certain JDL activities in America, they were also in contact with Jewish dissidents in the Soviet Union, sending them money and books and organizing some of their political protests. "We sent our brethren Hebrew books . . . and transmitted coded messages through a variety of clandestine channels, including the Finnish embassy," said Deutsch. They also surreptitiously channeled funds to subsidize an underground publication network through Soviet Jewish émigré groups in New York City, Switzerland, and England. The group also arranged to pay bribes of up to $50,000 for individual exit visas. Thanks to Deutsch and his associates, it was not uncommon to find refusenicks hurrying through the streets of Moscow and Leningrad with suitcases stuffed with Zionist and JDL literature.

---

* Although the SSSJ worked closely with the JDL, it resisted Kahane's repeated attempts to take over the organization. The FBI infiltrated the SSSJ believing it to be a JDL front group, according to documents that the SSSJ obtained under the Freedom of Information Act. The SSSJ was also infiltrated by operatives working for the Israeli consul in New York, who complained that the group had gone beyond the official Israeli line on the Soviet Jewish question, according to Biernbaum. Ironically, another official at the consul's office who was sympathetic to the SSSJ kept Biernbaum informed of Israeli attempts to disrupt the group.

On June 15, 1970, the KGB arrested scores of Jewish activists across the Soviet Union. Among them were nine Jews charged with plotting to hijack a Soviet airliner at Leningrad Smolny Airport and fly it to Sweden. American Jewish leaders accused the KGB of a frame-up. But according to Deutsch and other sources directly involved in the operation, the hijacking was planned by Kahane's control group in Israel, which had been secretly in contact with the plotters.

On Christmas Eve, 1970, a Soviet court sentenced two hijackers to death. The others received harsh prison terms. The death sentences were rendered not for the hijacking, but for attempting to leave the Soviet Union—a capital crime. On the day after the sentencing, concerned American Jewish leaders met in New York to organize an international protest. During the next two weeks, President Richard Nixon, Pope Paul VI, and hundreds of other religious figures, government spokesmen, and opinion leaders called on the Soviet leadership to commute the death sentences.

In the wake of the Leningrad trial, the JDL stepped up its attacks:

• On November 23, 1970, bombs exploded in front of Aeroflot and Intourist offices in New York.

• On January 8, 1971, a bomb exploded outside the Soviet cultural building on 18th Street in downtown Washington. Windows were shattered and an iron gate was hurled to a roof two hundred feet away. News agencies received calls that stated: "This is a sample of things to come. Let our people go. Never Again!" Three days later, the Soviet ambassador to the United States was abruptly called back to Moscow.

• On January 19, 1971, JDL members began to follow Soviet officials and their family members in New York and Washington, spitting and shouting epithets at them. The same week, three Soviet diplomats' cars were destroyed by firebombs.

• On March 30, 1971, a bomb exploded outside the New York Communist Party headquarters.

• On April 22, 1971, a bomb exploded inside Amtorg, the Soviet trade center, at 355 Lexington Avenue in Manhattan, gutting the nineteenth floor of the building. Sappers dismantled a second bomb, which nearly exploded while New York's chief of detectives and other officials looked on. Kahane sat in Deutsch's Wall Street office smiling as he listened to the radio broadcast speak of one bomb. "Two," Kahane said, raising his fingers in a "V" imitating a Churchill victory salute, according to Deutsch.

• On June 12, 1971, a bomb was found at the official Soviet residence at Glen Cove, New York. The explosive was safely dismantled.

• On December 5, 1971, a bomb exploded outside a Fifth Avenue gift shop in Manhattan specializing in Soviet goods. A store in Minnesota that sold Russian gifts was destroyed by a bomb.

In Europe, meanwhile, the JDL sent letter bombs to Soviet embassies, blew up a Soviet container ship in a Dutch harbor, and plastered London with thousands of flyers reading: "If you want a *full* body massage, call Sonia," and listed the number for the Soviet Embassy, tying up its switchboard for days at a time.

The JDL's membership grew with its increasing militancy. What began with a handful of hard-core activists and a mimeograph machine, by 1971 claimed more than ten thousand members in a least a dozen U.S. cities, as well as in England, France, and South Africa. The JDL had evolved into a mass movement, the likes of which Kahane and Churba had only dreamed about a few years before. "Kahane had the ability to take youth and give them incentives to become underground Jewish heroes," said Murray Schneider, a JDL founding member and the League's treasurer until 1975. "We looked up to him like a god. He had incredible charisma. He was brighter than all of us." But as the JDL grew, it became harder for Kahane to control. Soon handfuls of adventurous youths were carrying out violent operations without consulting the JDL leader. There were times when Kahane and his handlers had all they could do to guide the group in the direction they wanted. In the end, more JDL operations were carried out on an ad hoc basis by youths carried away by their own enthusiasm than were planned in advance by JDL leaders.

Although Kahane was harshly criticized by the Jewish establishment, he received a good deal of under-the-table financial support from segments of the Jewish community who championed him for bringing the plight of Soviet Jewry to the forefront of American Jewish concerns. Kahane's uncle, Isaac Trainin, who was then director of the Federation of Jewish Philanthropies, recalled: "I was at a Jewish Federation dinner in the early '70s with Max Stern [the multi-millionaire pet food prince], who told

me that at least twelve of the twenty or thirty people sitting on
the dais that evening had given Kahane $10,000 or more. They
would curse him in public, but give him money under the table."
One of the biggest Jewish philanthropists of the twentieth century once told Trainin that "we could use another dozen Kahanes!"

These Jewish movers and shakers would probably not want
to know how Kahane was using their money. According to U.S.
federal court documents, the rabbi illegally purchased weapons
with checks drawn on the account of Camp JEDEL, one of the
growing list of charitable, tax-exempt foundations that he controlled. Kahane even recruited his younger brother, Nachman,
who had moved to Israel where he was deputy minister of religious affairs, to help beef up the JDL arsenal. Nachman reportedly procured two hundred Karl Gustav submachine guns, which
he was to ship to America in a crate marked "religious articles—
talleisim and *tefillin.*" He went to Begin and asked for help in
shipping the weapons, but when Begin said no, Nachman
scotched the plan.

In late 1970, Mayor Lindsay ordered New York City Chief of
Detectives Albert Seedman to stop the JDL bombings. "It was
bad enough," Seedman wrote in his memoir *Chief*, "when the
JDL kids threw paint or eggs at Russian diplomats or followed
their wives around the supermarket shouting curses at them. But
. . . a bomb was a disaster for a city. The Mayor was acutely aware
that the United Nations did not have to be in New York . . . .
No one was more critical of New York than the Russians. The
JDL was out to make sure they liked it even less."

By the fall of 1971, the JDL's attacks against Soviet targets in
the United States had become so numerous that President Nixon
became concerned that Kahane would wreck the Strategic Arms
Limitations Talks. The Soviet press was filled with lurid accounts
of Kahane's anti-Soviet actions, and held Nixon personally
responsible for the "Zionist hooligan." A confidential State
Department memo at the time urged the Justice Department to
secure indictments against JDL troublemakers, arguing that it
would "measurably improve the ability of the United States to
deal with the Soviet Union on substantive foreign policy issues."
Another secret State Department memo to the FBI warned "that
further incidents of [JDL] violence would have damaging impact
on our overall relations with the USSR and possibly trigger reaction against Americans in the Soviet Union." On January 6, 1971,

Robbie Palmer, an American diplomat in Moscow, was threatened in the street after leaving the theatre by KGB goons. "How would you like to be treated the way Zionist thugs treat our diplomats in America?" they asked. "How would you like to have your car destroyed by demonstrators who are not under control?" For the next several months, U.S. diplomats and journalists posted in the Soviet Union came under increasingly frequent verbal attacks and sometimes violent physical harassment.

On November 30, 1971—just weeks after Jewish militants fired a high-powered rifle from the roof of Hunter College into the Soviet Mission in New York nearly hitting a diplomat's child—officials from the Justice Department, the Secret Service, and the FBI met in then U.S. Ambassador to the UN George Bush's apartment in the Waldorf Astoria to plan how to derail the JDL. Kahane's colleagues in Israel could not have been more pleased with the attention. "Kahane was the right man at the right time," said Deutsch. "We knew he was crazy, but . . . he got us on the front page."

The FBI, which had begun tapping JDL phones in October 1970 without a court order, had already foiled JDL plots to mortar the Soviet estate at Glen Cove and to assassinate Soviet Ambassador Anatoly Dobrynin in the driveway of the Soviet Embassy in Washington. With the help of a JDL informant, federal agents had also uncovered a sophisticated plot to detonate a car bomb in the underground garage of the Soviet Mission in New York. The most hair-raising scheme thwarted by the FBI was a plan to fly a remote control model airplane packed with dynamite into the Soviet Mission in New York. The fully operational drone, with a six-foot wing span, was parked at a JDL bomb lab at 4702 15th Avenue in Borough Park, Brooklyn. The building was raided by police, who confiscated the craft as well as an arms cache of twenty shotguns, twenty-one rifles, sixteen handguns, cases of cartridges, gunpowder, fuses, caps, and pipes suitable for the manufacture of bombs. Also seized were the floor plans of several UN missions, anti-Arab literature, and JDL materials. Kahane, who rented the apartment, listed its tenants on the lease as Mr. and Mrs. A. Stern. Abraham Stern was the founder of the Stern Gang, whose former colleagues, Geula Cohen and Yitzhak Shamir, were running Kahane.

By any measure the JDL was a strange brew of kooks, right-wing ideologues, and dreamers. There was a Jewish ex-CIA agent,

Jewish Vietnam War vets, ultra-Orthodox yeshiva kids with *payis* and long black coats, Brooklyn college students dressed in blue jean jackets and headbands, concentration camp survivors, a chemistry professor from MIT who had made explosives for the Stern Gang, an Israeli weapons expert who was an instructor at Camp JEDEL, a number of doctors, dentists, and Wall Street executives, as well as a cadre of JDL attorneys, who worked pro bono on an expanding list of JDL cases.

"We called a lot of the guys that joined the JDL 'Italian Jews,' " said a former JDL member who is now an attorney in Brooklyn. "These were guys with gold chains and hairy chests who talked like mobsters. They all seemed to be from Canarsie. We had one guy, an exterminator by profession, by the name of Herbie. He wore a leather jacket with 'Herbie the Exterminator' printed on the back. He used to pick up young JDL members by the neck and grunt, 'Jews gotta learn how to fight.' "

Kahane's manic energy amazed his older supporters and energized his young followers. "On the hottest day of the summer he'd be working in the office with the door and windows shut, a blanket over the window, wearing a jacket with no air conditioning—and sit down and write all day," said the JDL's former treasurer, Murray Schneider.

"I couldn't keep my kids away from Kahane," said Barry Leiben, head of Betar, who looked on helplessly as his organization began to merge into the JDL in the early 1970s. "Kahane is the closest thing on earth to Jabotinsky. I grew up reading the work of Jabotinsky. Then all of a sudden there was Kahane—an animated version of Jabotinsky right in front of you."

But Jabotinsky was not obsessed with Blacks like Kahane. Even at the height of the JDL's war against the Soviet Union, Kahane could not resist meddling in Black-Jewish affairs. After all, it was the fear that Black demands for equality would somehow sabotage Jewish achievements that had brought the clique of Revisionists, school teachers, Orthodox Jews, and wealthy businessmen together under the banner of the JDL in the first place.

In the summer of 1970, the JDL twice attempted to firebomb a Black community center in Crown Heights, Brooklyn in revenge for an alleged Black militant firebombing that gutted the Crown Heights Jewish Community Center. Friction between the neighborhood's poor Blacks and Hasidic Jews intensified that summer with Black complaints that Hasids controlled the area's federal poverty program. Kahane was so angry when he learned that the JDL firebombs fell harmlessly to the ground that he personally supervised the manufacture of pipe bombs and Molotov cocktails at Camp JEDEL. He even ordered JDL bombmakers to serrate the outside of the pipe to make it more lethal.

During this period, Kahane also harassed Nazis and anyone else who he felt threatened Jewish interests. In May 1970, for example, Kahane learned that the American Nazi Party was holding a meeting on Manhattan's Upper West Side. "The original plan was to wait for the Nazis to come outside, line them up against the wall, and shoot them," said Arnie Beiber. Instead, they attacked the Nazis with numchucks and baseball bats as they walked out of the meeting. "I hit one guy over the head with a numchuck," said Beiber. "I was pretty young and it was one of the first times I had hit somebody. I was stunned because he didn't go down. Our camp karate instructor kicked him, and he still didn't go down. Then there was this real madman of a *Chaya*, who smashed him in the head with the claw of a hammer. We just left the Nazi lying in a pool of blood in front of a posh building on Central Park West. There was this doorman huddled in the corner scared out of his mind."

Neither was the PLO immune to JDL hit-and-run violence. On May 22, 1970, the day after a murderous PLO attack on a bus carrying Israeli school children on a desolate stretch of road near the Lebanese border, the JDL invaded the PLO office in midtown Manhattan. "The men broke down the door and two of them began to beat [PLO executive Sadaat] Hasan with clubs," the secretary recounted to *The New York Times*. "The beating lasted six or seven minutes, I think. There was lots of blood." According to a CIA report obtained under the Freedom of Information Act, one of the JDL members who participated in the raid on the PLO office was also implicated in the burglary of the Soviet Trade Mission in Amsterdam.

In Jordan, PLO Chief Yasir Arafat vowed to retaliate against Americans if the U.S. government did not stop the JDL from launching similar attacks. "The Palestine Revolution cannot keep silent or accept such crimes," Arafat was quoted as saying in *The New York Times*. "The opportunities for retaliation are deep and wide."

Several months later Kahane planned the assassination of a notorious PLO terrorist. In retrospect, the scheme seems little more than a publicity stunt, though its consequences were very serious for the recently married young couple that Kahane had recruited for the mission. On Sunday, September 27, 1970, Avraham Hershkovitz, a tall, flabby, twenty-six-year-old concentration camp survivor and his nineteen-year-old wife, Nancy, attempted to board a 10 P.M. BOAC flight to London at Kennedy International Airport, concealing two loaded pistols and hand grenades, which had been handed to them moments before by two JDL men hiding in an airport bathroom. Nancy, a grenade taped to her thigh, was waved through by security, but Avraham—disguised as a Hasid and carrying a false passport—was arrested at the gate by alert policemen. When Nancy returned to look for Avraham, she, too, was taken into custody.

During his interrogation, police told Avraham that unless he cooperated, his wife would be sent to the infamous Women's House of Detention in Manhattan where, they warned, she would most likely be gangraped by other inmates. "They [the authorities] drew a lurid picture of lesbian attacks," Simon Chrein, Hershkovitz's Legal Aid Society lawyer told *The New York Times*. "Thereafter Mr. Hershkovitz made a statement." Hershkovitz confessed that he and his wife were members of the JDL, and that they were on a mission to hijack an Egyptian airliner in London and divert it to Israel. Although Avraham was carrying a check made out to him and signed by Rabbi Kahane, he denied that the JDL leader was involved in the plot. Federal agents later obtained a search warrant for the Hershkovitzs' cramped, $65-a-month apartment, where they found a scene of filth and chaos. "Heaps of clothing lay in a corner, a package of ice cream was melting in the refrigerator, and goblets and silver that appeared to be wedding presents lay in open packages," began a story in *The New York Times*. "Among the scattered papers in the room was a notice from a bank that a check for $159.77, made out to the couple on August 17, 1970 by the Jewish Defense League, had not cleared because of insufficient funds."

Were these hapless, would-be terrorists really on their way to London to hijack an Egyptian plane? According to Irving Calderon, one of the JDL men who had slipped the Hershkovitzs their weapons, "That was the cover story." Their real assignment, Calderon claims, was to assassinate Palestinian highjacker Leila Khaled who was then in a London jail. Calderon said a second JDL man-and-wife hit team had been sent to London ahead of the Hershkovitzs, but flew to Israel on false passports when they learned of the arrests.

Zweibon dismisses the entire episode as nothing more than a headline-grabbing ruse dreamed up by Kahane. If Kahane had really wanted to assassinate a heavily guarded prisoner in a London lockup, whey did he openly discuss the proposed attack in front of several dozen JDLers in the JDL office? Zweibon asks. "He mapped out the mission like a football coach diagramming a play at half time," said Zweibon. "We knew then that the government had agents in our ranks. Kahane must have wanted the FBI to find out about the plan."

A week after the Hershkovitzs were yanked off their flight to London, a young man carrying a tan, leather briefcase entered a building on 40th Street and Park Avenue where the PLO had its Manhattan office. The youth took the elevator to the third floor and deposited the briefcase outside the PLO's door. At 11 P.M. a powerful explosion ripped through the building, heavily damaging the PLO office. Fortunately, no one was hurt, although a cleaning lady was taken to a local hospital and treated for shock. Two days later, Kahane was a guest on "This Day," a radio news program on the Jerusalem Domestic Service in Hebrew. He was asked during the telephone interview if the JDL had bombed the PLO office. "Well, obviously if we were to say yes," he said, "we might have problems with the police, but I think that if one, perhaps as a conjecture, said that it might have been our group, then perhaps it might be a valid thought. . . . What happened to the PLO office . . . here happened because those terrorists who live by the sword should be ready to perhaps face the same fate. . . . What happened here will happen again!"

* * *

On May 12, 1971, Kahane and a dozen other JDL members were arrested by federal agents in New York for conspiracy to manufacture explosives. It was no accident that on the very next day Kahane publicly announced that the JDL was joining forces with another right-wing group—the Italian American Civil Rights League (IACRL). This unholy alliance was the first serious attempt to forge an ethnic fascist movement in modern American history.

The IACRL was founded by New York City Mob boss Joseph Colombo, Sr. to instill pride in Italian Americans and to counteract the notion that Italians in America were gangsters. It mattered little to Colombo's supporters that he had begun his career as a Mob hitman and worked his way up to control one of the five most powerful Mafia families in New York. For months at a time, Colombo and his followers, many of them burly teamsters and longshoremen, picketed FBI headquarters to demand among other things that the Bureau stop using the word "Mafia," which they declared was a myth created by overzealous federal prosecutors to justify their huge budgets. So powerful did the IACRL become that New York Governor Nelson Rockefeller, New York Congresswoman Bella Abzug, and New York Democratic Leader Meade Esposito, among other influential politicians, were guests at its parades, banquets, and demonstrations. Soon, IACRL stickers appeared on store fronts on Italian-American-owned businesses across the city.

On November 20, 1970, the IACRL sponsored a star-studded benefit at Madison Square Garden. Headlined by Frank Sinatra and Sammy Davis, Jr. and hosted by "Tonight Show" emcee Ed McMahon, the event raised more than $600,000 for the IACRL. Ticket holders that night included Mafia heavyweights Carlo Gambino, Russell Bufalino, and Raymond Patriarca, as well as political luminaries such as New York Deputy Mayor Richard Aurelio and Paul O'Dwyer, former Democratic candidate for the U.S. Senate.

Colombo even set up a political action committee through the IACRL, which endorsed and contributed to political candidates in New York. For example, Colombo's "Mob PAC" vigorously backed Edward T. Pulaski, a Democrat from Staten Island, in his 1970 effort to unseat New York State Senator John Marchi, an Italian-American who had repeatedly denounced Colombo as a "low-life thug."

Colombo's lawyer, Barry Ivan Slotnick, first told the Mob boss about Kahane. At a late night dinner in 1971, Slotnick mentioned to Colombo that he was representing Kahane at his arraignment on bomb-making charges. Slotnick said that the rabbi did not have much money and would probably have to fight his case from jail. Colombo, who according to Slotnick was attracted to Kahane's tough Jewish image, showed up in court the next morning with a bondsman to pay the rabbi's $25,000 bail.

Later, during an impromptu press conference with Colombo on the courthouse steps, Kahane told reporters that he welcomed the Mob boss's support, and promised to "picket the offices of the FBI if Mr. Colombo asks our [JDL] help.'' Asked by a *New York Times* reporter to discuss the implications of an alliance between the JDL and the IACRL, Kahane replied: ''It's human brotherhood. People of other faiths and backgrounds have come to help. It's the kind of thing which, had it been Blacks helping Jews, it would have drawn raves. The Italians are no worse than the Blacks.''

As a lawyer for both Colombo and Kahane, Slotnick was pivotal in setting up a working relationship between the IACRL and the JDL. And as a spokesman for both groups, Slotnick unswervingly trumpeted the organizations' virtues on numerous radio and television talk shows, declaring that their leaders were victims of racial and religious persecution by the government. At the time, Colombo's legal problems were certainly severe. He was implicated in a $750,000 jewelry heist; indicted for contempt of court; convicted in March 1971 of perjury; arrested one month later for interstate gambling; indicted twenty days after that on charges of controlling a $10 million-a-year gambling syndicate; and finally, he was awaiting trial for income tax evasion. When I interviewed Slotnick in 1986, during a time when he was reaping enormous publicity for his defense of subway gunman Bernhard Goetz, the flashy, self-proclaimed ''best defense attorney in America'' was still promoting the divisive racial politics of Kahane and Colombo. ''The major problem in this country,'' Slotnick told me, ''is not Americans of Italian descent overrunning unions, but the one Goetz confronted in the subway. Goetz was surrounded by four people. That's organized crime too, and a much more important kind of organized crime to be battled than [former] U.S. Attorney [Rudolph] Giuliani's so-called [Mob] Commission. I'm more concerned about the [James] Ramseurs of this world than I am about the so-called Mob.''* As for Kahane, Slotnick says historians will judge him as one of the great heroes of the Jewish people.

Judge Jack Weinstein saw more thug than hero in Kahane. On July 9, 1971, Kahane pleaded guilty to manufacturing firebombs. Prior to sentencing, the judge stated in court that he had received hundreds of letters on Kahane's behalf, some calling the JDL leader ''another Moses or Abraham Lincoln,'' ''a saint,'' ''the vic-

---

* James Ramseur was one of four Black youths who surrounded Goetz in the New York subway.

tim of another Dreyfus trial," "a Jewish Martin Luther King," "a modern day Maccabee," and a man "fighting for the blood of Jews that has been spilled down through the ages." Weinstein said that, while Kahane may have believed he was in a superior moral position, "so far as the law is concerned—when the JDL uses guns and bombs illegally they are not really distinguishable from the Weathermen or Black Panthers on the Left or the Ku Klux Klan on the Right." Despite Judge Weinstein's rebuke, he sentenced the rabbi to just four year's probation.

As part of Kahane's plea bargain agreement, he swore to have nothing more to do with weapons or explosives. Slotnick promised that the JDL would turn over its weapons stockpile to the government. Slotnick later phoned U.S. Attorney Thomas Pattison, saying that he had had a "dream" that the JDL had left a cache of explosives on the northbound Palisades Parkway, about one thousand feet south of the Alpine Lookout. Federal agents discovered 197 sticks of Trojan brand dynamite, the same brand used for the Amtorg bombing. The authorities closed the Parkway to traffic while an army bomb disposal unit from Fort Dix carted away the lethal explosives.

A few nights later, Slotnick told the U.S. attorney about another "dream." In this one, a JDL arms cache was located inside the East Side Air Terminal in Manhattan. Police who searched the terminal found gunpowder, fuses, and blasting caps in a locker directly behind a Delta ticket counter.

In the months that followed Kahane's conviction, the rabbi and the Mob boss became, Slotnick says, "close and good friends." The heart of the relationship as far as Kahane was concerned was easy access to illegal weapons and money. "The JDL got weapons and money, tons of money, from Colombo," said Irving Calderon. "Colombo thought he got respect from being seen with a famous rabbi, even though at the time most Jews didn't respect Kahane." Colombo got something more from his association with Kahane than "respect." Some of the JDL's toughest members worked as strong-arm men and loan collectors for the Colombo family, said Zweibon. "They wanted us to do muscle work for them like collecting loan shark debts," confirmed Calderon. "Our boys were unknown to the victims and didn't mind breaking kneecaps." Calderon also said that Colombo helped the JDL carry out several of its terrorist missions, though he will not say which ones. "Our relationship with Colombo gave us more clout," said Calderon. "People are afraid of the Mafia. It gave groups like the Black Panthers something to consider. One of the rationales Kahane used, and we promoted, was the precedent of Jabotinsky dealing with Mussolini before World War II. Kahane would say, 'If Jabotinsky could deal with Mussolini, we can deal with Colombo.' " Actually, the Italian Mafia has long had Jewish members. Some of Kahane's closest supporters were associates of the Colombo crime family, whose tentacles reached into a number of predominantly Jewish-owned businesses, from Manhattan's garment industry to jewelry and fur companies.

Kahane and Colombo assisted each other in other ways. For example, on June 8, 1971 at 7:00 P.M., according to an FBI surveillance report obtained under the Freedom of Information Act, Kahane joined Colombo, his son Anthony, and mobsters Joseph Brancoto, Nick Bianco, and Anthony Avgello in front of FBI headquarters in Manhattan to protest alleged Bureau harassment of Italian Americans. Later, Colombo helped Kahane organize a demonstration in Washington to protest the persecution of Soviet Jews. The demonstration, which Colombo and sixty of his followers attended, resulted in more than thirteen hundred arrests. Kahane later told me that Colombo paid bail and provided lawyers for some of those arrested. After the rally, Colombo "went on ABC-TV and said, 'We Italian Americans demand the American government cut relations with the Russians unless they let the Jews go,' " said Kahane. "I wanted to kiss him." (New York Congressman Mario Biaggi, who was recently convicted in separate trials in New York for accepting illegal gratuities and extorting money from a defense contractor, marched with Colombo and Kahane. Biaggi, still one of the rabbi's staunchest supporters, was awarded a medal of honor at a Kach dinner at Manhattan's prestigious Lincoln Square Synagogue in February 1988.)

Kahane and Colombo were often seen together. Kahane took the mobster to his favorite kosher deli on the Lower East Side and Colombo took the rabbi to his country club on Long Island to play golf.

To those who criticized Kahane for his friendship with a Mob boss, he replied: "I'll march with anyone if I think I can help a Jew." When Colombo was shot in the head by assassins while he was leading an Italian-American Unity Day rally at Columbus Circle on June 28, 1971, Kahane, who was to be a featured speaker, rushed to Roosevelt Hospital to visit his critically wounded friend. Chief of Detectives Albert Seedman recalled looking in on Colombo just before surgery: "The chief surgeon . . . showed me the X-rays of Colombo's skull. One bullet had lodged in the upper neck, two in the forehead. Incredibly, there was no sign of fatal subdural bleeding. So Joe Colombo was not going to die. . . . Just the same, it might have been better if he had passed away then. Those shots had made his brains into scrambled eggs." Following surgery, only Colombo's closest cronies were allowed into the hospital room. In addition to Kahane and Colombo's immediate family, entertainer Sammy Davis, Jr., and Howard Samuels, the unsuccessful gubernatorial candidate for New York, held a vigil at the Mob boss's bedside.

According to Irving Calderon and confirmed by a top Justice Department official, Còlombo's two sons, who are now in a federal penitentiary on racketeering convictions, asked the JDL to assassinate "crazy" Joe Gallo, a rival Mob boss who they believed had ordered the hit on their father. The intermediary conducting the negotiations between the Colombo family and the JDL was Nicky Bianco, a capo in the Colombo Mob on loan from the Patriarca family in New England. Bianco had met Kahane during a IACRL rally in front of FBI headquarters in Manhattan. Bianco thought that JDL members would have a better chance of getting close to Gallo because they would be unknown to him. "But the JDL didn't have the means to perform the hit," said the Justice Department official. "The JDL did say they were willing to supply logistics and information." Bianco also tried to recruit JDL people to assassinate the head of the Organized Crimes Strike Force in Brooklyn, said the Justice Department official. But Kahane rejected the proposal out of hand.

The Justice Department viewed the relationship between Colombo and Kahane as "an unholy alliance motivated by a need for mutual support," said the government official. "They each saw the other as a potential financial windfall. Colombo raised $3.5 million through IACRL, and Kahane hoped to cash in on it, claiming to have key contacts and political support within the Jewish political establishment, which Colombo could corrupt." The official noted, for example, that Kahane arranged to have New York gubernatorial candidate Howard Samuels picket the FBI for the IACRL. (There is no evidence that Samuels was corrupted by Columbo.) The JDL also helped Colombo launder

$2 million in IACRL funds that had been collected for a proposed children's hospital for which not even a cornerstone was ever laid. "The money went south with JDL couriers," said the government official.

Several months after Colombo was shot, the Bureau secretly met with Kahane hoping to recruit him as a source against the Mob. FBI officials thought that they might be able to "turn" the rabbi, because, "in wiretapped discussions with his own people following the Colombo shooting, Kahane said there was nothing to be gained from maintaining a relationship with the Colombo family," said the Justice Department official.

According to the top-secret FBI summary of the meeting with Kahane, the interviewing FBI agent wrote that he thought the JDL leader had the potential to become an excellent informant. "But nothing ever materialized," said the Justice Department official. "Kahane probably wasn't in a position to help in a substantial way."

Meanwhile, legal pressure continued to mount on Kahane through the summer of 1971. He faced upcoming trials for a violent protest in front of the Iraqi UN mission; for the December 1969 takeover of Tass in downtown Manhattan; and for rioting in front of the Soviet UN Mission.

The Nixon Administration continued to press law enforcement to clamp down on the JDL. Alarmed by Soviet threats against U.S. citizens living in the Soviet Union, the State Department turned to the venerable Rabbi Moshe Feinstein, then considered the foremost expert on *Halacha* (Jewish religious law) in the world. The State Department told Feinstein that many of the U.S. Embassy personnel in Moscow were Jewish. Feinstein summoned Kahane and ordered him to stop the JDL's harassment campaign. "You are jeopardizing Jewish lives," said Feinstein, whose position in the Orthodox world was such that even Kahane was forced to listen.

In August 1971, Kahane announced that he was moving to Israel. "It was impossible for me to tell people to go to Israel without going myself," he later told me. On a hot, sticky September morning, as he was on his way to catch an El Al flight to Tel Aviv, Kahane stopped at Joseph Colombo, Sr.'s house to pay his final respects. Kahane and his bodyguard Alex Sternberg were led into the basement where the Mafia don sat motionless in a wheelchair. Next to Colombo—who had been semi-comatose and on life support machines since the shooting—was a nurse, and "bodyguards galore, big beefy, deformed-looking brutes," said Sternberg. Kahane knelt at Colombo's side, softly cooing into his ear. The mobster stared blankly, without acknowledging his old friend's presence. "It was like he was in a catatonic state," said Sternberg. Later, as Kahane and Sternberg headed for Kennedy Airport, Kahane remarked that he believed Colombo was cognizant of what was going on around him, but would rather play brain dead than stand trial for a raft of indictments. As the Jewish militants turned onto the ramp leading to the airport, they heard a news bulletin about a JDL member who had been apprehended by federal authorities for making illegal weapons purchases. That afternoon, several young JDLers joined Kahane on his journey to Israel rather than face the feds. "That was the modus operandi," said Sternberg. "You get in trouble here and you go to Israel."

CHAPTER SEVEN
Hotel Zion

Although Meir Kahane declared that he moved to Israel out of pure Zionist convictions, the truth was more complex. First of all, the FBI had put him on notice that the next time he was convicted of a felony he would not be allowed to walk out of the courtroom on probation. The Nixon Administration was determined to rein in the JDL. Kissinger was not about to risk détente because of a pain-in-the-neck rabbi from Brooklyn. Kahane shrewdly calculated that federal prosecutors would not be able to lay a hand on him if his base of operations was in Israel, where he was immediately embraced by the Right and proclaimed a hero.

By February 1971, the entire seven-person JDL board was living under the shadow of a federal indictment. Bertram Zweibon, the JDL's chief legal counsel, began to make inquiries about moving his family and law practice to Israel. Dozens of JDL kids had already fled to the Jewish state, where Kahane offered them little or no assistance. Some turned to selling drugs. Two JDLers were arrested for extorting money from Israeli college students. A lucky few found temporary shelter with Nachman's family in Jerusalem. "We saw so many kids that joined the JDL get into serious trouble and were left floundering by my illustrious brother-in-law," Nachman's wife, Feiga, said contemptuously.

"We were the only ones around to help them. Thank God my own children stayed away from Meir. It was never forbidden, but they saw all the wrecks that came into our house."

Libby was equally determined that none of her children should wind up in a jail cell next to their father. "She made a deal with Meir," said Zweibon. "She would be the dutiful Orthodox wife and keep the home fires burning, but he couldn't have the children." But like many deals Kahane made, he later reneged. Libby had a ferocious fight with him after their twelve-year-old son Baruch was arrested at a 1971 JDL rally for Soviet Jews in Washington. She said that she was taking the children to Israel, and if he did not join them it would be the end of their marriage. In June 1971, Libby and the children moved to a small, drab apartment in Kiryat Itri, a West Jerusalem neighborhood. Around the same time, Libby's father, Joseph Blum, told an Israeli reporter that his daughter was distraught because of Meir's infidelities. He said that Libby was a "beaten woman" who moved to Israel because she feared for her children's safety in America.

Overwhelmed by their son's growing notoriety, even Kahane's aging parents reluctantly gave up their home in Brooklyn and moved to Israel. At a farewell dinner for Sonia and Charles Kahane held by Charles's synagogue in the summer of 1971, Meir managed to plug his own accomplishments while slyly chiding his father. "A week ago I was sitting in jail next to criminals," said Meir, addressing his father's congregants, the same ones he had ridiculed as a youth for what he perceived to be their brand of safe, middle-class Judaism. "I was afraid to close my eyes. What happened to this nice Jewish boy from Brooklyn? How did he end up in jail sitting next to common criminals? You are to blame!" he said, pointing to his father. "You taught me to fight for Jews. It's all your fault!"

In the final analysis, it was Kahane's appetite for power that brought him to Israel. "Meir has had one abiding dream that has motivated him since childhood," said Zweibon, "his desire to become prime minister of Israel. You can't get elected to that post from Brooklyn. Everything Kahane ever did was for that purpose. It was his overriding, maniacal ambition!"

But when Kahane arrived in Israel in September 1971, there seemed little chance of any right-wing politician becoming prime minister. Menachem Begin and his small, right-wing Herut Party had been political pariahs since the creation of the state in 1948. Ben-Gurion had forcibly disarmed the Irgun and Stern Gang and had hounded their members into the political wilderness. Herut-nicks, most of whom were veterans of the right-wing under-grounds, were passed over for promotion in the army and other state-run institutions. Begin himself was publicly ridiculed and openly despised by Ben-Gurion, whose Labor Party had domi-nated the government since the founding of the state.

Desperate for new heroes, the Israeli Right hailed Kahane as the universal symbol of the proud Jew fighting back. In a nation made up of survivors, nothing is more sacred than self-defense. As far as the Right was concerned, the JDL was the reincarna-tion of the self-defense group that Jabotinsky had founded in Odessa. To some, Kahane was the living embodiment of Jabotinsky.

"From far away Kahane looked like a real leader who modeled himself on Jabotinsky's humanistic philosophy," said Michael Kliner, a Likud Knesset member and head of its Immigration Committee, who, as chairman of the Israeli Student Union, pub-licly championed Kahane at an international convention of Jew-ish students in Philadelphia in 1969, provoking a furious debate in Israel. "We in Herut were all very much for the JDL."

More than anyone, Geula Cohen had high hopes for her Ameri-can protégé. "She was very enthusiastic about his arrival in Israel," said Yisrael Medad, Cohen's American-born legislative aide who had coordinated Betar's activities with the JDL in the late 1960s before moving to Israel. "She looked on him as the one who put the Soviet Jewish issue on the map. He was the anti-establishment fighter who had sabotaged Golda Meir's quiet diplomacy. She believed Herut needed someone like Kahane."

Begin agreed. The Herut leader touted Kahane inside the party's Central Committee and introduced him to the Israeli polit-ical scene. "The first time I met Kahane, Menachem Begin was leading him through the Knesset dining room introducing him to other Knesset members," recalled Uri Avnery, then head of a small, left-of-center party and now editor-in-chief of the Israeli magazine *Ha'olam Hazeh*.

"Begin was very high on Kahane," said Kliner, who some-times chauffeured Kahane to meetings with the Herut leader. "Begin agreed with Kahane that Jews had to fight for their civil rights, whether it was in the U.S. or the Soviet Union."

The best proof of Kahane's popularity was that Begin offered him a safe seat in his party. "I wouldn't say Begin and I were close," Kahane later told me. "But we had a relatively good relationship. I liked his work for the Irgun and he liked mine for the JDL.'' (So much so that Begin asked Kahane to write the introduction to the second American edition of his classic underground manifesto—*The Revolt.*)*

But Kahane said that he rejected Begin's offer for fear of having to compromise his principles. "We were shocked when Meir turned Begin down," said Kahane's New York lawyer and Kach supporter, Barry Slotnick. "But Meir told us to be patient—that he would be prime minister one day."

Kahane was also courted by the National Religious Party headed by Yosef Burg, who had been a guest in the Kahanes' home when Meir was a child. "Kahane told the NRP people that he would join the party if he was free to express his own opinions and vote according to his conscience," said a source close to Kahane who had firsthand knowledge of the negotiations. "But no party could accept that kind of lack of discipline, so the talks broke down."

Later, there were secret meetings between Kahane and two ultranationalist NRP Knesset members, Zevulon Hammer and Yehuda Ben-Meir (who was known as Jerry Meirson when he lived in the Bronx). Hammer and Ben-Meir considered breaking away from the NRP's aging leadership to forge a new settlement-oriented religious party with Kahane. The talks collapsed when

---

* The JDL was instrumental in distributing another classic Revisionist polemic, *Battleground: Facts and Fantasy in Palestine*, written by Samuel Katz, the former propaganda chief for the Irgun, who subsequently became the foreign press adviser to his mentor Prime Minister Begin. The crudely written tract's main contention is that most Arabs in Palestine arrived in the wake of the Zionist enterprise, and therefore are not entitled to national rights. "The physical reacquisition of the land from the handful of existing (Arab) inhabitants presented no moral problem of choice for the Zionists," wrote Katz. The JDL purchased 5,000 copies of the book, at a steep discount, directly from Katz, who had bought 30,000 copies from the publisher, Bantam Books. Katz wrote to Zweibon that the entire first edition was "covered in advance by the Israel-British Bank in Tel Aviv," which loaned the money against the guarantee of a well-to-do, right-wing Zionist. Thousands of copies of *Battleground* were subsequently distributed by Israeli embassies and pro-Israel lobby groups. The JDL consignment was sent to JDL member Fay Lloyd's house in Long Beach. William Perl, chairman of the JDL's Washington chapter, received 500 copies. Zweibon, meanwhile, contacted various libraries to make sure that they purchased the book. "*Battleground* is a fact-laden book constructed in such a manner as to afford the reader thereof with the intellectual ability to combat Arab propaganda in the United States and in particular on the college campus," Zweibon wrote to the American Jewish Committee's head librarian in February 1973. "It contains an analysis of the problem in an historical perspective which puts lie to much of the Arab myth."

Kahane demanded to head the party, according to several sources.

One of Kahane's most forceful advocates on the Israeli Right was Shmuel Tamir, a former high-ranking Irgun officer who then headed the right-wing Free Center Party, which had a single seat in the Knesset. Tamir had been one of the few right-wing politicians in Israel to openly support the JDL's ongoing terrorist campaign against the Soviet Union: "The real terror is being undertaken systematically by the authorities in the Soviet Union against Soviet Jewry," Tamir said in a conversation recounted in a confidential American Jewish Committee (AJC) memo. "It is our duty," Tamir continued, "to help to the utmost, and I stress utmost, to put an end to this situation and help liberate those Jews. All routine methods of declarations and conventions have failed. The system of harassing Soviet representatives and missions is a legitimate way of expressing public protest. As such it should be encouraged. The Soviets are sensitive to public opinion in the Free World. Any attempt to expose them in this area is helpful. Any denouncement ill serves Soviet Jewry."

Prime Minister Golda Meir was less than favorable toward Kahane, whom she viewed as an uncouth New York wiseguy. There were those in the Labor Party who even wanted to bar Kahane from becoming an Israeli citizen under the Law of Return as the state had done with gangster Meyer Lansky. In a way, the reaction to Kahane in Israel echoed the pre-state conflict between the left-wing Haganah and the right-wing Irgun and Stern Gang, which the JDL emulated. "Subconsciously we remember the disputes we had in the '40s," a prominent Jerusalem lawyer and Herut Party member told an AJC official who recorded the remarks in a confidential memo that I obtained. "The Labor government recoils from the League and the former [right-wing] underground members and their sympathizers incline towards it." The Israeli lawyer added that as long as the Arab world resorted to terrorism, Jews should counter with the JDL. "We can't always be good boys. When we object to something the Syrians have done, the Western world says, 'What can we do about those madmen?' Well, it's good to have some of our own madmen even though it disturbs the establishment."

Subscribing to the view that Israel needs its own madmen, Dr. Yisrael Eldad, one of the country's leading right-wing ideologues, had sought Kahane out even before he moved to Israel. Eldad,

who had been the Stern Gang's chief theorist, first heard about
Kahane from relatives in New York who were JDL members.
Eldad had always considered them apolitical. He was impressed
that Kahane had been able to shake his relatives out of their apa-
thy. On February 3, 1970, Eldad wrote to Kahane inviting him
to come to Israel and join him in his crusade to build Jewish settlements on the West Bank. The year before, Eldad had declined
an invitation to join Begin's list in the upcoming Knesset elections, and instead formed The Land of Israel Party. Though
Eldad's party polled only a few thousand votes, failing to win
the one percent necessary to enter the Knesset, his ideas stirred
the latent desires of many ultranationalists—who, like him,
dreamed of a Jewish super-state that would one day stand from
the Nile to the Euphrates.

Addressing Kahane as "flesh of our flesh, blood of our blood,
and soul of our soul," Eldad wrote: "It has occurred to those
of us who have long fought together in a common battle for the
salvation of our Land and our people—to bring you here to
demonstrate . . . *that the Jewish nationalist front is one*—and
that the battle for the wholeness of the people and the Redemption of the Land—is one war.

"We are willing to finance your visit and to organize some
rallies and to introduce you to the public and to also organize
a press conference and thereby to strengthen your organization
in the United States in the sense of its moral authority. During
your visit here we will also be able to discuss other ways we
can cooperate together. If this meets with your approval, please
answer promptly and your visit to Israel will be arranged. . . .
With honor and the blessing of the Kingdom of Israel, Dr. Yisrael Eldad."*

Overall, Kahane was delighted by his welcome in Israel. "The
response to the JDL is magnificent here," he wrote to Zweibon.
Kahane was even courted by several Labor Party mavericks, most
notably Moshe Dayan, who thought that Kahane would be good

---

* In 1987, Eldad received the Jabotinsky Prize, a $100,000 award given annually to
the person "deemed to have done the most for the defense of the rights of the Jewish
people," according to the New York-based, tax-exempt foundation's statement of purpose. Past awards have gone to Christian evangelist Jerry Falwell, former U.S. Ambassador to the UN Jeane J. Kirkpatrick, and Natan Sharansky. Judges have included two
past chairmen of the Conference of Presidents of Major American Jewish Organizations, Morris B. Abram and Kenneth J. Bialkin, and British media mogul Lord
Weidenfeld.

at persuaded American Jews to move to Israel. Following
Dayan's lead, Kahane founded *Habayta*, a short-lived organization dedicated to encouraging *aliya*, or immigration to Israel,
which was headed by Dr. Victor Ratner, an eccentric British neurologist whose patients included Elizabeth Taylor and Richard
Burton.

Kahane undoubtedly could have had a highly successful career
in right-wing Israeli politics if his overweening ego had not stood
in the way. He simply lacked the temperament to be a team
player. Kahane had grown accustomed to being a one-man show
in America, where he not only had the limelight to himself, but
a measure of autonomy as well. He believed that his exploits in
America entitled him to a top position in Begin's party, not a
mid-level spot, which is what he was offered. Kahane did not
relish the idea of being told by party bosses how to vote in the
Knesset or what to say to the press. And he had no intention
of spending years toiling in Herut committee meetings, clawing
his way up the party ladder. His anti-establishment behavior may
have been a virtue in the United States, but Herut, the anti-
establishmentarians of Israel, demanded party discipline.

Less than a month after arriving in Israel, Kahane opened a
JDL office in Jerusalem—the first step in setting up an independent political party. The move infuriated Eldad and his one-time
colleague in the Stern Gang Geula Cohen. "Listen, this is
Israel," railed Cohen. "We don't need the Jewish Defense League.
We have Zahal—the Israeli Army. Don't transplant the League
to Israel!"

Kahane promised that he had no intention of using the JDL
to enter local politics. He told his Israeli backers that he wanted
to start his own *Kirya*, or Jewish educational center. American
Jewish graduates of the center were to return to U.S. college campuses and form student groups that would counteract left-wing,
anti-Zionist activism in academia. Kahane had been given
$100,000 by well-to-do New Yorkers to set up the center, which
would also offer Israeli youth classes in Zionist ideology. Since
Betar had degenerated into little more than a sports club in Israel,
Eldad and Cohen decided that Kahane was the ideal choice to
build a new right-wing Zionist youth movement. Eldad himself
was recruited to teach courses in Zionist history.

Kahane opened the youth center in the Zion Hotel, which he
leased with money given to him by his American supporters. The

shabby, nondescript building was located on Zion Square, in what was then a seedy section of downtown Jerusalem near the border that divided the Arab and Jewish sides of the city. Kahane's young disciples often leaned over the hotel balcony, taunting prostitutes who plied the alleyways.

The Zion Hotel was an auspicious choice for Kahane's school, as the neighborhood was rich in Revisionist history. In a violent harangue from a hotel balcony overlooking Zion Square, Menachem Begin had exhorted an angry crowd in January 1952 to topple the government for accepting war reparations from Germany. "It will be a fight to the death," Begin shouted. "Today I shall give the command—Blood!" Begin and several thousand followers then stormed the Knesset, pelting it with rocks and bottles and setting fire to cars. Begin's speech and the subsequent riot ignited a wave of right-wing demonstrations and terrorist attacks across the country, including the attempted bombing of the Israeli Foreign Ministry by Herut Party member Dov Shilansky, who today is Speaker of the Knesset.*

Two decades after Begin whipped up right-wing fury from his perch in Zion Square, Kahane was using the Zion Hotel to ready a new generation of young extremists to follow in the footsteps of the Irgun and the Stern Gang. Kahane had the hotel converted into a warren of dormitories, classrooms, and offices. Eldad, who had maintained an office at the Zion Hotel for years, turned it over to Kahane. Students spent up to eight hours a day studying Zionism and religion. One of Kahane's students was Geula Cohen's son, Tzahe Hanegbi, who later became an administrative assistant to Israeli Prime Minister Yitzhak Shamir and now is an ultra-hard-line Likud Knesset member.

A select cadre of Kahane's disciples was taught more than Talmud and Jabotinsky's dictums. In a secret training camp near Jerusalem, they were instructed in terrorist tactics by some of Israel's best-known, pre-state underground fighters. One of the students was Alex Sternberg, a twenty-two-year-old Hungarian-

---

* One extremist group composed of Orthodox Jews and ex-Stern Gang members bombed Israeli army bases to protest inducting women into the military. At a secret meeting in May 1951, the group's leader, Rabbi Frank, who later became the Grand Rabbi of Jerusalem, authorized a plan to bomb the Knesset on May 14 while it was in session. Fortunately, Israel's internal security service, Shin Bet, thwarted the plot. Two years later, sixteen former Stern Gang members who conspired to overthrow the government were convicted by a military tribunal for a wave of terrorist bombings. But not until 1958, did Shin Bet eradicate the various right-wing extremist groups.

born Jew whose parents had survived the death camp at Auschwitz, who visited Kahane at the Zion Hotel in June 1972. "The Zion Hotel was like the JDL camp in the Catskills," recalled Sternberg, who had been one of Kahane's bodyguards and the JDL's ace karate instructor in America. "It was supposed to be used as a base to go into the desert and learn how to shoot Uzis."

Sternberg, a short, compact, powerfully-built man, had first met Kahane in 1968 when he was teaching karate in Williamsburg to yeshiva boys. Kahane heard about Sternberg's prowess, and asked him to train JDL youths. Sternberg was mesmerized by Kahane's brand of Zionism. "Kahane often said that when Moses saw an Egyptian taskmaster hitting a Jew, he didn't form a committee of concerned Egyptian Jews, but he went and killed the guy," said Sternberg. "As a Holocaust survivor's child—Kahane's message was tremendous. The Black Power movement was happening, and I felt, 'Why not a Jewish movement? We have rights too.' Kahane came along at a very opportune time in my development."

But Sternberg grew disillusioned with Kahane, who, he thought, seemed more concerned with getting his name in newspapers than with defending American Jews. Sternberg resigned his JDL post in America, and in June 1972 visited Israel, looking for a new start in the "Promised Land." He had intended to steer clear of Kahane. Yet there was some inexplicable force that drew him to the militant rabbi. Wistfully, he visited his former mentor at the Zion Hotel. Kahane was happy to see Sternberg. He was even happier to hear that Sternberg had publicly broken with the JDL in America. It was a perfect cover for Kahane's latest scheme. He recruited Sternberg to build a Jewish terrorist underground in the United States that would be made up of persons who had no previous links with the JDL. "He told me he wanted to start an underground group in American that would target various buildings and organizations for bombings," said Sternberg. "The three main targets were Arabs, Nazis, and Russians."

Kahane introduced Sternberg to Amihai "Giddy" Paglin, the brilliant chief operations officer of the Irgun, at a meeting in the back room of a kosher dairy restaurant on King George Street near the Central Synagogue in Jerusalem. Paglin had been secretly training JDL kids in the craft of terrorism for several years. "When I met him I felt I was shaking hands with a legend," said

Sternberg. "I remember feeling very psyched. I had read so much about Giddy in Begin's book *The Revolt*," the blood-and-fire tale of Begin's underground years.

Paglin hardly looked like an arch terrorist. He was a middle-aged man of medium height, broad shouldered, with a little bit of a paunch. A diehard Irgunist who had lived at the cutting edge of "the revolt," Paglin could not seem to adjust to a mundane life in his family's stove manufacturing business. His involvement with Kahane had as much to do with finding an outlet for his pent-up energy as expressing his commitment to the rabbi's hard-line ideology. That is not to say that Paglin was not ideologically motivated. He told Sternberg that he saw Zionist fervor fading in Israel, especially among the youth who, he said, were more interested in Tel Aviv's gaudy night life than in wresting the West Bank from the Arabs. He told Sternberg that Kahane was the natural heir of Jabotinsky and Begin—and that the JDL would inherit the Irgun's fighting spirit. "He thought the JDL was going to revive the fire of the old days," said Sternberg.

As the three men talked quietly over blintzes, Sternberg recalled some of Paglin's infamous exploits: the bombing of British headquarters at the King David Hotel, the mass breakout of Jewish prisoners from the British jail at Acre, the execution of two British sergeants in retaliation for the hanging of two Irgunists. The executions had particularly shocked the British mandatory authorities for their sheer cold-bloodedness, hastening their departure from Palestine.*

Kahane hoped that some of Paglin's ruthless efficiency would rub off on his followers. As the waiter served Turkish coffee, Kahane described the JDL's desperate situation in America. The militant wing of the JDL, he said, was on the verge of collapse.

---

* J. Bowyer Bell describes the execution in his book *Terror Out of Zion*: "Paglin pulled a homemade hood over his [the British sergeant's] head. He was hustled into the next room and lifted onto a small chair. A rope with a looped noose dangled from a hook in a rafter. As his wrists and ankles were bound, he spoke for the first time. 'Are you going to hang me?' No one answered. 'Can I leave a message?' Paglin told him there was no time. The noose was around his neck. Paglin gestured, and one of the men kicked the chair away. The body swayed back and forth, the hook creaking in the rafter. The rumble of British traffic searching along outside was the only sound. The sergeant's fingers grew limp, his trousers became stained by his voided bladder. Paglin made another signal. The second sergeant was brought out, hooded, bound, and placed on the chair with the second noose around his neck. Another signal and he too swayed at the end of a short rope, the hook creaking. The bodies were then hung from a tree in an orange grove, booby-trapped with anti-personnel mines."

Charles Kahane *(left)* and one of his brothers, shortly after their immigration to the United States.

An angelic-faced Meir Kahane at his Bar Mitzvah.

Meir Kahane's Bar Mitzvah. *From left to right*, Meir, Sonia,
Charles, and Nachman.

Allan Mallenbaum (*left*) and Joseph Churba (*right*) in
Coney Island, Brooklyn, 1949.

Meir Kahane, 1956.

Meir Kahane's wedding, 1956. *From left to right*,
Nachman, Charles, Meir, Libby, and Sonia.

Libby Kahane, 1956.

Nachman and Feiga Kahane at
their wedding.

TWA PILOTS PERIL AIR PEACE

—Story on Page 2

Clinging to Life. Patrolman John Conway supports Estelle Evans as Patrolman Vincent Miller handles life preservers. Police said Miss Evans, a 21-year-old model, leaped 135 feet from the Queensboro Bridge into the East River early yesterday. Alerted by other cops, Conway and Miller spotted girl and leaped into water for rescue. —*Story on page 3*

Police rescue Estelle Donna Evans, who leaped from the Queensboro Bridge into the East River on July 30, 1966, after Meir Kahane ended their affair. (Photograph by George Lockhart. Copyright ©1966, New York News, Inc., reprinted with permission)

Meir Kahane in the New York office of the JDL (*left*). Bertram
Zweibon, JDL cofounder and chief legal counsel from
1968 to 1974 (*right*). Photographs circa 1971.

Meir Kahane, police
mug shot, May 12,
1971.

Irving Calderon, police
mug shot, May 12,
1971.

Bernie Deutsch and Menachem Begin in Deutsch's
Brooklyn home.

JDL members break up a Communist book fair in Haifa, Israel
in 1979. Matt Liebowitz in a black leather jacket (*left*);
Avigdor Eskin wearing a white jacket and holding
a Hebrew sign (*right*).

Bernie Deutsch (*center*) and Geula Cohen (*far right*) with a group of
Soviet Jews who had recently arrived in Israel.
(Israel Press & Photo Agency)

Meir Kahane in his Jerusalem office, The Museum of the Potential
Holocaust, 1979. (Photograph by Robert I. Friedman)

Victor Vancier, convicted firebomber and head of the JDL in New York, 1986. (Photograph by James Hamilton. Courtesy of *The Village Voice*)

Alex Odeh, the Western regional director of the American-Arab
Anti-Discrimination Committee, who was blown apart by a pipe
bomb attached to his office door on October 11, 1985.
(Courtesy of the American-Arab Anti-Discrimination Committee)

Alex Odeh's office after the October 1985 bombing. (Courtesy of
the Santa Ana, California police department)

DID THIS MAN KILL ALEX ODEH?

**ANDY GREEN: ONE OF THE
FBI'S THREE SUSPECTS**

Andy Green, one of the FBI's three suspects in the
Odeh bombing, *The Village Voice,* July 12, 1988.
(Photograph by James Hamilton. Courtesy of *The Vil-
lage Voice*)

Meir Kahane raising money among Brooklyn's Syrian Jewish community, 1987. (Courtesy of Ralph Betesh)

Meir Kahane is carried through the streets of Jerusalem by supporters following the announcement of his election to the Israeli Knesset, July 24, 1984. (The Associated Press/Wide World Photos, Inc., reprinted with permission)

Most of the high-profile people were on trial, in prison, or fugitives in Israel. What was needed, Kahane declared, was a professionally trained Jewish underground in America that would go beyond the demonstrations and violent acts that had characterized the JDL in the past. He envisioned a shadowy army of unknown assassins who would murder their victims in well-planned, smoothly executed attacks and then disappear back into the yeshivas, the synagogues, and the suburbs.

Over a two-month period during the summer of 1972, Sternberg met Paglin several times a week at Paglin's oven factory outside Tel Aviv. After the workers had gone for the day, Paglin taught Sternberg the fundamentals of terrorism. During one session, Sternberg complained about the JDL's ineptitude. "It was especially embarrassing to tell a consummate professional like Giddy what amateurs we were," said Sternberg. "But he told me that many of the Irgun's operations also went haywire." Once, Giddy recounted, the Irgun blew up a building in Jaffa used by Palestinian guerrillas, killing many innocent Arabs in the neighborhood because they had used too much dynamite. "It made me feel a lot better about our lack of professionalism," said Sternberg.

One day Paglin arrived at the factory, hauling a milk box laden with bomb-making devices. There were wires of different sizes and thicknesses, timing devices, fuses, "all kinds of goodies to make bombs from material that you could pick up in most paint stores," said Sternberg. Paglin demonstrated what to do with the bombs once they were assembled. "He showed me how to collapse a building like a house of cards by placing a bomb next to a support beam in the basement."

Paglin also taught Sternberg how to make timing devices from an eye dropper, acid, paraffin, and prophylactics. Unlike a timer built from a clock, this ingenious contraption would be untraceable if the bomb failed to go off. On at least one occasion, police in New York had been able to apprehend JDL bombers by tracing a timing device in an unexploded bomb back to the Radio Shack electronics store where the parts had been purchased. "The discussion about how to build a timing device was pretty funny because of the language problem," Sternberg recalled. "The word for condom in Hebrew is *gummy*, which literally means rubber. He kept saying, 'You get a *gummy*.' I thought he meant a rubber band. It didn't occur to me he meant a prophylactic. 'If you're twenty-three years old, why don't you understand what a gummy is?' cried Paglin. Once he began to elaborate, I caught on."

Paglin even devised a blueprint for an underground army in America. "He told me to keep a public distance from the JDL when I returned to America," said Sternberg. "At the same time, I was supposed to look for young Jews who had strong right-wing Zionist views, but who had no previous ties to the JDL. 'You're like a producer looking for a certain face to cast in your movie,' he told me." Once Sternberg found his featured players, his task was to organize them into three-person cells. "I would be the only link between the cells," said Sternberg. "That way if one of the kids became a government informant, he could only turn in the other two and me."

Kahane had his own set of detailed instructions for Sternberg. First, he told Sternberg to use synagogues and large yeshivas for cover because they were an inexplicable universe to the FBI, let alone to most Jews. "Put on a black coat and hat and walk into a yeshiva library and no one will question you," Kahane told Sternberg. Yeshiva libraries, Kahane said, were filled with musty shelves of seldom used religious texts—a perfect place for a message drop. Most importantly, Kahane counseled, only Orthodox youths should be recruited into the underground. Not only could they inconspicuously navigate inside a yeshiva, but they also had characteristics that he thought were often lacking in secular Jews—self-discipline and adherence to a higher authority. "He believed that if an Orthodox kid is committed to something," said Sternberg, "he will do it with religious fervor."

Kahane had already worked out the financial end of the operation, as well as a clever way to relay instructions. When Sternberg needed money or wanted to communicate with Kahane, he was to leave a message in the Oran Hakodesh (the arc of the covenant) near the Safer Torah in a certain Brooklyn synagogue. He was to receive money and messages in the same way. The courier was a prominent New York businessman.

Meanwhile, Kahane continued to shuttle back and forth between Israel and America throughout the fall and winter of 1971, carrying out increasingly violent anti-Soviet operations. Although familiarity with Kahane's personality began to breed contempt, his covert backers in Israel knew that there was no one else with Kahane's stature who was willing to stage daily demonstrations in America on behalf of Soviet Jews, not to mention risk a prison sentence. "Begin wanted daily headlines about Soviet Jews in the American newspapers," said Yisrael Medad, Tehiya Party leader Geula Cohen's Knesset aide. "Kahane still appeared to be the best man for the job."

But while Cohen, Shamir, and the others applauded the JDL's fits of violence and Jewish machismo in America, they were enraged when Kahane imported the same tactics into Israel. Despite promising his patrons that the Israeli JDL would be a nonviolent educational organization, it was soon firebombing Christian churches and bookstores in Jerusalem and staging violent demonstrations against a sect of Black American Hebrews that had settled in Dimona. "The [Israeli] government is in the midst of a real crackdown . . . since the missionary office on the Mount of Olives passed into oblivion," a JDL member who had jumped bail in America and fled to Jerusalem wrote to Zweibon in 1972. "While many Israelis are upset by the alleged actions of the League, there are those who support it morally and some businessmen who give substantial financial support. There is a lot of money spent on bail lately."

Less than a year after arriving in Israel, Kahane seized on what would become his overriding obsession—expelling Israel's Arabs. On November 1, 1971, the Israeli JDL staged its first anti-Arab demonstration. A group of Kahane's young American followers, with long hair and dressed in black leather jackets and blue jeans, jostled Arabs at Damascus Gate in East Jerusalem's Old City, warning them to leave Israel if they valued their lives. "They [the JDL] are more unwelcome and more dangerous to Israel than a whole . . . network of Fatah agents . . .," editorialized *The Jerusalem Post* after the incident. "As far as I'm concerned," Jerusalem's Mayor Teddy Kollek said on a New York radio talk show, "Rabbi Kahane is an unwanted import and you can have him back as quickly as possible."

In late 1971, Kahane instructed Robert Fine, a JDL thug and part-time strong-arm man for the New York Mafia, to attack PLO targets in Europe, according to ex-JDL officials. Left to finance the operation himself, Fine set up an extortion racket that preyed on students at Bar Ilan University near Tel Aviv. When an Israeli student who had been victimized threatened to go to the police, Fine beat him up so badly that he required hospitalization. Fine and a second JDL man were arrested and ended up with six-month jail terms. Geula Cohen fired off a letter to Zweibon begging him to try to control Kahane and his young followers. "He'll destroy what I'm doing in Israel and what we're doing in the States," she complained.

On January 26, 1972, the anti-Soviet violence that Cohen and her cohorts had helped set in motion some two years earlier finally ended in tragedy. On that date the JDL claimed its first victim—a Jew. A squad of JDL youths firebombed the Manhattan offices of Jewish impresario Sol Hurok, who brought Soviet performers to the United States. Iris Kones, a twenty-seven-year-old secretary in Hurok's accounting department, choked to death on the fumes. According to the autopsy report, her lungs were filled with black soot mixed with mucus. Within hours of the bombing, an anonymous caller phoned NBC News and UPI in New York claiming credit for the bombing in the name of the JDL.

Given the JDL's proclivity for violence, the tragedy seemed inevitable. Still, no one in the JDL thought the group's first fatality would be a defenseless Jewish woman. Kahane, then in Jerusalem, deplored the bombing, although when I asked him about it in 1979, he admitted that the bombing was the work of the JDL. "I once asked Begin how he felt when he learned that thirty or forty Jews were killed in the [Irgun] bombing of the King David Hotel," Kahane said. "Begin told me he felt horrible. That's exactly how I felt after the Hurok bombing."

It was Zweibon who called Kahane from a JDL member's house on Long Island with news of Kones's death. "He went bananas," Zweibon recalled. "He was terribly upset, as we all were. I said to him: 'Meir, we have nothing to do with this—you and I. We are completely free of any guilt. But there is a moral guilt because we advocated violence and we singled out Hurok as a target and somebody listened to us. It's not traceable to us. But it is our moral responsibility.' "

Zweibon said that he urged Kahane to exploit the tragedy to promote the JDL's agenda. Until now, Zweibon argued, JDL violence had been intended to win headlines, not body counts. "I told Meir that the Hurok bombing is our ticket into the dark world of terrorism," said Zweibon. "It enhances the image we're trying to project. It was like talking to the wall. He just stuttered away like crazy. The next time I saw him in person he foreswore ever using amateurs in physical violence.''

Zweibon said that he viewed Kones's death as an acceptable if unfortunate by-product of a greater struggle for the freedom of Soviet Jews. ''My father was a union organizer in the 1920s,'' said Zweibon. ''He was beaten up and he had people beaten up. He told us when we started the JDL that when you use violence some people get hurt. What the hell did Meir know about violence? Or his father? They were rabbis from a long line of rabbis. The most violent thing they could do is slam their *Gemorrah* shut. When it finally happened that which had to happen, he couldn't tolerate it. . . . He is as much equipped to be an underground leader as I am to be the first man to sit on Pluto.''

As he had done in other JDL bombings, Kahane allegedly advised those involved in the Hurok incident to flee to Israel. Zweibon strongly denies that he helped anyone connected with the Hurok bombing to slip away. But one former JDL member who says he helped some of the accomplices leave the United States, claims that Zweibon had worked out the details of the escape, handed out cash and plane tickets, then swallowed the paper with the written instructions. At least four suspects were allegedly spirited out of the country this way, two to Israel and two to Canada.

On June 16, 1972, a federal grand jury in New York indicted three JDL members for Kones's murder. The government's case ultimately collapsed when one of the defendants, Sheldon Seigel, the JDL's premier bombmaker who had secretly agreed to cooperate with the government in return for immunity, refused to testify. Seigel's defense attorney, Alan Dershowitz, discovered that his client had been coerced into becoming a police informant after his identity became known to the authorities from illegal wiretaps that had been placed on JDL phones. Dershowitz successfully argued that because the taps violated Seigel's Fourth Amendment rights, which protected him from illegal search and seizure, all the evidence that flowed from them was tainted. The fact that Seigel, a tall, gaunt twenty-five year old, had confessed to making the bomb that killed Kones and had implicated his friends in the conspiracy, was now irrelevant because the government could no longer force him to testify.

The case was finally dropped in 1975, after two more potential witnesses refused to testify and the government failed in its attempt to extradite two suspects from Israel.

One was Jerome Zeller, whose girl friend, Gitti Masowicki, told her parents that Zeller had planted the bomb in Hurok's office, lit the fuse, and ran. She even told them that Zeller had gotten lost in the building and had to ask a security guard for directions to Hurok's office. Gitti's parents, both Holocaust survivors, forced her to give a signed statement to the FBI implicating Zeller. But just before she was to appear in front of a federal grand jury, a relative drove her to Canada, where she left for Israel. When she finally arrived in Israel, both Zeller and Kahane called her a traitor and refused to have anything to do with her. Estranged from the JDL, her boy friend, and her family, Gitti ended up living on the streets for a while. In the summer of 1973, FBI agents tracked her down to Herzelyia, where she was living, and unsuccessfully tried to get her to voluntarily return to the United States and testify. Masowicki, thirty-five, is now living in Sheepshead Bay under her married name.

Zeller found a safe haven in the home of Nachman Kahane, then Israel's assistant minister of religious affairs. He was subsequently arrested at the request of the U.S. government and imprisoned in Tel Aviv, but was released on $1,200 bail while he fought extradition. On May 15, 1973, Meir Kahane wrote to Zweibon asking him to send $1,000 for Zeller's lawyer. "I emphasize that Zeller is as much a part of the Hurok case as the others and I would like to see money before the lawyers quit and Zeller goes back." Several months later, Zeller was wounded in a tank battle on the Golan Heights during the Yom Kippur War. When the United States made another request for Zeller's extradition, "the reply was you can make it and hold your breath until you die 'cause you ain't going to get him because he's a national hero," said Joseph Jaffe, one of the U.S. attorneys who prosecuted the case. During the extradition proceeding Kahane asked Chief Rabbi Ovadiah Yosef to issue a ruling prohibiting Israel from surrendering Jews to other countries, citing Maimonides. Impressed with Kahane's efforts to protect Jews from extradition, gangster Meyer Lansky, who was tossed out of Israel as an undesirable, gave Kahane a large donation to keep up his good work. Zeller is now living in a West Bank settlement with his family.

The JDL's popularity plummeted after the Hurok bombing. Kahane's tactics, long tolerated among some segments of the American Jewish community, were increasingly condemned. Ironically, Meir Kahane's first cousin, Rabbi David Kahane of the posh Sutton Place Synagogue on Manhattan's East Side, presided over the Kones funeral, calling her death the "bitter fruit of the climate of violence."

Yevgeny Yevtushenko, the Soviet poet who had immortalized the Nazis' mass slaughter of Kiev's Jewry in the poem "Babi Yar," was in New York for a poetry reading when Kones was killed. Moved by the tragedy, he composed a poem called "Bombs for Balalaikas":

Poor Iris,
Victim of the age,
You've fallen
Fragile,
Dark-eyed
Jewish girl suffocated by smoke
As though in a Nazi gas chamber.
It's hard to vent out poisoned air.
Damn you, servants of Hell
Who seek coexistence between peoples
By building bridges of cadavers.

Yet when Kahane's covert backers in Mossad finally broke with him, it was not because of Iris Kones's senseless murder, or because of his Wild West behavior in Israel. The relationship ran aground primarily over the issue of money, or more precisely, allegations that Kahane had misappropriated funds earmarked for terrorist operations. "The break had nothing to do with Kahane's politics in Israel," said Deutsch. "It had to do with money we gave him for specific activities."

According to Deutsch, Zweibon, and other sources connected to the operation, in early 1972 Kahane was given $70,000 to stage a number of violent demonstrations in England, France, and North America. The climax was to be in Canada, where Kahane was supposed to arrange the kidnapping of Soviet Prime Minister Alexei Kosygin, scheduled to arrive on a state visit that summer. However, not a single action was carried out. Kahane refused to return the money, using it instead to finance his first unsuccessful run for the Knesset in 1973, according to Zweibon and others who at the time backed the militant rabbi. At a stormy meeting on August 12, 1972, in Deutsch's suite at the Tel Aviv Hilton, Geula Cohen and several others confronted Kahane about the money. "I spent every penny on logistics, surveillance, and salaries," insisted Kahane. "I hired good people. It's not my fault the mission failed."

"We called him a thief and a liar," said Deutsch. "At that point, we wished he had stayed in the U.S."

A few days after the meeting, covert group member and attorney Pessach Mor wrote to Zweibon, explaining that the break with Kahane appeared to be irrevocable. The letter began: "I am afraid that we (Geula and myself) had some harsh words with Meir on various subjects (his 'school,' his activities, etc.), and he left the discussions rather in a 'huff.' As things now stand we see no way that we can cooperate with him in any way nor with his 'organization'. . . . The result is that, as long as the conditions we complained about continue, we will give no support to him in any form whatsoever (financial or otherwise). Bernie [Deutsch] was present at the discussion and will give you some details; but it is really a long story and I would prefer not to deal with it on paper.

"I cannot say of course where this puts you personally vis-à-vis us; you know our line and activity, our ideas and our methods and it is up to you to decide. From our point of view we look on you as one of us to the extent we are and can be active but of course wish in no way to put our noses into affairs that concern Meir and yourself. Unfortunately, Bert, if the last year is an indication, Meir seems to us to have gone off on a tangent which makes him so useless and harmless that, in a little while, people will forget what he was."

Zweibon sided with Mor and Cohen. "Meir betrayed Cohen and the others from the beginning," Zweibon told me during an interview at Cheers, a kosher restaurant in Manhattan. "The money just went through his pockets. Why didn't Geula see it coming? She is an idealist of the worst order. Kahane's duplicity boggled her mind. She was an expert in underground warfare, not judging people. But given the fact that he was willing to expose himself in the U.S. to prison and public repudiation, she made an assumption that he was one of us and could be trusted." Cohen adds now, "His place was in the U.S. fighting for Jews. . . . The break destroyed our group."

Regardless of how the unruly rabbi spent their money, he did get the issue of Soviet Jews onto the front pages of *The New York Times*, and that is all Cohen, Shamir, and the others wanted, said Zweibon. By late 1972, the American Jewish establishment, which had played down the Soviet Jewish question, had set up well-funded bureaucracies to deal with the problem. In 1969, the year Kahane began his Soviet Jewish campaign, less than 3,000 Jews were permitted to leave Russia. In the two-year period between 1972 and 1973, more than 66,000 Russian Jews emigrated. The Soviets certainly did not let their Jews go in order to accommodate Kahane, but to promote détente, which was jeopardized by Jewish groups and their congressional allies who tied improved relations with the U.S.S.R. to human rights issues.

Perhaps the most telling example of Kahane's impact occurred in 1972 when the JDL leader was invited to stand on a New York City stage with Washington Senator Henry "Scoop" Jackson, who was campaigning for the Democratic presidential nomination. Jackson had asked Kahane to join him against the wishes of his advisers, saying that he admired the rabbi's concern for his brethren. Earlier that year, in September 1972, Jackson had proposed linking U.S. trade benefits to emigration rights from the Soviet Union in a speech before the National Conference on Soviet Jewry. He later cosponsored the Jackson-Vanick Amendment, which withheld "most favored nation" status from Socialist countries that restricted Jewish emigration. The bill, which was bitterly opposed by Nixon and Kissinger as a threat to détente, is now hailed by many American Jewish leaders as having been instrumental in prodding the Russians to release greater numbers of Jews. Significantly, the bill's principal architect was Jackson's Senate aide Richard Perle, who had worked closely with Deutsch's ILRRJ on Soviet Jewish issues. Many Jewish leaders privately say that the JDL was the real impetus behind the bill, however. As for Jackson, he often said that his own strong support for Jewish rights was solidified after he visited a Nazi death camp. "Never Again!" he used to tell friends—echoing the slogan that Kahane had thrust into the national lexicon.

CHAPTER EIGHT
Letters from Israel

^^

In August 1972, Meir Kahane dropped leaflets throughout the West Bank Arab town of Hebron, announcing plans to hold a mock trial of the Hebronites for the 1929 massacre of more than sixty Jews there. Shock waves swept across Israeli occupied Arab lands. Although Kahane's proposed trial was condemned by the Labor government, to some Palestinians it heralded a disturbing, new Israeli policy. While Kahane was officially reviled and occasionally jailed for his increasingly violent harassment of Arabs, there seemed to be a fair amount of sympathy for him in certain government circles. For his part, Kahane sensed a deepseated racial hatred of Arabs lurking just beneath the surface of public discourse in Israel. The rabbi theorized that he could harness that atavistic rage to catapult himself to power.

The massacre of eleven Israeli athletes at the 1972 Munich Summer Olympics following their kidnapping by Palestinian terrorists presented Kahane with a chance to test his theory. The massacre had triggered mass national hysteria in Israel, undermining, Kahane believed, the country's image of strength. It struck at the very spirit of the *New Jew*—someone proud, defiant, not afraid to fight back. After all, fighting back is what Kahane and the JDL stood for. Terror against terror. Revenge is not a mindless or heedless act, Kahane often said, but a lesson in political logic—cut off the hands of your tormentors before you end up in Auschwitz.

In perhaps the most bizarre and sensational episode in this phase of his career, Kahane claims that he planned to blow up the Libyan Embassy in Brussels in retaliation for the Munich massacre. The Libyans had publicly announced that they had trained and financed the Palestinian Black September commando group that had stormed the Israeli athletes' compound at Munich. Kahane told me that a JDL hit team was supposed to assassinate Arab diplomats throughout Europe and America after destroying the Libyan Embassy in Brussels. According to a report published in Israel, Kahane also ordered a dozen JDL men to storm the Libyan Embassy in Rome, murder half its staff, then negotiate a return flight to Israel using Libyan hostages as bargaining chips.

Once again, Kahane turned to Amihai Paglin for help. Paglin had already masterminded some of the JDL's most brazen exploits. In 1970, bombs Paglin had hidden inside three stoves and smuggled to JDL agents in Europe ripped through the Soviet cultural center in Amsterdam. Around the same time, he engineered the bombing of a Soviet container ship in Rotterdam, sent a letter bomb to the Soviet Embassy in London, and orchestrated attacks on Palestinians living in Europe, according to European and American intelligence sources. In one incident outside a train station in Paris, two JDL men trained by Paglin threw acid in the face of a well-known PLO supporter.

Following the Munich massacre, Paglin ingeniously crated grenades, automatic weapons, and ammunition to be smuggled as oven supplies to Chaim Stern, a New York furniture manufacturer and fervent Kahane supporter. A second weapons crate was to go to Shlomo Tidhar, Betar's representative in Belgium.

But Mossad sniffed out the plan, and two JDL operatives were arrested at Lod Airport with the weapons. Paglin was arrested two days later for smuggling arms abroad; Kahane was also picked up, but was released the same day. On October 1, 1972, Kahane was arrested on an arms smuggling charge as he was about to board a plane to America. When he was released from prison on bail five days later, Kahane told reporters that he had been on his way to the United States to urge his Mob contacts to help him set up an anti-Arab terrorist underground. Declaring that his arrest was due to "wickedness on the part of certain government quarters," he vowed to continue his war against Arab terrorism. He also announced plans to form a political party and enter the 1973 parliamentary elections. As a Knesset member he believed he would be immune from prosecution in pending criminal matters.

It was certainly no coincidence that Kahane was arrested so soon after his break with his Israeli patrons, themselves prominent members of the country's intelligence community. They had helped the JDL in the past, but they were not about to let Kahane operate independently. And Israel hardly needed Kahane to avenge its slain athletes. It had every intention of teaching the PLO that terrorism was a game that two could play. Mossad hit teams dispatched by Golda Meir tracked down and murdered Black September operatives from Beirut to Paris.

Pessach Mor, one of Kahane's ex-handlers, summed up the feelings about the Munich tragedy of many Israelis that summer: "We are in a black mood here today because of the Munich killings and both the heart and head seek vengeance," Mor wrote to Zweibon. "But as the French say: vengeance is a dish that should be eaten cold. And I subscribe to that dictum. . . . I keep telling people that we are in a perpetual battle from many sides and there is no time for niceties and so-called 'humanitarian' weaknesses. In the final analysis, both Fatah and the Russians are doing us a favor—for both remind us (and many want to forget) that the sword cannot be sheathed yet."

Kahane needed no reminding. Unfazed by his arrest for arms smuggling, he continued to work on plans for building a Jewish terrorist underground in America that would operate apart from the JDL. "The need to create the kind of professional Jewish defense group that will fight . . . growing Arab and Nazi and Soviet terror is clear," Kahane wrote to Zweibon. "I spoke to Jan Okan, our former West Coast coordinator [who was then living in Israel], and he is willing to come back to America to devote *full time* to building the kind of group needed. Only you and 1-2 other people will know why he returned, and he will have nothing to do with JDL at all."

At a meeting in a Brooklyn safe house in late 1972, Okan showed Alex Sternberg a letter from Kahane, instructing the two to work together on the Jewish underground. "I was shocked," said Sternberg who had already begun recruiting potential terrorists from outside the ranks of the JDL. "No one besides Paglin was supposed to know about this. I turned to Jan and said, 'You can do the whole thing. Tell Meir I'm out of it.' "

Sternberg, who had just celebrated his twenty-third birthday, had no intention of spending the next one in a federal correctional institution for violent offenders. Just a few months before his meeting with Okan, he had been yanked out of line by Israeli security agents as he boarded a plane at Lod Airport. They told Sternberg that they knew about his training sessions with Paglin and warned him not to come back to Israel. Luckily for Sternberg, a powerful explosive called jellynite, which he was supposed to carry back to America concealed inside a toothpaste tube, had not been delivered to him by Paglin as planned. "It began to dawn on me that I could end up in the slammer," said Sternberg, who had already stood trial in the United States for buying guns under an assumed name and conspiracy to blow up a building. He was acquitted each time. "This is serious business. It's not like being an Irgun freedom fighter making a speech in front of a British court during the Mandate."

In November 1974, Paglin and Kahane were brought to trial in Jerusalem for attempted weapons smuggling. Shmuel Tamir, their lawyer, who later became Israel's justice minister during the first Begin Administration, argued that they had acted out of patriotism. The judge agreed, lavishly praising Kahane for his struggle on behalf of Soviet Jews and for his commitment, however misguided, to fighting Arab terrorism. "Of course, they [Paglin and Kahane] are not to be blamed for these objectives and for the fact that they are devoting their lives to working in the service of the public at large," the judge declared. They received a two-year suspended sentence.

Paglin, the arch-terrorist, was hardly penalized for his misadventures with Kahane. In 1977, newly-elected Prime Minister Menachem Begin appointed Paglin to the powerful post of Adviser to the Prime Minister on Counter-Terrorism—a position that he held until he died in an automobile accident in 1979. Reporting directly to the prime minister, the office on counterterrorism functions much like the National Security Council in America. (One of Paglin's successors as adviser on counterterrorism, Amiram Nir, worked directly with Colonel Oliver North and John McFarland, initiating and then helping to implement the Reagan Administration's ill-fated Iran-contra policy. It was Nir who devised the scheme of shipping four thousand

American-made TOW missiles to Iran and using profits to fund joint U.S.-Israeli covert operations.)

Kahane's arms smuggling caper was just the first of three controversial trials that he became entangled in during his first year and a half in Israel. In April 1973, the Israeli attorney general charged Kahane and his plump, bearded, American-born aide Yoel Lerner with sedition for mailing thousands of letters to Israeli Arabs urging them to leave Israel. The form letters offered to purchase their property and to help them emigrate to America. Kahane later told me he received three thousand positive responses to seven thousand letters.

Kahane's lawyer, Aaron Papo, who under Begin became director of Israel's Broadcast Authority, threatened during a pre-trial hearing to call to the stand each of the three thousand Arabs who had expressed interest in the resettlement scheme. Papo also asserted that he would prove that Kahane was only repeating statements that had been made by leading mainstream Zionists who also favored a population transfer (the euphemism in Israel for the mass expulsion of Arabs). "If the Arabs are incited by anything, your honor, it is by the fact that this courtroom was built in [Arab] East Jerusalem and that an Israeli flag flies out front," said Papo. "What bothers the Arabs, your honor, isn't Kahane, but the fact that there is a Jewish state." The judge threw the case out of court for "lack of evidence."

Papo was certainly correct when he said that the idea to expel Israel's Arabs did not originate with Kahane—although until Kahane popularized the notion few dared mention it in public. "Transfer" is an idea as potent as it is disturbing. For Kahane, an Arab majority in "Greater Israel" is no mere paranoid vision, but an inevitable, scientifically verifiable, demographic fact. As he sees it, an explosive Arab birth rate in Israel and the Occupied Territories combined with the increasing emigration of disaffected Israeli Jews spells an Arab majority in "Greater Israel" by the beginning of the next century—that is, unless someone takes steps to solve the "Arab problem."

The notion of Israel devoid of Arabs is nearly as old as the Zionist dream itself. Israel's founding fathers naively believed that they were establishing a national home in "a land without a people for a people without a land." In 1902, Theodor Herzl wrote *Altneuland*, a utopian novel about a liberal, enlightened Jewish state in Palestine, where a grateful Arab minority paid homage to the Jews for bringing them modern science and technology. Instead, the Zionist pioneers were confronted by an indigenous Arab community that for the most part tenaciously clung to the land. From the earliest days of Zionist colonization there were repeated, violent clashes between Jewish settlers and local Arabs. By the 1930s, Zionist leaders were acutely aware of the demographic threat that a large and hostile Arab population posed to a future Jewish state in Palestine and considered various formulas for solving the problem. They even negotiated for the purchase of land on the East Bank of the Jordan River for Arab resettlement. Labor Zionists, influenced by the massive population transfers in Europe after the First World War, believed that financial incentives would suffice to entice Arabs to leave Palestine. Not surprisingly, Kahane's hero, Ze'ev Jabotinsky, also supported the idea. "We should instruct American Jewry to mobilize half a billion dollars in order that Iraq and Saudi Arabia will absorb the Palestinian Arabs," Jabotinsky wrote a supporter in November 1939. "There is no choice: The Arabs must make room for the Jews in *Eretz Ysrael* [the land of Israel]. If it was possible to transfer the Baltic peoples, it is also possible to move the Palestinian Arabs."

During Israel's 1948 War of Independence, thousands of Palestinians were forcibly evicted from their homes by the Israeli army. Hundreds of thousands more fled. In all, more than 750,000 Palestinian Arabs were uprooted and became refugees. Following the war, David Ben-Gurion appointed what became known as the "transfer committee" to study means of limiting the Arab population to no more than 15 percent of the Jewish population of Israel. "I am for compulsory transfer; I don't see anything immoral in it," Ben-Gurion told the Jewish Agency. For tactical reasons, however, he never advertised his views or put them into action.

In the tumultuous days following the 1967 Six Day War, the Israeli Cabinet discussed various ways of ridding Israel of the Palestinian refugees that it inherited when it swallowed the Gaza Strip and the West Bank. Menachem Begin, then a Cabinet minister, recommended demolishing the refugee camps and transferring their residents to the Sinai, according to the private diaries kept by Yaacov Herzog, then the director-general of the prime minister's office. Finance Minister Pinhas Sapir, backed by Foreign Minister Abba Eban, called for resettling the refugees in nearby Arab countries. Deputy Prime Minister Yigal Allon proposed that Palestinian refugees be moved en masse to the Sinai Desert and that other Palestinians in Israel should be persuaded to move abroad. According to Herzog's notes, Allon said: ''We do not do enough among the Arabs to encourage emigration.'' Soon after the Six Day War, the Israeli government set up a covert unit that gave financial assistance to Arabs who wished to emigrate from Israel. Hundreds of Palestinian refugees moved to farms and homes that the secret Israeli unit had purchased in Paraguay, Brazil, and Libya.*

Therefore, when Kahane first announced his plans to transfer Israel's Arabs, he was not out of step with mainstream Zionist thinking—though he was clearly out of line. ''Transfer'' was to be encouraged quietly, or under cover of a general war, but it was not to be openly discussed to the detriment of Israel's image abroad.

Kahane unveiled his masterplan to rid Israel of its Arabs at a press conference on March 1, 1973 in Tel Aviv. He was joined by William Perl, head of a JDL shell corporation called ''New Horizons,'' which had been established in the United States to underwrite the costly venture of transferring Israel's Arabs to America. The idea, Perl told reporters, was to sell shares of the corporation for $2 each—the money going to buy the property of prospective Arab immigrants. The Arabs could take their profits and relocate in America.

At the time, Perl was one of the few highly respected Revisionists who still publicly supported Kahane. As joint chairman of the Revisionist Zionist Organization in Vienna in 1939, Perl had helped to rescue nearly 18,000 Jews from Nazi Europe. His daring, face-to-face negotiations with Adolf Eichmann nearly resulted in his own internment in a Nazi death camp. After fleeing Europe just one step ahead of the Gestapo, he joined the U.S. Army and was later posted to military intelligence in Europe. In 1945, as a special assistant to the prosecutor of the U.S. War Crimes Commission in Germany, Perl, then a lieutenant colonel, was one of the military interrogators assigned to investigate the murder of U.S. prisoners of war by a German S.S. unit in Malmedy, Belgium. Perl was accused by German POWs of using torture and murder to extract confessions. Though there was

---

* The 1967 Israeli Cabinet debate about what to do with the newly conquered Arabs was first revealed by Yossi Melman and Dan Raviv in *The Washington Post*.

a great deal of publicity surrounding these allegations, no formal military charges were brought. Perl left the U.S. military in 1958, finding employment as a psychologist at American and George Washington Universities. A specialist in disinformation and psychological warfare, Perl became head of the JDL's Washington, D.C. chapter in 1971 and national chairman of the JDL in 1973 and 1974.*

Perl and Kahane recruited Emanuel Houri, an Israeli Arab who had been an agent for the Haganah during Israel's War of Independence, to travel to the United States as a spokesman for New Horizons. "I wrote to Dave Fisch [the JDL's national director] about the Arab Houri coming to America," Kahane wrote to a JDL board member, adding that New Horizons "will buy Arab land and be a very nice profit-making thing." But the Israeli government refused to issue Houri a passport, and when he sued successfully in court to obtain it, the American consul refused to give him a visa.

To make matters worse, the JDL board showed little enthusiasm for New Horizons. "The refusal of the JDL board to get off its incompetency and make this Arab emigration plan a success is not only inexcusable but a thing that they will carry on their consciences in years to come," Kahane wrote to an American JDL member . . . "I hope they will yet realize the tragedy of their actions and just how they are—in the end—as myopic as the Jewish Establishment we have come to attack with such delight."

A few months after unveiling his Arab deportation plan in Tel Aviv, Kahane ordered his followers to step up their violent activities in America. On May 17, 1973, Kahane, from his Jerusalem office, wrote the following letter to an associate in New York:

> Dear Josh: If we can't find some Jew(s) willing to blow up the Iraqi Embassy in Washington . . . and if we can't get

* Perl was the JDL's master of disinformation and dirty tricks. For instance, it was his idea to put stickers in topless bars and public rest rooms around Washington listing the Soviet Embassy's phone number as a prostitution service. The embassy was flooded with calls, tying up its line for months. "New York functioned as the commandos and we as propaganda," Perl's son Raphael has said. In recent years, William Perl has helped found Americans for a Safe Israel, a pro-Israel, right-wing lobby group, and CAMERA, a Middle East media watchdog group, which has strong ties to the Israeli Embassy in Washington, D.C. and to AIPAC, America's most formidable pro-Israel lobby. A book authored by Perl called *The Holocaust Conspiracy* was published in 1989 by Shapolsky Press. U.S. Senator Claiborne Pell, chairman of the U.S. Senate Committee on Foreign Relations, wrote the foreword.

someone to *shoot* a Russian diplomat (anyone), we are Jewish pigs and deserve what we get.

P.S. For this you can try to get money from Joe Alster, [Chaim] Stern, etc. *You* don't go but send someone trustworthy with this letter—then burn it!

In another letter, Kahane outlined his plan to sabotage détente between the United States and the Soviet Union: "All possible efforts have to be made to stop Brezhnev's trip to America or, failing that, to ruin it. A successful visit will make détente an unstoppable thing and the Russians will then turn on their Jews. . . . I suggest an immediate kidnapping or shooting of a diplomat."

Kahane named the Soviet diplomat, his Virginia address, and the model, make, year, and license-plate number of his car.

Kahane ordered a JDL member to place "a bomb at the offices of Occidental Petroleum to warn Armand Hammer and any other people against deals with the Russians. Similarly, at a Chase Manhattan Bank since David Rockefeller opened a bank in Moscow."

Kahane also ordered a shooting attack on the Soviet Embassy in Washington. He instructed an American Jewish high-school student who belonged to the JDL to arrange for her teacher to invite a Soviet diplomat to speak to her class so that the JDL could assassinate him. "This is urgent for the survival of . . . Jews or else I would never ask you to risk things. After anything is done," Kahane cautioned, "wait to hear the news broadcast and if no innocent person is killed, phone the press."

The letters never reached their destination. They were intercepted by the Israeli military censor, and on June 7, 1973, Kahane was arrested for conspiring to commit acts of violence in a foreign country and for attempting to harm relations between the United States and Israel. After a long, tedious, and expensive trial, Kahane was convicted—and once again received a suspended sentence. According to court records, Judge Yaacov Bazak said that he doubted the seriousness of Kahane's criminal intent because the rabbi had sent the letters "by regular mail, without using any form of code. It seems more likely that this was an emotional and noisy presentation than it was an actual underground plan," said Bazak.

* * *

While Kahane's activities in Israel generated headlines, the JDL in America was rocked by scandal. In 1972, allegations surfaced that Kahane was taking money meant for the JDL school at the Zion Hotel and using it to finance his campaign for the Knesset. "When I got to Jerusalem . . . I found that the school was Kahane's campaign headquarters," a distraught JDL official told *The New York Post.* "Let's face it. The man is a fraud!"

Hoping to head off the conflict, Kahane wrote to Murray Wilson, a wealthy New York businessman and key JDL activist who had given him $50,000 for the school. "We worked like dogs this spring and summer—with a *minimum* of help—to put out the best summer program Israel has ever had," Kahane wrote to Wilson. "If . . . you are disillusioned, tell me now, so I will know how to function. This school is going to put out Jewish leaders the way we want them." Kahane sent Wilson a canceled check for three thousand dollars drawn on his own personal bank account and made out to the school—a sum, Kahane wrote, that represented his "total personal savings."

But the school soon collapsed and Kahane sold the lease on the Zion Hotel for a hefty profit. Wilson wanted to prosecute Kahane in an Orthodox Jewish court for the alleged diversion of funds, but says that he was voted down—four-to-three—by the JDL board. "They didn't want us to wash our dirty linen in public," said Wilson.

In the wake of the scandal—and with allegations that he had pocketed $70,000 meant for JDL terrorist operations still fresh—Zweibon sent Kahane a blistering letter condemning him for taking advantage of the JDL's key financial backers. "Is there some requirement that we alienate friends . . .?" Zweibon wrote on September 7, 1972. "Must we be so obdurate that we are always alone?"

For the first time in the group's short history, the JDL board began to scrutinize Kahane's use of funds. Kahane always had had carte blanche to use JDL money as he saw fit. In any case, the board really had no way to gauge how much Kahane raised or spent because all the major financial backers dealt directly with him. "You want JDL to do things?" Zweibon wrote to Kahane. "Remember that every contact JDL made, be it for money or at the Jewish Agency, you kept to yourself. No one here was privy to the meetings; all the strings are in your hands."

Zweibon estimated that Kahane had raised nearly $10 million by 1972. Yet the JDL never had enough money to pay lawyers or printers, and was chronically late with the rent check. Nothing aggravated Zweibon more than Kahane's insistence that tax-exempt money collected under a variety of guises was his to use no matter what else was pressing. The money had been raised to pay the fines of two JDL members who had been convicted for the 1970 bombing of the Amtorg office. Kahane, who had also pleaded guilty to the bombing, had already paid his fine with JDL contributions. "What will I use to get them out of jail when they are arrested for not paying their fines?" asked Zweibon. "Raise additional money," Zweibon said Kahane replied.

In another instance, Kahane instructed Nancy Hershkovitz, the young woman who had attempted to fly to London with guns and grenades in a Don Quixote-like quest to assassinate Palestinian terrorist Leila Khaled, to flee to Israel after she was released from jail on bail. As usual, Kahane expressed little concern about reimbursing those who had put up her $50,000 bail. Zweibon wrote to Kahane:

> It is our responsibility to develop relationships with people who don't necessarily give money to JDL but who will be willing to post bail. Our people are entitled to know that they will not sit in jail waiting for bail to be posted. Without this assurance their exposure is criminal. Do it, you say? The fact of the matter is that every money person from Bradish, in the beginning, to Wilson, most recently, has not been used but abused. There isn't even a mention of the moral duty to repay loans, to make good the losses incurred when Nancy fled. In the process we cut ourselves off from every available money source. We obtain from each of them some small momentary advantage only to lose not only them but those in their circles. The list is imposing and the [Zion Hotel] school group will be added to it. . . .

Kahane even belittled the lawyers who took JDL cases, often for little or no fee. Once Kahane wrote a nasty letter to Nathan Lewin, a prominent Washington attorney (whose clients today include former U.S. Attorney Edwin Meese), accusing him of exhibiting a "lack of sufficient interest" in Avraham Hershkovitz, whose weapons violation and false passport convictions Lewin was appealing for a reduced fee.

Unlike many others, Lewin was not intimidated by Kahane. In a stinging rebuke, which offers insight into how Kahane conducted JDL business, Lewin wrote:

You . . . forget that because of the proceedings in the Brooklyn Federal District Court concerning wiretaps, I had access to notes and transcripts of conversations that you had on JDL telephones during the period of time following Avraham's arrest. I could find in those many pages precious little discussion on your part or attempts on your part to see to it that he was properly represented in the charges being brought against him. Your principal concern at the time seemed to be additional speaking engagements.

I ask you . . . to consider what the effect has been of your own actions on the future of Avraham Hershkovitz. I can tell you that—ranging from the remarks you made after sentencing before Judge Weinstein, through your call for the arming of Jews in East Flatbush, through your threats in Israel to kill Soviet diplomats if harm would befall any Jew in the Soviet Union, and including whatever participation you may have had in the shooting into the Soviet Mission— all these measures have made it *far*, *far* more difficult for Avraham Hershkovitz to be released from jail than was true last July. I ask you whether you can expect any rational person to believe that you have 'very warm feelings for Avraham' when, in fact, your own acts have consistently added to the padlocks on his jail cell. . . .

I represented you—without fee and, quite typically, without even a 'thank you'—in a case you had here in the District of Columbia when you were arrested in front of the Soviet Embassy. You may rest assured that your letter of October 28 satisfies me not to make that error again.

Your letter also confirms all the worst fears I have ever had about how the JDL is conducted. I find this particularly regrettable since I have come to have some affection and regard for Bert Zweibon, who I think is a sensitive and sensible fellow.*

* Ironically, Lewin is currently representing Kahane in his attempt to retrieve his U.S. citizenship, which he voluntarily surrendered on the eve of the 1988 Knesset elections. Lewin would not return repeated phone calls for comment.

But no one was more maligned by Kahane than Zweibon, who became a scapegoat for the JDL's declining fortunes. The two men had a complex relationship that was more often than not like sibling rivalry. Their backgrounds were fixed at the opposite ends of the American Jewish experience. Kahane was the ambitious son of an Orthodox rabbi, raised with a sense of Messianic purpose. Zweibon had grown up on Manhattan's Lower East Side, a wisecracking kid who spent more time hustling pool than studying. His father was an official of the American Communist Party, who was expelled with Jay Lovestone and other dissidents in a 1928 factional dispute. Like Lovestone, the elder Zweibon became a hard-line anti-Communist.

Bertram obtained his law degree from New York University Law School in 1954. Unlike Kahane, he passed the bar. Though he had grown up in a non-traditional Jewish home, Zweibon turned to Orthodoxy, later joining the Young Israel Synagogue in Laurelton, Queens after moving there in 1959. He often drew snickers in synagogue when he read prayers in halting Hebrew that everyone else could recite perfectly from memory. During one Saturday service, "having witnessed my most recent humiliation, Kahane stood up, held a prayer book high, and read a blessing that he had known by heart since he was four," recalled Zweibon. "He did it to cover me. It was an extremely kind act." The two men had not spoken a word to each other before then. As they got better acquainted, their strong anti-Black, anti-Left, and pro-Israel views bonded them.

Zweibon's politics were at least as extreme as Kahane's. But he was the more stable and disciplined of the two, and he helped to anchor the impulsive rabbi. Perhaps for that reason Zweibon was not as well respected as Kahane was by younger JDL members. An estate lawyer by training, he defended many JDL criminal cases, much to the consternation of some clients. "Zweibon was an egotistical, intelligent man running a mediocre law firm who gained immeasurable publicity and notoriety from his involvement with the JDL," said Alex Sternberg. "If not for JDL, Zweibon would be just another fat, mediocre Jewish lawyer who trudges to the office day after day, making good money though never rising to any kind of brilliance. I will say on the record that I wouldn't want him defending me in a legal action. Nobody [in the JDL] wanted him."

Many in the JDL detected a zany quality to Zweibon's militancy. Sternberg recalls: "He came into the JDL office one day and said with tremendous glee that he had just convinced his sixth client of German descent to cremate a recently deceased loved one. He was trying to get even by burning his share of Germans. Who wanted a lawyer like that representing you in a serious criminal matter?"

Whatever JDL youth thought of Zweibon, he was ultimately more concerned with keeping them out of jail than was Kahane. The increasingly bitter differences between Zweibon and Kahane over the JDL's direction were played out in a remarkable exchange of angry, mean-spirited letters.

Typifying the exchange was a letter that Kahane wrote on August 13, 1972, in which he lashed out at Zweibon for the "irresponsibility, indifference, and lack of talent" that had characterized the JDL since Zweibon had taken over the American operation. Complaining that Zweibon had not organized a single militant action that had captured the attention of the American Jewish community, let alone the news media, Kahane wrote:

> Despite all this, JDL is the best hope for Jews. . . . *Everything* JDL has done came about because of a vigorous, militant, semi- (and not-so-semi) violent policy. That policy was motivated by me and I tried to carry out its teachings *in the States*. That is why it worked.
>
> The reason, I am afraid, that imaginative and violent actions are not initiated in my absence—thus eroding our morale, image, and Jewish defense— is because there may be a subconscious drawing back on your part. When I am away you are responsible for JDL policy and actions and militancy, which could bring down the wrath and indictments of the federal government on the whole Executive Board—already a possibility (or it was in February 1971).

In another letter, Kahane chastised Zweibon for cancelling a terrorist act because he feared that it would jeopardize the outcome of the Iris Kones murder trial, then underway in New York. "What if the trial—and sentencing—last a year or more?" wrote Kahane. "Does JDL close down except for limited activities? Do you really believe that the people who have done things want this paralysis?" Kahane urged Zweibon not to obstruct future

JDL operations. "*Otherwise, other people will be asked* [to supervise militant activities] *and the results will be the same. Please answer me on this immediately.* I care for the kids as much as anyone . . . you should know that things here in Israel did not stop because of my upcoming trial." Kahane said that he appreciated Zweibon's need to insulate himself from illegal activities because it could lead to his disbarment and jail. Nonetheless, he instructed Zweibon to resign if he feared the legal ramifications of running an outlaw organization.

Even as Kahane criticized Zweibon, he was totally dependent on him for a host of favors. Kahane's most pressing problem was getting back his passport, which had been confiscated by the Israeli government in 1973. "The problems here are really nothing," he wrote Zweibon. "To the contrary, they have gained the League tremendous support. What concerns me enormously is the thought that I will not be able to come back to America. I *must* go back. The Soviet Jewish issue is of paramount importance and there will be *pogroms* unless immediate action is taken now. . . . Bert, I *must* get back to America. Please move heaven and earth."

Kahane outlined a series of steps that he wanted JDL attorneys Barry Slotnick and Robert Persky to take on his behalf, including asking pro-JDL Brooklyn Congressman Bert Podell (who was convicted for fraud and conspiracy in 1974 by a young assistant U.S. attorney, Rudolph Giuliani) to get Attorney General John Mitchell's help in retrieving his U.S. passport from the Israeli government. Kahane also instructed them to persuade prominent Jewish Republican fundraiser Max Fischer to intervene on his behalf with President Richard Nixon. "Point out my anti-McGovern articles," he wrote. Moreover, fearing that his arrest in Israel for arms smuggling would lead to the revocation of his probation in the United States, he implored Zweibon to try to manipulate Judge Weinstein by appealing to his loyalty as a Jew. "See Judge Weinstein discreetly and informally," wrote Kahane. "Tell him as a Jew what my absence will mean for Russian Jews, Aliya, etc. . . . Tell him I spoke at a press conference in Israel about the need to create a group that would meet the terror of the Arabs, but never spoke about guns or bombs."

As far as Zweibon was concerned, this latest communiqué was yet another example of Kahane's astounding megalomania. Once again it seemed that Kahane had confused his own fate with the

destiny of the Jewish people. That Kahane would ask his lawyers to try to put a fix in with a highly respected federal judge
was a total misreading of what his lawyers were willing to do
for him, said Zweibon. As for Kahane's desire to recruit Max
Fischer, "He wouldn't even sit on the same toilet seat that Kahane
had sat on in the distant past," snorted Zweibon, adding that
he put the letter into his files, never acting on a single request.
Zweibon felt that Kahane was treating him the way an abusive
father treats his child. "He'd slap me in the face, then he'd figure I'd say don't slap me again, let me help you."

Whatever their personal problems, Kahane continued to
shower Zweibon with demands for money. "I insist on JDL
allocating a MINIMUM of $500 a month to us here," Kahane
wrote in one letter. "I am no longer able to sit back and raise
money by long distance when every other Israeli group which
has sister groups in America receives money from them. . . ."
Kahane's appeals for money became so outrageous that he even
had Libby telegram the JDL office in New York demanding
$2,000 from the Estelle Donna Evans Foundation. In a follow-
up letter, Kahane explained that the $2,000 had been "loaned"
by the foundation to a JDL member for bail—and he wanted it
back!

In an attempt to reassert control of the JDL board, Kahane
began appointing to leadership positions young surrogates who
would take orders directly from him without asking too many
questions. One such youth was David Fisch, who was studying
political science at Columbia University and went on to become
the JDL's national director, before heading Herut-USA.* Kahane
wrote to Fisch complaining that the adults in the JDL were a
bunch of "lice" who were oblivious to how desperate the Jewish predicament in the United States had become in his absence.
Kahane explained that Jewish survival in America depended on
Fisch's replenishing JDL ranks with "new blood" from the
nation's high schools and college campuses. "The lack of identity among young Jews which leads to the Left, drugs, Zen, Jesus
and *all* the rest cannot be met unless a major, well-funded drive
to get a full-time JDL campus and high school (network) is
begun," wrote Kahane. He continued:

* Now an ultra-Orthodox rabbi in Woodland Hills, California, Fisch made a minor stir
in 1983 when he wrote a fawning book about Ariel Sharon, which was published during
the Israeli general's highly publicized libel trial against *Time Magazine*.

The school in Israel was aimed at that and was destroyed because of the garment-worker types, and others suffering psychological glaucoma. . . . The death of that school is a tragedy for world Jewry and there are people on the present board whose silence and inability to understand it makes them unqualified for leadership in an organization whose major strength must be the ability to see problems where others may not; the ability to call for solutions, no matter how bold or difficult. The Jewish youth must have such a leadership school and JDL must have such a school for its own ideological training since it is lack of ideology that has led to the reaction of certain (JDL) leaders.

Kahane's anger was fueled by his allies in America, who fed him reports about how Zweibon was constantly undercutting him. "Meir, my father asked you not to let JDL go down the drain, and he feels if you resign, or take some honorary position, thus giving the United States to Bert, this is exactly what will happen," wrote Raphael Perl, whose father, William, was head of the JDL's Washington, D.C. chapter. "Our chapter is growing in size. And for the first time we have a problem in spending the money we have. We even have been RECOMMENDED for membership in the local Jewish Community Council by their executive membership board." (On April 26, 1973, the Jewish Community Council of Greater Washington rejected JDL's bid to join by a vote of 49 to 31.)

Kahane and Zweibon were clearly heading for a showdown. The JDL leader decided to dispose of the rebels at a national convention that he would call as soon as he retrieved his passport and returned to America. "I want JDL to be more than a Grossingers weekend group and a T-shirt seller," he wrote Zweibon. "JDL needs new, vigorous leadership, and I am asking that a national convention—LONG OVERDUE—be called. . . . I have become reconciled to the fact that JDL will not do anything to get me back to the United States and I regret this because Jews suffer for it."

By now Zweibon was sure that American Jewry would suffer more with Meir Kahane around. "One must always keep in mind that no matter how important one becomes, no matter how much notoriety one obtains, it is the height of egomania to equate what is good for the Jewish people with what is good for oneself,"

Zweibon wrote to Kahane on November 21, 1972. "I believe that the last four and a half years have given me the right to ask one favor. Forget my address, my telephone number, and my name. For my part you no longer exist."

One week after receiving this missive from Zweibon, a despondent Kahane announced his resignation from the American branch of the JDL. Characteristically, he compared the event to a cataclysm of Biblical proportions. In a note to Zweibon on December 5, 1972, he declared:

> I resent the fact that people walk around with the impression that I steal their money. I don't live in the lap of luxury in Israel. When the *Jewish Press* check is late, that's the end of the thin edge between money and none. I work for JDL with no compensation at all (unlike you); I put in *full* time for JDL (unlike you); I got JDL into politics because FOR ISRAEL it is good for JDL and for the Jews. I regret that you do not have the vision to see this but that is no sin. What is a sin is that you also believe that I do things for personal profit and make this view heard to others. It has not only ruined my reputation and value to the organization but I am no Moses or Samuel who could take this kind of conduct from people to whom they dedicated their lives. You may tell the Board to ignore all that I sent them. I am tired of fighting little people. I resign from the JDL in the United States. I am just tired.

The tirade was hardly fair. Contrary to what Kahane had written, Zweibon drew no salary from the JDL. Moreover, he was deep in debt and his law practice was in shambles.

Perhaps realizing the foolishness of totally alienating someone he still depended on, Kahane sent Zweibon an apology of sorts on December 10, 1972. "I hope to see you when I come back to America for visits and am reserving a Shabbos at your home," wrote a somewhat humbled Kahane. "Please let me know if that is not agreeable because I am making no other plans and would hate to sleep in the street."

* * *

In less than a year and a half after breaking with the Cohen-Shamir group, Kahane had been tried in Israel for arms smuggling, sedition, and conspiracy. At the same time, he introduced his Arab emigration plan, while battling with disaffected JDL members in America who accused him of stealing. Incredibly, none of these events stopped Kahane from running flat out for the Knesset in 1973. Indeed, he used the trials in Israel to harvest free publicity for his Knesset bid, which, according to some of his followers, had been his goal all along. Campaigning under the banner of the JDL, Kahane was the first politician in modern Israel to run on a platform that openly called for the expulsion of Israel's Arabs. He was so certain that he would win two seats that he began to campaign on the slogan "give us a third seat." Though Kahane had constantly pleaded poverty in his letters to Zweibon, his campaign was lavishly funded. Geula Cohen estimates Kahane spent more money on media advertising than Begin's Herut Party.

On election eve, Kahane threw a victory celebration at the Grand Beach Hotel in Tel Aviv. Dr. Victor Ratner, the well-known British neurologist, toasted the Brooklyn-born rabbi as the next prime minister of Israel. Ratner, who financed much of the campaign, believed himself to be the descendant of the ancient Canaanites and adorned his house with ancient amulets and statues, which he said would bring him good luck. But the gods failed Kahane. When the ballots were counted, the JDL leader had 12,811 votes, just 0.81 percent of the electorate—less than the one percent minimum necessary to enter the Knesset. Deeply depressed, the rabbi withdrew from public view, turning to the Talmud for solace.

CHAPTER NINE
The Jewish Idea

∧∧∧∧∧∧∧∧∧∧∧∧∧∧∧∧∧∧∧∧∧∧∧∧∧∧

Meir Kahane had been subject to wild mood swings and crippling bouts of depression since childhood. Now, having been simultaneously rejected by the Israeli electorate and by key JDL members in America, he suffered what some of his closest supporters described as a nervous breakdown. But after briefly disappearing from public view, Kahane reemerged more determined than ever to build a viable political party in Israel.

His manic energy combined with his wounded pride never let him rest. He woke each morning at 4 A.M. to study Torah, prayed and studied again. Then he would go to his office at the Museum of the Potential Holocaust in Jerusalem, returning home around 10 P.M. He was seldom in bed before midnight. "I don't think he even dreamed at night," recalled Matt Liebowitz, a young American-born Kach supporter. "Everything he did was geared toward achieving his vision. I think he had such total control over his thoughts that he could even control his subconscious. He believed the Apocalypse was coming, so he was willing to do desperate things."

Kahane was swept up in a kind of Messianic passion. Jewish destiny, he believed more than ever, was in his hands. Words like apocalypse, redemption, and Messiah took over his political vocabulary. He rationalized his Knesset defeat on the grounds that Jews did not yet understand that he was working from a divine plan. While the JDL in America was supposed to be concerned with helping Jews achieve greater temporal power, in Israel it was rapidly evolving into a fundamentalist cult with Kahane—like some medieval cabalist—twisting and turning the Torah to explain why expelling the Arabs would usher in the Messiah.

Kahane soon discovered that he did not have a monopoly on fundamentalist fervor. As he turned increasingly to Jewish mysticism for salvation, an earthquake on the Israeli Right shattered the political spectrum. The upheaval was set off by Gush Emunim (the Bloc of Faithful)—a mystical-Messianic movement that would not only radically transform Israeli politics, but would have a profound impact on the Arab-Israeli conflict as well.

Gush Emunim was based on the teachings of Rav Zvi Yehuda Kook, then the eighty-year-old head of Yeshiva Mercaz Harav in Jerusalem. The son of Rav Avraham Isaac Kook, founder of modern religious Zionism and the first Ashkenazi Chief Rabbi of Israel, he had devoted his life to preserving and expounding his father's teachings—foremost among them that the Jewish return to Israel and the flowering of the land signify the beginning of the Messianic Age. Contending that the Occupied Territories are part of the "holy inheritance" of lands given by God to the Jews as recorded in the Bible, Kook declared that they must be secured and defended at any cost.

Rav Kook and his religious school became the nucleus of Gush Emunim, which was born in 1974 following the Yom Kippur War. It was organized by seven middle-aged students from Yeshiva Mercaz Harav who sought to Judaize the West Bank.

Jacob Levine, then a forty-one-year-old, soft-spoken, unemployed Talmud student, and one of the movement's early leaders, believed Zionism had become sterile and self-destructive during the years of Labor Party rule. Gush Emunim, he said, was created as an antidote.

He explained: "There was a lack of clarity in Israel after the '73 war. The dominant spirit was one of depression. The Labor Party and the country didn't know what to do about the Arab territories. We stepped into the breach."

So Gush Emunim began what it regarded as its holy crusade to settle and build up Judea and Samaria, the land of the ancient Hebrews now known as the West Bank. Infused with a selfless dedication and an almost cosmic awareness of self and mission similar to Israel's early pioneers, Gush Emunim captured the imagination of many war weary Israelis.

Jaded young Sabras who were born long after the pioneering ethos had died and who had never before identified with political Zionism, émigrés from the corrupt and disintegrating Labor Party who were looking for a more meaningful ideology and lifestyle, and Orthodox Jews who decided to keep the promise flocked to Gush Emunim. A handful of new immigrants, mostly Russian and American, also joined the fold. Though Gush Emunim viewed Arabs as intruders in the land of Israel, it had no systematic program to drive them out. Instead, Gush leaders stated that Arabs who were willing to live without political rights in the Jewish state would enjoy a protected minority status similar to the second-class status that Jews historically held in Islamic countries.

Gush Emunim's West Bank settlement program grew slowly during the years the Labor Party was in power. Labor's policy was to build settlements in the Jordan Valley for security purposes, while avoiding the occupied areas largely populated by Arabs—these, according to such leaders as Yigal Allon, were to be held as bargaining chips in future peace talks. But as early as 1970, a bitterly divided Labor government allowed a group of ultranationalist Orthodox Jews led by Rabbi Moshe Levinger to build Kiryat Arba on a hilltop overlooking Hebron, the site of King David's first throne, and home to 78,000 fiercely nationalist Palestinian Arabs.

Most of the Gush Emunim's attempts to settle the West Bank during the Labor government era were stopped by the army. Gush members would arrive at a site in a caravan of trailers in the middle of the night without government permission. When the army came to expel the settlers—which it almost invariably did—the right-wing parties would charge the Labor government with betrayal of Israel and compare it to the British Mandate government before Jewish independence. Either way Gush Emunim bested the Labor government.

But when Labor was voted out of office in 1977, and Likud's Menachem Begin became prime minister, he organized a right-wing coalition government that was strongly influenced by Gush Emunim. Immediately after his election, Begin journeyed to Elon Moreh, a settlement near Nablus that Gush Emunim had tried and failed seven times to settle extralegally before the Labor government finally gave in. Holding a Torah scroll aloft, Begin vowed that he would establish "many more Elon Morehs."

Begin, the former commander of the Irgun, which had called for a Jewish state on *both* banks of the River Jordan, was true to his word. Between 1977 and 1984, successive Likud governments invested more than $1 billion in Jewish West Bank settlements—a huge sum for an economically hard-pressed nation that depends on more than $3 billion in annual aid from America. Today, Gush Emunim is the spearhead of Israel's West Bank settlement program, which totals more than 150 settlements comprising some 75,000 settlers. Gush Emunim currently boasts important enclaves of support in the right-wing Likud and Tehiya parties, as well as in several of the religious parties. Among its most potent supporters is Ariel Sharon, who through a Gush Emunim real estate front, purchased an apartment in the Muslim quarter of East Jerusalem's Old Walled City. Sharon moved into the apartment on the first day of Passover in 1988, sparking an Arab riot.

Gush Emunim had everything that Kahane and his movement lacked, observed Professor Ehud Sprinzak, an expert on extremist groups at Hebrew University. It was a cohesive cultural and social entity; it had a skillful, yet modest, collective leadership, as well as an effective membership. A spiritual movement led by the scion of the founder of religious Zionism, Gush Emunim was fully backed by Israel's leading rabbinical authorities in addition to being very Israeli in character. In contrast to the rather fringe-like nature of Kahane's mostly American-born followers, Gush Emunim attracted thousands of well-educated, middle-class supporters and settlers, whose outposts in Judea and Samaria soon obliterated the 1949 armistice line that had separated the modern state of Israel from the core areas of the Biblical Hebrew nation.

"In view of the emergence of Gush Emunim and its prestigious and highly publicized activities, Meir Kahane had to reassess his political strategy," said Sprinzak. But in 1974, Kahane was no more capable of joining Gush Emunim than he was Begin's party or the National Religious Party. So Kahane staked out a position to the right of Gush Emunim. If Gush's role was to settle and build the land of Israel, then Kahane would concentrate on driving out the Arabs living there. The JDL leader set about subverting Gush Emunim's declared goal of coexistence

with the local Arabs by instigating conflicts between Jewish settlers and the Palestinian Arab population. He purchased an apartment in Kiryat Arba, which became a base for his goon squad's
increasingly violent forays into the Arab West Bank. "They [Gush
Emunim] don't realize what nonsense it is to put a settlement
of fifty people in a sea of Arabs," Kahane told me in 1979. "What
do they think they are going to do with those Arabs?"

Since Gush Emunim's philosophy was firmly rooted in Halacha
and the normative Zionist tradition, Kahane countered with his
own selective quotes from the Torah and Jabotinsky. In a book
he published in 1974 called *The Jewish Idea*, Kahane challenged
Gush Emunim's view that redemption could come with Arabs
living in the land of Israel.

According to Kahane's view, Arabs are more than just a demographic and physical threat. Their presence pollutes the very
essence and spirit of Judaism. Therefore, their expulsion is a
necessary precondition for redemption. "Zionism, the establishment of the State of Israel, the return of millions of Jews home,
the miraculous victories of the few over the many Arabs, the
liberation of Judea-Samaria, Gaza and the Golan, the return of
Jewish sovereignty over the Holy City and Temple Mount are
all parts of the divine pledge and its fulfillment," wrote Kahane.

He argued that Messianic redemption would have taken place
if the Israeli government had expelled the Arabs, destroyed the
Dome of the Rock Mosque, which was built on top of the ruins
of the Second Temple, and annexed Judea and Samaria. "Had
we acted without considering the gentile reaction," Kahane
wrote, "without fear of what he may say or do, the Messiah
would have come right through the open door and brought us
redemption."

Kahane insists that redemption is guaranteed simply because
God picked Jews as his Chosen People. "We are different," said
an article in a JDL publication also called the *Jewish Idea*. "We
are a Chosen One and a Special One; selected for purity and holiness, and to rise above all others and to teach them the truth
for purity and holiness that we have been taught. There is no
reason or purpose to being a Jew unless there is something intrin-
sically different about it. No. We are not equal to the Gentiles.
We are different. We are higher."

Gush Emunim also is disdainful of gentiles. Its leaders main-
tain that Israel will become "a light unto the nations" only after
it has attained complete political and spiritual isolation from the

rest of mankind. Then, they prophesy, Israel will build its moral and military strength until it is powerful enough to destroy Arab opposition. "We must overcome the goys and dominate the spiritual world," said Gush activist Jacob Levine as we sat in his apartment with its spectacular eighth-floor view of Jerusalem's magical countryside.

But even the mystics of Gush Emunim have hard-headed political priorities. Their primary goal has been to confiscate Arab land a *dunam** at a time—and to build settlements stone by holy stone. They believed that this "divine process" would be far easier to accomplish without deliberately inflaming the local Arabs (not to mention the Zionist Left), who in any case would never be reconciled to their presence in Judea and Samaria.

In response to Gush Emunim's more pragmatic brand of Messianism, Kahane stepped up his attacks on Arabs, ignoring government pleas that he was undermining Israel's democratic image.

"The irrational Jew is the rational one," Kahane once told me. "Democracy and Western humanistic values are foreign implants, which are meaningless to authentic Judaism. The Jewish people didn't survive for two thousand years by being rational. Had we been rational we would have been done for. We survive because there is a clear promise that the Jewish people will never be destroyed." So long as Jews fulfill their covenant with God their destiny is assured, said Kahane. Therefore, it makes no difference if America breaks diplomatic relations with Israel for deporting the Arabs. God, not Uncle Sam, will provide, he declared.

If, as a child, Kahane daydreamed about becoming the saviour of his people, he now openly presented himself as a modern day prophet. He claimed to hold the authentic Jewish spark, which had fractured into a million pieces at the Creation. Like his great grandfather who was a cabalist from Safed, Kahane preached that it is man's task to recover these sparks and make the world whole again. Kahane claimed that the divine spark was within him and that he could find it in others.

Kahane's militant Messianism began to affect his relationship with his followers in America. He warned them that American Jews faced the twin perils of assimilation and annihilation if they did not return to Israel. Those who do not melt in America's melting pot would ultimately melt in America's ovens, he

---

*A *dunam* is a approximately a quarter of an acre.

predicted. He compared the United States to the Weimar Republic, declaring that American Jewry was as blind to its fate as were the German Jews before Hitler took power.

Much of Kahane's Messianic fury was aimed at America's 400,000 Orthodox Jews, who, according to Kahane, are worse than blind—they are hypocrites. "The tragedy is that most observant Jews in America are practitioners of Jewish ritual and folklore," Kahane once told me. "A religious Jew is one who does the really hard *mitzvah* [commandment], and that's settling the land. My purpose in life, therefore, is to say the things that no other Jewish leader is saying—that the fate of the Jewish people in the *Galut* [exile] and in Israel rests upon their being Jewish again. This can only be done in Israel. Only then will God shine his light on Zion."

He insisted that, just as there cannot be a Jewish state in the Messianic sense unless the Jews return to the land of Israel, a Messianic Jewish state cannot exist with an Arab minority. Jews must be alone in the land to rebuild their moral fiber—which is another reason for this emphasis on Arab deportation, he says.

"I'm not a racist," he declared. "A racist is a Jew who says Arabs can be equal citizens in a Jewish state."

* * *

Soon after stepping down as American JDL boss, Kahane realized that he needed access to JDL's coffers in order to fund his Messianic-minded activities in Israel. That meant a bloodletting.

On July 3, 1974, Kahane wrote to the JDL board instructing them to steep themselves in the revelations contained in his Messianic manifesto—*The Jewish Idea*. The instrument of this ideology would be a new group called Kach—Hebrew for "thus" or "this is the way." He wrote:

> It is no secret that JDL has long since lost both its vitality and purpose. Lack of talent, funds and above all—failure to grow in ideology—have made it one more Jewish group. In Israel, we are planning to announce the formation of a group known as Kach-Thus, which will carry the JDL ideology to its highest level. It will take a Jewishness that is dynamic but limited in what it can do permanently and add Judaism which is the cement and truth of our people.
>
> The Jewish people need the JDL idea—in its total form— very much. Because of that, I want to revitalize JDL [in

America]. I would like JDL to be in the Exile what Kach will
be in Israel.

Kahane announced that he would present his program at a JDL
national convention to be held in New York in September 1974.
"If I do not hear from you," he threatened in a letter to the JDL
board, "I will call a conference of key people in the JDL for the
purpose of organizing . . . JDL-Kach. For the good of the *Idea*,
please let us not have to do this."

Kahane returned to New York on August 14, 1974, after having been detained in Israel for more than two years without his
U.S. passport. He was paler and thinner than anyone had remembered; his eyes twitched and he stuttered badly when he talked
about his chief nemesis Bertram Zweibon, whom he called a "fat,
sweaty, suburban lawyer."

Zweibon, meanwhile, was attempting to gain control of JDL
front groups, which had become money feeders for whatever
Kahane wanted to do in Israel. One such group, which had been
a considerable source of funds, was Jewish Operation Youth
[JOY], a charitable, tax-exempt foundation incorporated in New
York by Kahane, Zweibon, and Morton Dolinsky. Zweibon wrote
to Dolinsky, who had moved to Israel where he was then director of public relations for the Hebrew Institute of Technology
in Haifa, asking him to sign over his proxy. Zweibon claimed
that Kahane had used JOY to illegally finance his Knesset campaign, in violation of IRS tax codes governing charitable organizations. "I want to make sure, since my name is involved with
it [JOY], that it does not become a vehicle for further rip-offs
which sooner or later will be picked up by the federal government and result in giving me some grief," wrote Zweibon. "I
trust that I can rely upon you not to reveal the contents of our
correspondence to Meir."

On September 27, 1974, Kahane staged a putsch. He obtained
a court order enjoining Zweibon and eight others from representing themselves as the JDL and collecting funds on behalf of the
JDL. "He manipulated and maneuvered until he was in control,
even though it meant discarding people who were important,"
said Sue Caplan, a New York attorney and former JDL activist,
whose husband, David, a scientist at Bell Laboratories, was a
member of the board. Kahane announced his victory in *The Jewish Press*: "A general housecleaning has taken place and the brief

era of mindlessness is over. We return to the mature days of strength with sanity and militancy with normalcy.''

What Kahane meant by normalcy was not difficult to decipher. On October 30, three JDL men broke into the PLO office in Manhattan. They pummeled the assistant director, ripped out the telephones, smashed furniture, rifled the office files, and emptied a clip from an Uzi submachine gun into the wall. A JDL cell calling itself Jewish Armed Resistance Strike Unit claimed credit for the attack in a call to the media. A few days later, the JDL's new executive director, Russel Kelner, a former school teacher from Philadelphia, was arrested after he gave a television interview in which he threatened to assassinate Yasir Arafat when he came to New York to speak at the United Nations.

On January 19, 1975, Kahane returned to New York to spur the troops. That same day two shots were fired into the Soviet UN Mission; Kahane and forty-seven others were arrested during a violent protest outside the Mission in which six persons, including two policemen, were injured. Later that week, JDL activists stole the printing presses of Philadelphia's only Arabic-language newspaper, which the JDL claimed was spreading anti-Israel propaganda.

With Kahane at the helm, the JDL spewed out its own propaganda and raised money through a dizzying array of front groups, including Jewish Political Action Committee, Democracy in Jewish Life, Conference of Presidents of Major Activist Jewish Organizations, Committee Against Israeli Retreat, the Jewish Identity Center, and the Jewish Idea. *Shuva* (The Return) was set up to promote immigration to Israel. Its office was located in the Catskills near Grossingers and funded by the Jewish Agency.

Other fronts included SOIL (Save Our Israel Land), which was set up by Kahane in 1974 and placed under the control of Dov Hikind, today a New York State assemblyman from Brooklyn's Forty-eighth District. SOIL, a group that demonstrated against returning Arab land captured by the Israeli Army in the 1967 Six Day War, was intended to attract people who would not want to be associated with the JDL. ''The use of front groups should be encouraged within limitations,'' Kahane wrote to a JDL board member.

''SOIL, under Dov H., is a good example of what can be done. I think Dov should be invited to the next Board meeting to explain what has been done and what is being done. All SOIL names should be discreetly funneled to JDL, which in turn should be careful to contact these people only many weeks later and without saying that they were gotten from SOIL. Work closely with Dov; I told him that he is to listen.''

In the same letter, Kahane recommended the formation of a JDL front group to be named *Yiud* (Destiny) as a way of attracting young people between the ages of ten and seventeen who, in Kahane's view, would be more stable emotionally than many of the members of the JDL. Kahane also suggested that the JDL organize a *shul* (synagogue). He explained: "A *shul* is never bothered by the IRS and it can be held in a store front in Brooklyn. . . . It is a great investment because then tax deductible contributions can be made with no trouble and the store can be used for meetings.''

Though neither Yiud nor the JDL *shul* got off the ground, Kahane effectively used SOIL to needle the Israeli government, which he feared would negotiate away the Occupied Territories in a peace treaty with the Arabs. "I know what a mental block it is for Jews and JDL to publicly criticize the GOVERNMENT of Israel,'' Kahane wrote to the newly installed JDL board, knowing that they considered the Israeli government a sacred cow. "But if we do not have the courage to do what is unpopular *AS WE ALWAYS DID AND FOR THE SAKE OF ISRAEL*, then we are not worthy of the name JDL.''

In one instance, Kahane instructed JDL under the cover of SOIL to occupy the Manhattan office of the Religious Zionist Organization of America to protest the National Religious Party's alliance with the Labor government, which had called for trading territory for peace with the Arabs. "Stay in there and make sure that Israeli TV and the Jewish Telegraphic Agency cover it,'' Kahane wrote to Kelner. "Have picketers outside too in decent numbers. . . . At the press conference please make it clear that the Israeli government is the main target and that those who love the *State* of Israel must save it from disaster at the hands of the government. Contact Dov Hikind on this immediately!''

During this period of sniper shootings and sit-ins, Kahane took a kind of devilish delight in flagrantly violating the terms of his probation stemming from his 1971 felony conviction for manufacturing firebombs. As a special condition of that probation, Kahane had been instructed that he was to have nothing to do, directly or indirectly, with guns, bombs, dynamite, or other weapons. On May 15, 1972, a federal court had found Kahane guilty of violating the terms of that probation. Though Judge Jack B. Weinstein ultimately restored Kahane's probation, he warned the rabbi that if he were caught even encouraging anyone to use violence he would go to jail.

"Even inside Israel?" Kahane asked the Judge.

"Right," said the court.

"Even to the Israeli army?" asked Kahane.

"Yes," said Judge Weinstein.

"Fine," replied Kahane.

On February 21, 1975, the U.S. government revoked Kahane's probation at a hearing in a Brooklyn federal court, citing the letters he wrote from Israel directing his associates in America to assassinate Russian and Arab diplomats. The probation revocation hearing was noteworthy for the luminaries that attorney Barry Slotnick paraded on the witness stand to vouch for Kahane's sterling character. The list included JDL supporters Dr. Samuel Korman, the chief of the Cancer Division of the Kingsbrook Jewish Medical Center, and Rabbi Avraham Weiss of the Hebrew Institute of Riverdale, who told the court that he volunteered to testify because he found Kahane to be "extremely sincere, highly motivated, understanding and compassionate, and self-effacing." Several Russian Jewish activists living in Israel also flew to New York to testify for Kahane. Their expenses were covered by Menachem Begin, according to Irving Calderon, then a JDL official who went to Begin's house in Jerusalem to help with the arrangements.

This time around, however, Judge Weinstein was not buying the "Kahane as saviour of the Jewish people" routine, nor did he cave in to the hundreds of letters from Kahane's disciples. Kahane self-righteously postured in court up until the moment of sentencing.

"The letters—all the violence that the JDL . . . has used . . . was not a mindless violence or a heedless violence," Kahane said to the court before sentencing. "It was a lesson in political logic." The letters had been written in response to Munich, which "struck at the very spirit of what people like to call 'The New Jew,' " and against détente, which, he said, "doomed" Soviet Jews.

> What I did I did, but I certainly never did it with a contempt for law, never. I did what I did. I will do what I may do again, because I love the law and there must be law with justice and there must be law with freedom and there must be law for all the people. If I ever stopped doing what I have to do, my wife would break up the family. I have the most wonderful wife and I spoke to her last Friday by telephone. She said, 'Whatever happens, you just do what you have to do.'
>
> So I can only end by saying that I don't envy you, Your Honor. I did what the government says I did and I violated probation and you will have to do what you have to do and do it with a good conscience and know that that which I did I did with a good conscience.

Kahane was sentenced to one year in prison. He served eight months in a Manhattan halfway house, which he was allowed to leave every day to eat in kosher restaurants. Kahane actually used the time to conduct JDL business. Fed up with Kahane's antics, Weinstein ordered the rabbi to serve the remaining four months of his sentence in a minimum-security federal penitentiary in Allenwood, Pennsylvania.

"Prison was a real joy," Kahane later told me. "I read the Torah all day."

CHAPTER TEN
The Gerri Alperin Affair

By the time Kahane's cell door at Allenwood Federal Penitentiary slammed shut behind him, the JDL was in disarray. The national membership rolls had dipped to well below two thousand, and the JDL's New York chapter had no more than four hundred, $25-a-year dues paying members. The League had changed, one observer noted, from an organization bustling with unruly youth into a group staffed by a frightened secretary hiding behind a locked office door in Brooklyn. "The JDL had a very bad reputation," admitted Bonnie Pechter, an obese, curly-haired twenty-six year old, who was appointed JDL's national director not long after Kahane went to prison. "The media didn't want to hear from us. They would throw our press releases in the garbage. And remember, the JDL's whole game is press. Without it we couldn't exist—and the press just wasn't interested in our sit-ins at the Israeli Embassy."

On June 19, 1975, a few weeks before he entered Allenwood, Kahane held a press conference at Gefen's Restaurant in Manhattan to announce the formation of a Jewish terrorist underground that he said would combat "the sworn enemies of the Jewish people with hard-core violence." At the time, Kahane was being held at a federal halfway house in Manhattan that he frequently left to conduct JDL business. He was so flagrant in his disregard for the rules, which prohibited him from engaging in JDL activities, that on one occasion he even left the halfway house to lead three hundred JDL demonstrators through an Hispanic enclave of predominantly Jewish Borough Park in Brooklyn, shouting over a bullhorn that two Hispanics would be attacked for every Jewish victim of street crime. Now at Gefen's Restaurant, Kahane declared that the JDL would aid the new Jewish terrorist underground "in whatever way that we can. . . . We hail their creation as a tragically needed thing. I wish them well and I hope they have the Jewish head to go with the Jewish fist."

For nine months in 1975 and 1976, JDL extremists calling themselves the Jewish Armed Resistance attempted to emulate past glories. In New York, pipe bombs exploded outside the Iraqi Mission to the UN, the Polish Consulate, and the Amtorg office. Shots were also fired into the Soviet residential complex in the Bronx; into the homes of two Soviet diplomats in suburban Maryland; and into the Soviet Mission to the UN, piercing two fifth-floor windows in the Ukrainian section. On May 2, 1976, in the early morning hours before a march for Soviet Jewry in Manhattan, five low-yield pipe bombs caused minor damage to the American Communist Party national headquarters, two midtown banks that did business with the Soviet Union, a Russian-language bookstore, and a subway exit near the United Nations Library. On June 23, 1976, vehicles belonging to Pan American Airlines were destroyed by incendiary bombs. In Washington, D.C., a bomb blew a hole in the retaining wall at the State Department, shattering several plate glass doors and windows, causing more than $15,000 in damage. A JDL spokesman announced that the explosion was to protest the "sellout of Israel to Sadat."

The flurry of activity stopped when the FBI arrested twenty-one-year-old Steven Ehrlich, seventeen-year-old Steven Rombom, and Thomas MacIntosh, a thirty-six-year-old convert to Judaism, as they drove across the Goethals Bridge between New Jersey and Staten Island with four pounds of gunpowder. MacIntosh, who turned state's witness, testified against his friends and also implicated thirty-five-year-old JDL leader Russel Kelner and one other person in the spate of Jewish Armed Resistance terror bombings. The JDL men were subsequently convicted and received prison sentences. According to government documents, at least two dozen people were investigated for their roles in the JAR bombings, including Kahane, who was named as an unindicted co-conspirator.

Steven Rombom was a particularly tragic example of the sort of psychopaths Kahane attracted to the JDL. The violence-prone youth, who, according to court records spent eight years in psychiatric institutions from the age of six, joined the JDL when he was twelve years old over the frantic objections of his doctors and social workers who called JDL officials, begging them not to allow Rombom to get involved in the militant organization. Following Rombom's conviction, his mother spun into a deep depression. His father, Abraham, wrote to the judge pleading for his son's early release from prison, saying that "my marriage has been completely ruined. There is no interest in marital relations on the part of my wife. I cannot talk to her about any subject but Steven." As late as 1985, Rombom, who now works in New York as a private investigator, was handling security on the East Coast for Rabbi Kahane.

JAR activities in Washington, D.C. ceased after William Perl, the seventy-year-old architect of Kahane's Arab deportation plan, was convicted of conspiring to shoot into the homes of two Soviet diplomats in Hyattsville, Maryland. Perl claimed at his November 1976 trial that he was lured into the plot by a man named Levtov, who pretended to be an Israeli intelligence agent. In fact, the man turned out to be an undercover operative for the FBI. Perl received a two-year suspended sentence and a $12,000 fine. At the request of the FBI, one of Perl's sons was picked up by police in Italy in connection with the JAR crime spree but was subsequently released for lack of evidence.

The trials depleted both the JDL's bank account and manpower. According to Pechter, as many as forty JDL members in New York were involved in the Jewish Armed Resistance bombings. As soon as Rombom and his cronies were arrested, dozens of JDL members and their families fled to Israel. In the meantime, attorneys' fees ran into the tens of thousands of dollars. "There were many people who carried out violence for the JDL because they were dedicated and devoted to Kahane," said Pechter. But Kahane, by then out of prison and barnstorming for money, disavowed the JDL bombers, even though he had sanctioned their terrorist activities, according to Pechter and several other ex-JDL officials.

As Kahane wrote JDL board member Larraine Schumsky:

As far as the JDL people facing trial are concerned, I made it clear that I will devote a weekend to raise money for them. Let me again say that I consider their actions terribly *harmful* to Jews (not just stupid, though that certainly is the case). Let me tell you why:

. . . assuming that the charges against Russ, Rombom, and MacIntosh are true (which I pray they are not), then we are dealing with the idiocy and irresponsibility of people acting 1) on their own; 2) despite the fact that they know that all active JDL members have to be idiots to think that they can be open members of a group that is watched by the FBI and at the same time James Bond underground operatives; 3) amateurs who were certain to be caught and doing things that five years after the big events no longer carry the same weight; 4) thrust on us the burden of destroying all our plans and projects for the vital things that must be done today by mortgaging our funds, our people, our resources to help them.

What happens tomorrow when some other kid decides to do a crazy and senseless act? Are we always to be bogged down in these things that we not only did not order and plan but which are not good or vital now? . . . And why didn't JDL empty its treasury every time we knew that there was a Jew in Israel who needed a kidney machine or faced death (which is almost daily)?

JDL has to keep existing and planning projects and actions that are 1) important and 2) sensible. It cannot die because of every other need, let alone insane act. And so I will help them and especially Bill Perl. But since JDL has now reached a point where it not only does not do things that have to be done but begins to hurt my efforts to do things that should be done, I wish to get out of an . . . obligation to help.

Dismayed JDL board members were too cowed by Kahane to demand that he do more to help his jailed comrades. ''We were timid people,'' said Stanley Schumsky, Larraine's husband, who was also a JDL board member. When Kahane was in trouble, Stanley noted, he got lawyers like Barry Slotnick—the best money could buy. When JDL kids were arrested, they usually had to make do with mediocre legal talent—or "dog-bite lawyers" as they were dubbed by JDL members. "I don't think Kahane ever saw the JDL as a 'defense organization,' " said Schumsky, who had used his position as president of the Young Israel Synagogue of Coney Island to funnel thousands of dollars to Kahane in Israel. "He saw it as a vehicle to reach the press and raise money. When these kids got into serious trouble and we needed to use the phones to raise money, that's when you got *no* Kahane participation. If you were a kid taking risks, minimally you wanted to know that your costs were going to be covered if you got arrested. Russ Kelner was in jail for three years. He was certainly entitled to a weekly stipend. We took care of it. Kahane wouldn't even visit him in prison when he was in the States on his tours to raise money for his Knesset campaign."

Although Kahane refused to aid his American followers, he nonetheless demanded that they do his bidding. "He had us do all kinds of activities that were supposed to hurt the Israeli government and gain him publicity," Pechter recalled. "He wanted us to harass Israeli diplomats—he told us to get their license plates and follow their cars to harass them. We used to stage sit-ins at the Israeli Embassy. We did it very half-heartedly because there was a consensus within JDL that that's not why we joined. We had joined to fight anti-Semites—and we really didn't think the Israeli government was our enemy, even though we took issue with many Israeli government policies."

The hard-core residue of the JDL stuck with Kahane even though his anti-Israeli actions pained them nearly as much as his lack of regard for the JDL youngsters who ended up behind bars. Moreover, it seemed that no matter what Kahane did, or how much he was vilified, politically conservative Orthodox rabbis continued to invite him to speak and raise money in their temples and community centers. In certain New York neighborhoods it was even fashionable during the late 1960s and early 1970s for politicians to stump on pro-JDL platforms. Bronx Congressman Mario Biaggi boasted about his friendship with Kahane and attended JDL functions. Dov Hikind won his first State Assembly seat as an avowed former JDL leader. Harry Smoler, a Brooklyn stockbroker, ran twice for a State Assembly seat on an unabashedly pro-JDL platform, before finally capturing a seat with their backing. In 1969, Leon Katz successfully ran for the Brooklyn City Council with the open support of the JDL. In the early 1970s, the JDL also quietly supported Liberal Party Councilman-at-large Kenneth Haber, who later became executive assistant to Brooklyn Borough President Howard Golden. In 1970, Hy Dechter ran a rabidly pro-JDL campaign for a State Assembly seat representing the Lower East Side of New York, taking in more than $10,000 in political contributions raised by Kahane. Dechter lost by just forty-seven votes.

The entire 39th Assembly District Democratic political machine was permeated with right-wing Herutnicks who saw no perceptible difference between Herut and JDL. George Meissner, Brooklyn powerbroker Meade Esposito's personal attorney, was a gung-ho Kahane man. Barry Fox, the JDL chair of Sheepshead Bay, was also the United Federation of Teachers chapter chairman. And Andrew Stein, now the powerful president of New York's City Council, supplied the JDL with microphones and speakers for Soviet Jewish rallies when he was a state assemblyman.

So politically precocious did the JDL become that in 1972 it fielded its own candidates, who unsuccessfully ran against liberal Democratic New York State Assemblyman Steven Solarz and U.S. Congresswoman from New York Bella Abzug. JDL member and attorney Harvey Michelman ran a redbaiting campaign against Abzug, accusing her of having ties to the Communist Party, the PLO, and the Black Panthers. "For voters of the 19th Congressional District," said one of Michelman's flyers, which was penned by Kahane and run off on JDL presses, "this is not an ordinary election. It is one that pits Moscow against Jerusalem."

* * *

Yet even Kahane's most stalwart supporters reeled when news of his sexual indiscretions surfaced shortly after he got out of Allenwood. They could forgive the Orthodox rabbi his Mafia ties, his megalomania, and certainly terrorism—but illicit sex? To them Kahane was a holy man; he had to set an example. After all, adultery is proscribed by the Ten Commandments, and even Kahane was not above laws made for mortals. Despite all of Kahane's failings, his followers never had repudiated him because they agreed with what he stood for. But they had little inkling that he had an obsessive weakness for women.

For those who looked closely, of course, there were plenty of clues that the rabbi's behavior was far less pious than his preaching pretended. The JDL was perpetually rife with rumors about Kahane's womanizing, partly because there were so many women in the group who dreamed about making love to the skinny, nervous, constantly blinking rabbi. "There wasn't a woman in Laurelton who didn't fantasize about him," said Edith Horowitz, who along with her husband, Fred, had befriended Kahane and Joseph Churba in the 1960s. Kahane's probation revocation hearing in 1975 drew rows of swooning Jewish matrons, recalled Fay Lloyd, one of Kahane's minions. "Women were gaping," Lloyd said. "One fifty-year-old woman stood on the courthouse lawn under a tree. Her eyes lit up like a pinball machine whenever he walked outside."

During the JDL's formative years, Kahane spent weeks at a time on the road, crisscrossing the United States to raise money and build new chapters. Reports began to filter back to the board about Kahane's alleged sexual liaisons, but no one wanted to believe them. When Kahane was in New York, he maintained a facade of strict probity. Once, at a JDL Legal Defense Fund benefit in Queens where the great jazz musician Lionel Hampton and Borscht Belt comic Jackie Mason performed, Kahane bolted from the theater when a scantily clad belly dancer appeared on stage to perform between the main acts.

Still, there was constant office gossip about Kahane and Renee Brown, a New York City school teacher and Kahane's personal secretary. Brown, who former JDL members describe as a severe, matronly-looking woman with a domineering personality, is five years older than Kahane and was very protective of him. "Renee used to call me day and night mooning over Kahane," said Bonnie Pechter. "She wanted him desperately. She was obsessed with him. People tended to dismiss her as emotionally unstable. Just because he sent her flowers and spent a lot of time with her didn't mean they were sleeping together. But Renee did tell people she was sleeping with him. We just didn't want to believe it."

After Brown complained to friends in the JDL that Kahane had jilted her for another woman, the rabbi dismissed her and hired Gerri Alperin—an attractive, busty, outgoing twenty-nine-year-old Manhattanite who was a JDL hanger-on. Alperin had dated Russ Kelner before becoming Kahane's personal secretary. "People in the JDL office started making little jokes about Gerri and Meir," said Pechter. "Board members would say, 'Don't be ridiculous.' But we were suspicious."

The JDL's inner circle tried to ignore reports about Kahane's philandering. They lived in fear that a scandal would destroy the JDL. A collection of ordinary middle-class Orthodox Jews from New York City's outer boroughs, they craved the excitement that Kahane brought into their lives. They believed him when he declared that together they would save the Jewish people. "I lived and dreamed JDL," said Fay Lloyd, who operated one of several JDL printing presses from her basement in Long Island. "I couldn't imagine my life without it."

On the other hand, Libby Kahane must have dreamed of a life free of the JDL. One reason she had moved to Israel in the first place was to distance herself from her husband's political and sexual affairs. Now she was receiving anonymous letters replete with lurid details about her husband's alleged relationship with Gerri Alperin. The letters were mailed to her office at the Hebrew University where she worked as a librarian. Kahane's brother and sister-in-law received similar letters. When Nachman confronted Meir about Alperin, he simply told his younger brother to keep out of his business. Incredulous, Nachman refused to talk to him until their father became terminally ill almost a year later.

Kahane was not much better at being a caring father than he was at being a loving husband and brother. "When he was traveling in America, he would sometimes call long distance to study Talmud with his sons," said Feiga, Nachman's wife. "Occasionally, he'll play with his grandkids. He takes out his stopwatch and plays a few minutes. At family affairs the minute you sit next to him it's politics. He's only interested in immediately swerving the conversation to how horrible the world is and how he's going to save it."

Kahane was just as perfunctory in his relationship with his parents. "He visits his mother every Friday," said Feiga. "He's in and out of Sonia's house in thirty minutes—the time it takes to wolf down some cheese blintzes. She's very high on him, but she gets very low when he's in trouble. She knows most people are not pro-Meir. But she gets a lot of positive reinforcement from his friends. Most Kach people have enough sense to know she's an old lady and not to tell her things that will upset her.''

Early in 1977, Charles Kahane collapsed in his apartment and was rushed to the hospital. Nachman called Meir, who was in America on a fundraising tour for his Knesset campaign, and begged him to rush home. ''No, it's not the right time for me to come home,'' replied Meir, who was traveling with Gerri Alperin.

Kahane campaigned feverishly in Israel through the winter and spring of 1977. Kach's party platform promised to solve the Arab problem and Israel's economic and social problems in one fell swoop:

> Imagine in your souls what an enormous contribution to the economy of Israel our Arab deportation plan would bring . . . imagine what could be done if all the millions of dollars that we spend today on the development of towns and villages in the Arab sector were summoned back and used for Jewish ends . . . if the Jews lived in the thousands of vacated Arab homes . . . if we saved all of the wasted money that is spent on security for the prevention of attacks from a hostile population . . . the imagination goes wild! . . .

Kahane directed his pitch in Israel primarily at members of Gush Emunim, whose spiritual leader, Rav Zvi Yehuda Kook, endorsed the Kach leader. ''The presence of Rabbi Meir Kahane and his uncompromising words from the Knesset platform will undoubtedly add strength and value to the obligatory struggle on behalf of the entire land of Israel,'' declared Kook in a widely publicized letter of support. Kook had been a staunch supporter of the National Religious Party, but broke with them in 1974 when they joined the Labor government coalition. The influential Gush leader even posed for a photograph with Kahane in front of the Wailing Wall. Kahane had the photo made into flyers, which he used to raise campaign funds. Kook's motive for backing Kahane may have transcended ideology: for years Kahane had been funneling money to Yeshiva Mercaz HaRav through a JDL front group, Jewish Operation Youth (JOY), according to cancelled checks that I obtained, which were made out by Kahane to the ultranationalist yeshiva.

Begin, so supportive of Kahane in the past, was annoyed that the American rabbi was running on an independent list for the Knesset. In the light of the public's growing disenchantment with the scandal-ridden Labor Party, which was widely blamed for nearly losing the Yom Kippur War, Begin's right-wing bloc had for the first time a solid chance to capture the Knesset. As far as Begin was concerned every vote for Kach was at his expense.

Ex-JDL official Irving Calderon said that Begin asked him to try to inveigle Kahane into withdrawing from the race for the good of the Israeli Right. But Kahane refused to listen. "Kahane told me he was going to be prime minister of Israel," recalled Calderon. "I wondered then if he had two minds—a rational one that knew he had no chance of even getting into the Knesset, and a Messianic one that was getting the word from God."

Although polls showed that many Israelis went along with some of Kahane's ideas, none except his ultra-hard-core followers and the fanatical fringes of Gush Emunim approved of his confrontational tactics. And while those tactics had won him widespread publicity and some support, they did not help him gain his long-coveted Knesset seat. In the elections of 1977 that propelled Begin into power, Kahane was thumped—winning 4,396 votes, a mere 0.25 percent of the electorate.

Once again, Kahane's addiction to publicity had come back to haunt him. Like so many times in the rabbi's life, his unrestrained behavior was his downfall. "One week before the May 1977 election, I lost 5,000 votes in a single day," Kahane admitted reluctantly. That was the day that Kahane and a group of his followers, carrying Uzi submachine guns, stormed the offices of Nablus's pro-PLO mayor, Bassam Shaka, in an attempt to drive him out of the West Bank. "There was a backlash," he told me. "I got thousands of angry letters and phone calls. It cost me the election. But, as usual, I was simply ahead of my time."

Shaka well remembers Kahane's attack. "Kahane sent me a telegram warning that he was coming to Nablus to help me pack my bags," Shaka recalled in a 1980 interview. The mayor gave the telegram to Colonel Joseph Cohen, then military governor of the West Bank. The colonel told the mayor that because Israel was a democratic country, he could not prevent Kahane from "visiting" Nablus.

The rabbi and his goon squad were barred from entering Nablus's municipal building by a crowd of angry Arabs. Shaka left his second-floor office to confront Kahane, who was chanting in Arabic "*ma fish Filastin*"—"there is no Palestine." The mayor offered to pay the rabbi's way back to America. The Arabs burst out laughing and a shoving match began. The Israeli military arrived only moments before a full-scale riot erupted.

"Kahane is allowed to stir up trouble because the present Israeli government wants the Arabs to get fed up with life on the West Bank and leave," the mayor told me. "His politics are a logical extension of the Likud's."

Kahane said that he agreed with the mayor's analysis in at least one respect: he claimed that he had many influential friends in the Begin government who wanted to deport the Arabs from Israel and the Occupied Territories, but feared hostile international reaction. Despite his own defeat, Kahane said that he was jubilant after Begin's surprise victory in May 1977. Finally, he thought, Israel had a prime minister who claimed *both* banks of the Jordan River.

"So I came to him with a plan," Kahane recalled. "I told him I'd gather thousands of my supporters and create anti-government riots across the country. Then Begin could tell the White House that he was a moderate—as witness all the pressure from the Right. I thought Begin could use this as a smokescreen to annex Judea and Samaria." Begin rejected the plan, prompting Kahane to denounce his one-time hero as a traitor to the Jewish people.

Kahane returned to America in June 1977 to begin raising money for his next Knesset campaign. As usual, he employed the JDL as his personal public relations tool. Egyptian President Anwar Sadat's historic 1977 journey to Israel sowed panic among Israel's radical Right, who feared their government would appease him with territory. Kahane used Sadat's visit as a pretext to stage demonstrations against the Israeli Consulate in New York. "I thought O.K., it will give him something to do," said Pechter, who had phoned Kahane soon after his Knesset defeat to express her support and sympathy. "I knew he would feel deflated and my heart went out to him," she said.

Although she reluctantly went along with Kahane's plans to demonstrate against the Israeli government, she had her own ideas about how to run the JDL. In March 1977, neo-Nazi Frank Collins had won court permission to stage a march through Skokie, Illinois—an affluent Chicago suburb that was home to many Holocaust survivors. Pechter began raising money to charter buses to Skokie for a counter-demonstration. It was the first real act of "Jewish self-defense" that the JDL had contemplated in years. But incredibly, Kahane vetoed the plan, explaining in a *Jewish Press* column that a counter-demonstration would fail and make Jews look the worse for trying.

Pechter ignored Kahane and continued to scrape together funds to charter buses. Kahane countered, sending out flyers on JDL stationery asking that donations for the JDL's Skokie march be mailed directly to his personal post office box in Brooklyn. Pechter said that the JDL never saw a penny of the money he collected. Meanwhile, a letter bomb was mailed to Collins's home. According to several ex-JDL officials, the bomb, which failed to explode, had been authorized by Kahane, who hoped it would upstage Pechter's march.

On a sweltering July 4th afternoon, in 1977, about a dozen Nazis marched through downtown Chicago, having abandoned their plans at the last minute to march in Skokie. More than two thousand counter-demonstrators from around the country, including Communists, Socialists, and a large contingent from the JDL, pelted the Nazis with rocks and police horse droppings. It was the first time that the JDL had cooperated with leftists. For his part, Kahane spent the July 4th weekend in New York with Gerri Alperin—trying to summon up the courage to leave his wife.

Rabbi Kahane often went to Elyakim and Trony Rosenblatt's home for the Sabbath when he was in New York. Trony had known Libby and Meir in B'nai Akiva, an Orthodox Jewish youth group, and she later became an ardent JDL supporter. Elyakim, who was dean of the Rabbinical College of Queens, had been convicted in 1976 for conspiring to use his school's bank account to launder an estimated $180,000 in stolen postal checks for a fee. The conviction was subsequently overturned by a U.S. appeals court on a technicality. Kahane, who himself was allegedly receiving funds funneled through Rosenblatt's school, defended him in his *Jewish Press* column. Before long, Kahane was bringing Gerri Alperin to the Rosenblatts's for "religious instruction." Though Alperin was Jewish, Kahane told the Rosenblatts that she knew next to nothing about "authentic Judaism." Kahane and Alperin often spent the weekends at the Rosenblatts's, sleeping in separate bedrooms. The Rosenblatts's maid claimed to have once seen Kahane creeping out of Alperin's room late at night, but Trony refused to believe the story, calling her a liar. It took Kahane himself to convince her otherwise.

As Alperin sat in the Rosenblatts's dining room after the Sabbath meal on the July 4th weekend, Kahane matter of factly told his friends that he and Gerri had been seeing each other for a long time, that they were in love and wanted to get married. This was the real reason why, he said, he wanted to expose Gerri to Orthodox instruction—so that she would make a good *rebbitzin* (Orthodox rabbi's wife). Kahane asked the Rosenblatts to help him with his divorce and the wedding plans. If he could not get a divorce from Libby, he said, he would simply have two wives, claiming bigamy was acceptable from a Halachic point of view.

The Rosenblatts were flabbergasted. Orthodox Jews might use their yeshivas to launder money; the practice dates back to Czarist times. But "gods" don't screw around. After all, it was Kahane who was always screaming Torah! Torah! Torah! and using religion as a bludgeon to enforce his puritanical codes of behavior. Now here was Kahane trying to rationalize his adultery, even as the JDL's New York contingent was clambering aboard the Skokie-bound buses to battle the Nazis. Trony was particularly devastated because she still had a schoolgirl crush on Kahane. When the shock wore off, Trony phoned JDL officials with the news.

Twenty-four days later, shellshocked JDL board members piled into Larraine Schumsky's Manhattan office to consider the next move. For years the board had been nothing more than a rubber stamp for Kahane. "If his spirit was blowing in one direction the board would blow with it," said Howard Barbanel, then national student director of JDL and today publisher of *The Miami Jewish Tribune*. "He was sort of like the Ayatollah."

This time it was an ill wind that blew against Kahane. The board overwhelmingly voted to expel him from the JDL. The only dissenting vote was cast by Stanley Schumsky, who told me that he thought they could use the affair to blackmail Kahane to do whatever they wanted. "It was not pleasant to learn that a man we had devoted our lives to was a sham, a scoundrel, a world-class fraud," said Schumsky.

Just as suddenly, they realized that they could not account for as much as a dime of the millions that they had raised on his behalf. Gerri had confided in Trony that Kahane had bought her expensive jewelry, paid rent on her Manhattan apartment, shuttled her back and forth to Israel, and had run up thousands of dollars in phone calls to her home. He even had her install a private phone line exclusively for their conversations. "We realized that all this money was coming from funds Kahane had diverted from the JDL," said Pechter. "How could JDL have no money, while Alperin is getting expensive pearl necklaces, designer nightgowns, and who knows what else?"

Fearing the worst, Kahane scrambled to catch a flight to Israel. The board dispatched a three-person delegation to the airport to intercept him. They found the rabbi sitting alone reading a magazine in the lounge. "Kahane became very agitated," said Pechter, who was briefed about the confrontation by the delegation. "He declared that what he did with his personal life was his business. His departing words were that the JDL was nothing without him—and that we were nothing without the JDL." "I own the JDL," Kahane hissed, stalking away.

"I was shocked and hurt," recalled Bob Duchinoff, a restauranteur and one of the three board members who confronted Kahane. "I thought maybe he needed emotional help, so I called his brother in Israel. But Nachman said he had already given up on Meir."

The board members no longer cared what happened to Kahane. But they feared that a scandal would ruin what was left of the JDL. At the board's behest, Fay Lloyd visited Alperin at her Manhattan apartment, hoping to dissuade her from continuing her relationship with Kahane. "Kahane is a world Jewish leader and this will be terribly damaging if it gets out," Lloyd told her. "It will hurt the rabbi and the movement. Pack your bags and disappear!"

Alperin merely shrugged, saying that she would never leave the rabbi. "She was truly in love," said Lloyd. "She told me she never knew a religious person could touch her in such a sensual way. I nearly went through the floor!"

Lloyd tried to make her face facts. "You're not his first mistress," Lloyd lectured. "You won't be the last. He won't marry you. He'll never divorce Libby. Disappear fast or the [JDL] kids will kill you."

Soon after Lloyd's visit, Alperin began receiving telephone death threats. "They scared the shit out of her," Lloyd said. "She kept saying 'I can't imagine anyone would hurt me.' " Finally, Alperin fled from New York. When Kahane found out what the board had done to Alperin "he went crazy," Lloyd recalled.

" 'What do you mean threatening the poor girl?' he screamed."

Just a few days after voting to expel him, the board publicly disassociated itself from Kahane, proclaiming the break in *The Jewish Press*. "As of July 5, 1977, Rabbi Meir Kahane is no longer associated with JDL, the Jewish Identity Center, and affiliated organizations," said the announcement, signed by the JDL's executive board.

Nevertheless, Pechter realized that Kahane and the JDL were synonymous in most people's minds. Kahane's name had marquee value and without him, she knew, the group was in danger of becoming just one more relic from the Sixties. JDL needed a dramatic new direction if it were to survive, Pechter concluded. Instead of attacking the Israeli government and Jewish liberals, she decided that it should focus on fighting Nazis. Shortly after the television mini-series "The Holocaust" was broadcast, Pechter emptied the JDL bank account to pay for an ad in *The New York Times*, announcing that the group was embarking on a campaign against Nazi war criminals living in America. Pechter said that the ad, which cost $2,500, brought in more than $10,000 in contributions.

For starters, the JDL launched a series of well-publicized demonstrations in front of the homes of alleged Nazi war criminals in the New York area. At the time, the Justice Department was not very interested in tracking down the many hundreds of Nazi war criminals who had entered the United States after the war. The most violent incident in the JDL's new anti-Nazi campaign was an attack on Boleslaws Maikovskis, a Mineola, Long Island man who had been condemned to death in absentia by the Soviet Union in 1965 for participating in the mass slaughter of Jews in Riga during the Second World War. On a Sunday morning in 1977, Maikovskis was shot below the right kneecap by a gunman who trailed him home from mass. The assailant left behind a cloth patch bearing the insignia of the Jewish Defense League. Suddenly, the JDL's coffers were bulging.

Kahane fumed as Pechter tracked down Nazis—probably the one task that most Jews could at least privately sympathize with if not publicly support. In the fall of 1977, Kahane announced that he was touring America with his wife to start a new militant, religious group called The *Chug* (Circle). Around the same time, *The Jewish Press* published an article by Libby Kahane about how wonderful it was to be Meir Kahane's wife. JDLers speculated that Kahane had actually written the article and affixed Libby's byline.

Shortly before his return to America, Kahane wrote a conciliatory letter to Larraine Schumsky in which he compared his expulsion from the JDL to the destruction of the Warsaw Ghetto:

> I write this letter after a long discussion with Bill Perl. It is clear to both of us that tragedy of unprecedented dimension is coming to Israel and world Jewry. His call for unity is something that brings to mind the senseless refusal of both the Revisionists and the Left in the Warsaw Ghetto to join together even as the Ghetto was going up in flames.
>
> I have no interest in any personal relations with JDL or its members. Indeed, even had nothing occurred on a personal level, I am convinced that for me the JDL was a dead end. Be that as it may, if there is any meaning to the protestations of people about loving Jews, that means the ability to work together DESPITE differences and dislikes. Lashing out at each other guarantees nothing except hurting the Jewish people.
>
> I am returning to America with my wife . . . regardless of what JDL decides to do. But I strongly urge you to have us work—if not together—then at least complementing each other's efforts. If JDL is not prepared to do this, then it deserves to be condemned. I am convinced that you and those whom I have known for so long, will not have descended to the level of those who place pettiness over the Jewish people.
>
> I strongly urge you to meet with me . . . and work out a program whereby Jewish activist strength can grow. I will be working alone, setting up The Chug and, hopefully, from it an umbrella organization. I urge you to remember what is at stake here. We need not like each other but we must surely love the Jewish people.

No matter how hard he tried, the usually persuasive rabbi was still *persona non grata* with the JDL. For the first time ever, the JDL did not need Kahane. Its Nazi-bashing was attracting sympathy and financial support from more mainstream segments of the Jewish community.

Moreover, Kahane's harpy-like attacks on Begin for signing the 1978 Camp David Accords—which returned the Sinai to

Egypt and pledged that Israel was willing in principle to extend autonomy to the Palestinians in the Occupied Territories—were making him unwelcome even at *The Jewish Press*. Klass went so far as to threaten to fire Kahane after receiving pressure from the Herut Party about Kahane's smear campaign against Begin, which was partly conducted in his *Jewish Press* column. "There was once a man, and his name was Begin," Kahane railed. "Now he prostrates himself in front of the *goy* [Jimmy Carter] in the White House. Begin, the big ex-extremist, thinks I'm an extremist now. He didn't think I was so extreme when he gave me tacit support in my letter writing campaign which urged the Arabs to leave Israel." Though Kahane declared that the Camp David Accords would lead Israel to the abyss, it was clearly the rabbi himself who was teetering on the brink of political extinction.

Begin was disgusted by Kahane's behavior. "Before he moved to Israel, Kahane said the laws of Israel should not be broken," said Calderon. "He kept modifying his views until he said he would only obey his own interpretation of Halacha. He hid behind the shield of Halacha to justify all kinds of behavior. That's when Begin turned against him." "He doesn't believe in law," Begin told Calderon. "He doesn't believe in party discipline. He's no longer an asset." Indeed, after Camp David, Kahane never again recognized the legitimacy of the government of Israel.

Charles Kahane died in March 1978 of a heart ailment. The Kahane family sat *shiva* (the traditional seven-day period of Jewish mourning) at Sonia's Jerusalem apartment. "Meir sat in the bedroom with his cronies," said Feiga. "I couldn't see intense grief. He was constantly on the phone making political calls."

But when Libby brought up Meir's affair with Gerri Alperin, she finally got his undivided attention. This time, she vowed, she was leaving him. Kahane knew that the publicity surrounding a messy divorce would ruin his reputation—especially among the morally conservative American Orthodox Jewish community from which he drew most of his financial support. "He promised Libby that it wouldn't happen again," said Irving Calderon, who witnessed the encounter, which took place in front of stunned mourners in Sonia Kahane's living room. "It was horrible," added Feiga. "Charles had just died and here was Meir, juggling his wife, his Knesset campaign, and his mother like nothing made any difference but him." Although Libby and Meir briefly separated, she decided not to divorce him. Instead, she laid down strict rules about whom he could bring to the house, and what he could do or say around the children. "Orthodox Judaism is a very conservative society," said Feiga. "The kids would certainly be scarred by a divorce. Libby's not a martyr."

Kahane's seemingly self-destructive behavior continued into the summer of 1978, when he and several followers broke into the Russian Orthodox Church in Jerusalem with cans of spray paint and vandalized it. Kahane told reporters that he attacked the church because it was "a nest of KGB espionage in the Holy Land."

A few days later, Bonnie Pechter took out an advertisement in *The Jerusalem Post* denouncing Kahane for religious intolerance. The advertisement appeared at the lowest point in Kahane's political life. Isolated in Israel, where his small band of followers was increasingly targeted by the government for prosecution, and condemned by more and more of his American supporters, something inside Kahane snapped. Here was Bonnie Pechter, whom he had dismissed as a "fat circus clown," ridiculing him on his own turf. Whatever misgivings he still had about attacking his fellow Jews evaporated with the broadside in *The Jerusalem Post*. Kahane declared unconditional war on Pechter. Fighting anti-Semites had never aroused his wrath like this vicious campaign against Pechter.

Kahane recruited Victor Vancier—a short, pimply-faced militant who specialized in arson bombings—to hound Pechter and her allies from the JDL. "Victor, I don't care w-w-what it takes," cried the rabbi. "You get her out! I've h-had it!"

"This was music to my ears," Vancier recalled during a 1987 interview in Manhattan. "It was an all-out war; it was a war on her apartment building; it was a war on her family; I drove her out of her mind," he laughed demonically.

Vancier had joined the JDL in 1971 when he was a junior at Jamaica High School in Queens. Three years later he was convicted for his first felony—a JDL firebombing of a Soviet diplomat's car in Manhattan. Vancier served two months on Rikers Island, then he joined SOIL. Borough Park Assemblyman Dov Hikind, who was SOIL's leader, remembers Vancier as being "extremely sincere, dedicated . . . and devoted to Jewish causes."

Vancier was also one of SOIL's most notorious bombers. After committing a wave of arson bombings for which he says he was never arrested, in December 1978, Vancier and JDL member Bruce Berger were convicted of firebombing eleven Egyptian diplomatic targets in New York, Virginia, and Maryland, including cars, homes, and office buildings. The bombings were carried out to dramatize Kahane's disapproval of the Camp David Accords. Vancier served sixteen months of a twenty-one month sentence in federal prisons in New York and Florida.

If Vancier was good at terror bombings, he was unsurpassed at harassment. "I heard Rabbi Kahane once say: 'Victor Vancier is the most dangerous Jew alive today,'" recalled Howard Barbanel. "When you're harassed by Victor Vancier you don't even want to go out and buy a carton of milk. It's that frightening. He drives you to a level of paranoia. If you change your phone number, he will find it. If you move, he'll find you."

Vancier enlisted an odd collection of JDL misfits to help him unhinge Pechter, including Bruce Berger, who happened to be Pechter's ex-husband. "They were the cream of the crud," said Pechter. Berger, a somber, hulking man, knew Pechter's fears and vulnerabilities. "Bruce was an unstable guy and Vancier used him like a rag," said former JDL member Yaacov Rodan, now a journalist in Jerusalem.

Berger and Vancier spent hours in phone booths making threatening phone calls to Pechter and to her family in Philadelphia and California. "They would call up my grandmother at 2 A.M. to tell her there was a bomb in her apartment," said Pechter. "Bruce gave Victor access to everyone in my family." The FBI later told Pechter that Vancier charged more than $5,000 of harassing calls to the Egyptian UN Mission's credit card number.

The harassment did not stop with telephone death threats. Berger gave Vancier a nude photo that he had taken of his ex-wife one night while she was asleep. They had it made into posters and flyers, which they mailed to JDL members as well as to Pechter's family. They even slid the photos under the doors of her Manhattan neighbors' apartments.

Next, Vancier made racist phone calls to Black tenants in Pechter's apartment building. "Nigger, you better watch your black ass or it will be shot off by the the JDL," Vancier would say. Pechter's second husband was punched in the face by an irate Black tenant who had received many such calls.

But Pechter did not give in until Vancier began to torment her younger sister, who had a form of multiple sclerosis. Though she had lost 80 percent of her vision, the disease had not affected the rest of her body. The family doctor never told Pechter's sister the diagnosis, fearing that the knowledge might impair her chances of leading a normal life. She was a student at a Philadelphia community college when Vancier, posing as a relative, called the dean and said that Bonnie had been in a fatal car accident. "My sister had a nervous breakdown and had to be rushed to the hospital," says Pechter. "The next day Vancier called my mother and said, 'see how we can reach your daughter. If Bonnie doesn't resign in the next twenty-four hours we're going to tell your daughter she has multiple sclerosis.'"

Pechter says she had no choice but to capitulate and resign from the JDL. Within six weeks of Kahane telling Vancier to dispose of her, she was thrown out of her Manhattan apartment because of the harassing phone calls to her neighbors; one sister had a nervous breakdown; two other sisters who lived in Southern California had to be escorted to school by police because of death threats; her second marriage collapsed; she had a miscarriage; and she was operated on for ulcers.

"I knew these people were dangerous," Pechter says now. "It was only a matter of time before a bomb went off in my grandmother's apartment. How far can you fight them before it ends in bloodshed?"

As Kahane had promised, a new era of "strength and sanity and militancy with normalcy" had dawned on the JDL.

CHAPTER ELEVEN
Portrait of a Young Fanatic

~~~~~~~~~~~~~~~~~~~~~~~~~~~~~~~~~~~~~

On a fog-shrouded road between Jerusalem and Ramallah in the Israeli-occupied West Bank, two young American supporters of Rabbi Meir Kahane put on their prayer shawls to *daven* (pray), then pulled ski masks over their faces, slipped on black leather gloves, and loaded a U.S.-made M-16 automatic rifle.

Around 5:30 on that chilly March morning in 1984, the men watched an Arab bus wind around a steep curve. As it approached, they jumped from a ditch that ran parallel to the road and opened fire on the driver's window and the bus's right side. The volley lasted three to four seconds. While nine Arabs lay wounded inside the blood-spattered vehicle, the Jews ran a quarter of a mile to a prearranged spot, where a friend from New York City waited in a Hertz rental car. When the youths were later arrested by the Israeli police, Kahane told a press conference that his followers were "good Jewish boys" and that the machine-gunning was "sanctified by God."

Kach supporter Matt Liebowitz, a bearded, disarmingly soft-spoken twenty-four-year-old who served twenty-six months in an Israeli prison for the bus attack, epitomizes the kind of American kids who joined the JDL after Kahane wrested control of the organization from Bonnie Pechter.

Liebowitz's career in "Jewish activism," which began in Chicago, where he was raised, and led to New York and later to the West Bank of the River Jordan, is similar to the path taken by many young American Jews who get hooked on Meir Kahane's sinister vision of ridding Israel of its Arabs. "Violence is a tool," Liebowitz told me during a 1987 interview at a yeshiva in Far Rockaway, Queens where he sometimes studies. "Kahane says violence is not a nice thing, but that it's sometimes necessary. For me and for others there was a certain mystical attachment to blood and violence. This was the violence that drew us to the JDL and bonded us together in the struggle. . . . Kahane taught us that what we were doing was true and correct according to the Torah."

Liebowitz was not always interested in the "Jewish struggle." He was raised in an assimilated, middle-class Jewish home where Judaism had more ritual than meaning. Like many future JDL members, he was embarrassed by his religion. "I had no connection to Judaism," Liebowitz told me. "When I was a kid I used to hang out in the inner city and saw old Jews harassed by Black gangs. I had a very bad image of Jews—that they were weak, that they were worms."

Matt was thirteen when his parents divorced. He moved in with his mother, then later with his father, a family therapist in Chicago. Eventually, he returned to his mother's house because he did not get along with his stepmother. Matt became, according to his mother, "a street child." Uninterested in school, he began to hang out with white street gangs, she recalled, until he discovered the JDL and found religion. "He just looked for some authority, someone who would tell him how to live, who would tell him what to do, someone who would decide for him what was good and what was bad," she told the Israeli publication *Koteret Rashit* when she was in Jerusalem for her son's trial. "He was very restless."

Matt says that he discovered Kahane and the JDL when he read Kahane's militant manifesto, *Never Again*. The book's title, which became the JDL's rallying cry, was a warning that Jews will never again be led like sheep to the slaughter. The message was meant as much for passive, liberal-minded Jews as it was for gentiles. "I read *Never Again* and it hit me right in the heart," said Matt. "I found what I was looking for." His first illegal act inspired by Kahane's philosophy, he said, was to place a homemade bomb under the car of Arthur Butz, an engineering professor at Northwestern University. Butz had written a book in 1978 claiming that the Holocaust was the hoax of the twentieth century. "The bomb never went off," recalled Liebowitz. "I learned how to make it from a book by Abbie Hoffman."

Liebowitz was soon studying in a yeshiva and working out with members of the small but violent JDL chapter in Chicago. "I started training with sticks, knives, hand-to-hand combat. We were trained by a guy who was a Navy SEAL. . . . It was cool for a fourteen-year-old high-school freshman to see Jews do this stuff. Even though most of the JDL members weren't religious, they put on *kippos* [skullcaps] whenever they fought anti-Semites. I hung out in neighborhoods where everyone was fighting, so it took a lot to impress me. The JDL really impressed me!"

But Kahane impressed Liebowitz even more than the street fighting. The Pied Piper of confused Jewish youth, Kahane has a knack for convincing youngsters that violence in the name of Greater Israel or Soviet Jewry is heroic in the tradition of the Bible. "I got to know Kahane when he came to Chicago in 1979. I thought he was it. He had unbelievable charisma. I came to him for advice and guidance, and depending on his answer I would have switched schools or made major changes in my life."

Shortly after meeting Kahane, Matt moved to Israel to be with the fiery rabbi. At the time, Kahane was a political pariah in Israel with no more than a few dozen young followers from the United States. Like many American Jews who arrived in Israel for the first time, Liebowitz was shocked that Israeli Jews bore so little cultural resemblance to the Jews he had left behind. This fast-paced, chaotic, and intense new world on the Mediterranean was both strange and a little frightening. "I am at an *ulpan* [an intensive, Hebrew-language training institute]," he wrote to his mother soon after arriving in Israel. "We sing Chanukah songs. . . . I had to leave the room because the songs reminded me of you and I long for you so much. . . . I did not realize it would be so difficult."

There was little time, however, for reflection when one's days and nights were devoted to Kahane. There were almost daily vigilante attacks against Arabs, Christian missionaries, Black Hebrews, and U.S. diplomats whose cars were firebombed. Once Matt and a compatriot, laden with satchels of explosives, even scaled a wall that encircled the Dome of the Rock Mosque, intending to "purify" the Temple Mount. But the two scurried away when they heard an approaching Israeli army patrol.

Not surprisingly, Matt gained a reputation inside the JDL as one of Kahane's most dedicated "crazies." "Kahane was asked by a reporter why he had so many crazies around him," Liebowitz recalled."He replied that he needed crazies because they were the first to cross the barricades. Everybody in the JDL joked that *I* was the crazy Kahane was talking about."

In 1980, burned out from the frantic militant activity, Liebowitz borrowed money from his mother and returned to Chicago. He jumped from yeshiva to yeshiva before he moved to New York City, where Kahane had reasserted control of the JDL, after successfully crushing Bonnie Pechter. The JDL, which had claimed as many as ten thousand members in 1970, was now a shell of its former self. Without Kahane's constant guidance and charismatic presence, it foundered, breaking into small, competing factions. Kahane continued to milk the organization for publicity and money for his affiliated party in Israel. By the time Matt arrived in New York, the JDL had just a few dozen hard-core activists in New York and Los Angeles.

During a brief revival in 1981, however, the JDL began a paramilitary training camp in the Catskills, similar to the one that it had run during its heyday a decade earlier. Matt was one of some fifty youths who spent the summer training with automatic weapons and in martial arts. "Matt was a sweet, good-hearted kid," recalled Gary Moskowitz, a New York City policeman who was the JDL camp karate instructor. "He loved training. He used to run ten miles a day. But he was easily manipulated and extremely prone to violence."

Liebowitz rose to become the head of JDL security during a period when the organization was implicated in a number of terrorist attacks, including the bombings of Soviet and Arab diplomatic missions in New York and the firebombing of an Arab-owned restaurant in Brooklyn in which a woman was killed. During the summer of Israel's 1982 invasion of Lebanon, armed JDL militants raided the Manhattan offices of the November 29th Coalition, a pro-PLO group. A week later, the JDL training loft at the intersection of West 34th Street and Broadway in Manhattan was bombed. A JDL security guard asleep inside narrowly avoided injury. "It was a crazy summer," Liebowitz recalled.

"The camp produced fifty good, dedicated JDL people who would prowl the streets of New York at night in search of Arab or Russian victims. That summer there were twelve to fifteen bombings. We had an underground bomb lab in a house in Borough Park crammed with explosives, Tommy guns, Uzis. . . . We knew a grand jury was investigating us and that federal indictments were coming down. Then one of our people was arrested in Israel for shooting a West Bank Arab and was convicted and went to prison. We were very bummed out by that."

As a federal grand jury weighed indictments against a number of JDL militants, about forty suspects, including Liebowitz, suddenly moved to Israel in the winter of 1983. According to a federal law enforcement agent involved in the JDL probe, that effectively stymied the investigation. Weary of police investigations, Liebowitz tried to keep away from Kahane and his followers in Israel. He moved to a military base in the Negev to work as a volunteer. "It is wonderful to be in my country," he wrote his mother. "There is some poetic justice in this scene of lighting the Chanukah candles in a military base in the Negev. It is a dramatic scene. The sun shines softly and religious soldiers light a large menorah and say prayers. I am home. I have never felt better in my whole life in any other place."

A few weeks after Liebowitz wrote to his mother, a bomb planted by the PLO in the back of a bus in Jerusalem exploded, killing several passengers, including two young Jewish girls. "I feel as if I had lost my own sister," he wrote in another letter home. "I can't stand this. . . . I am very upset. . . . Jews are dying here only because they want to live here. . . . I must see Rabbi Kahane."

But Liebowitz got mixed signals from Kahane. On one hand, he says, Kahane told him not to do anything illegal and risk going to jail. However, he said Kahane also constantly preached that vengeance is holy. "The bombing of the [Jewish] bus was like a sign," Liebowitz told me. "I knew what road I had to take. I swore I was going to avenge Jewish blood." He says he met four other Kach Party members from the United States who, like him, itched to strike back at the Arabs. Craig Leitner, whose father is a top official with the New York City Board of Education, was responsible for co-planning the attack. Liebowitz went to Kahane for money to finance the operation without telling

him what they were planning. "I said, 'We need money fast,' "
Liebowitz recalled. "Kahane took $600 from his pocket and gave
it to me without asking any questions."

Prior to the attack, Leitner wrote to Randy Medoff, the JDL
boss in New York, instructing him that when he received a collect phone call from a "Mr. Gray," it would be a signal to phone
the Israeli media with the news that a Jewish terrorist organization had machine-gunned an Arab bus. The Kach kids were
arrested minutes after Leitner placed the call to Medoff. Liebowitz
claims that he learned during police interrogation that Shin Bet
had them under surveillance for twenty-four hours prior to the
shooting.

Craig Leitner, who turned state's witness, not only
documented the close links between terrorism, the Kach Party,
and Rabbi Kahane, but also told Shin Bet a chilling tale of Ku
Klux Klan-style violence. In a signed confession, he told Israeli
officials:

> One day, toward the end of July 1984, (we) agreed to take
> some action against the Arabs. About midnight we saw an
> Arab in his early twenties walking along the Hebron road. . . .
> I left the car and gave the Arab a blow with my fist and
> kicked him. . . . He escaped into the night. . . . We drove
> to Hebron and decided to set fire to Arab cars. We had two
> plastic bottles filled with gasoline. (We) took the fuel and
> poured it under a number of cars. We set them on fire, but
> we didn't wait to see what happened. There were many
> dogs around and I was afraid they might wake up the neigh-
> bors, or they might bite us and we would get rabies.

Several days later in Jerusalem, according to his confession,
"We took some empty bottles and rags, then we went to the
Kach office because I knew that Rabbi Kahane had left his car
there and a fuel tank was in the back of the car. We made Molotov
cocktails and drove to an Arab neighborhood. We threw two
Molotovs at one of the Arab houses chosen at random."

Leitner then contacted an American friend from Kach who
lived in the West Bank settlement Beit El. "I knew he spoke
Hebrew [Leitner could not] and could be relied upon not to
inform the police. I asked him to phone the news media and
inform them that the attack in East Jerusalem was carried out
by TNT [the name for the Kach terrorist underground in Israel]."

Kahane hired an attorney for his young machine gunners and occasionally visited them in prison. He appointed one of the youths imprisoned with Liebowitz, Yehuda Richter, from Beverly Hills, to be his chief deputy in Kach. Leitner, who somehow managed to flee from Israel, was later arrested by U.S. marshals at the White Plains, New York campus of Pace University Law School, where he was studying. He returned to Israel after lengthy legal maneuvering, served a year in prison, and is once again a law student at Touro College in Manhattan.

Liebowitz now says the machine-gun bus attack was a cathartic experience and that he is grateful that confinement in prison gave him the personal discipline he lacked. After spending more than two years in prison, he returned to the United States in 1986 to promote *aliya* (immigration to Israel) as an emissary of the Eretz Yisrael Movement, which is affiliated with Gush Emunim. He is currently working for a Manhattan-based security firm. He told me he helped install a security system for the Albanian Mission to the United Nations.

Matt says as soon as he saves enough money he will move to Israel permanently. His wife, Judy, a twenty-three-year-old nurse, would like to live in a quiet Jerusalem neighborhood and raise a family. Matt wants to move to the fiercely nationalist Palestinian West Bank city of Hebron, where ultranationalist Jews have carved a foothold in the heart of the city's squalid, fly-blown Casbah.

A young man who still values violence, Liebowitz says Kahane's radical philosophy continues to guide him. "I think the Arabs should be moved out of Israel," he said, echoing Kahane. "My parents can't believe that the bus attack had anything to do with ideology. They still think it happened because they got a divorce," he said, laughing softly.

CHAPTER TWELVE
Kahane in the Knesset

~~~~~~

Thanks in large part to Meir Kahane, more and more Israelis began to share Matt Liebowitz's desire to expel Israel's Arabs. During the early 1980s Kahane kept Jewish anxieties in Israel churning with a potent mix of Messianism, anti-establishment rhetoric, and anti-Arab vigilante violence. It proved to be a powerful elixir to thousands of mystical settlers in Kach and Gush Emunim, to young malcontents like Liebowitz, and to increasingly large numbers of Israel's Sephardim, who emigrated from Islamic countries with no democratic legal traditions and who have a profound hatred of Arabs. Kahane used this angst and anger to catapult himself to power.

Three times Kahane had run for public office in Israel and failed. But in July 1984, the fifty-five-year-old American-born rabbi won a Knesset seat with 25,907 votes, 1.2 percent of the electorate. Kach, which had been perceived by Israeli political analysts as a radical fringe party, overnight had blossomed into a mass movement. Kahane's election stunned the nation. A man who had left the Talmud academies of Brooklyn to become, in turn, a sportswriter, an FBI informer, a rabbi spurned by his New York congregation, Jewish Defense League founder, and friend of Mob boss Joseph Colombo, Sr., was now a legitimate member of Israel's parliament.

"Kahane is a stain on Israeli democracy," groaned Jerusalem's mayor, Teddy Kollek, after Kahane's victory-drunk supporters carried the exultant rabbi through the Arab neighborhoods of East Jerusalem, smashing shops and heads with equal abandon, while shouting "Death to the Arabs!"

After so many failures, how did Kahane manage to win a seat in the Knesset? Even his most dedicated supporters thought his career was over after he was repudiated by the JDL board in America in the wake of the Gerri Alperin sex scandal. Then, suddenly, like a hero in one of his mushy-minded, high-school short stories, the gates of the Knesset opened and he walked into its hallowed chambers, at last having a prestigious base from which to spread his anti-Arab venom.

Kahane owed much of his surprising success to Menachem Begin and Ariel Sharon, who legitimized right-wing extremism in Israel. When Begin wanted to implement his vision of "Greater Israel" in 1977, he had called in Sharon, who, as minister of agriculture, spearheaded Israel's West Bank settlement drive, unleashing long suppressed dreams of nationalist glory. And when Begin decided to annihilate the PLO—which he referred to as the "Nazi horde"—it was Sharon, the war's architect, who drove the Israeli army to the gates of Beirut in June 1982. Ironically, Sharon failed to finish off the PLO, which emerged from the rubble of Beirut a more potent political force. The war did, however, demoralize the Israeli army and ruin the Israeli economy, neither of which has recovered from Sharon's adventure.

The polarization and coarsening of political rhetoric in Israel that followed the war led to the stirrings of anti-Arab racism, while accentuating the sharp differences between the Israeli Right and Left. "Since the war was waged to smash the PLO, all those who opposed it were immediately labeled and denounced as pro-PLO traitors [by the Right]," says Professor Ehud Sprinzak. "Then the war went wrong. While that made many rational people question its planning and conception, for the emotional, the irrational, the defeat and the awful losses were all part and parcel of the great betrayal—by the Left, by the media." Soon crude anti-Arab racial slurs once associated strictly with Kahane and his followers became commonplace among "respectable" right-wing Israeli politicians. Rafael Eitan, now a hard-line, ultranationalist Knesset member and the army's chief of staff during the Lebanon War, referred to West Bank Arabs as "drugged cockroaches in a bottle." Begin called Palestinian members of the PLO "two-legged beasts." (Shamir would call Palestinian Arabs "grasshoppers" during the *intifada*.) One poll in *Ha'aretz* in 1984 revealed that 32 percent of Israeli Jews felt that violence towards Arabs, even terrorism, was justified; more than 60 percent of young Israelis polled believed that Arabs should not be accorded full civil rights.

By war's end, thanks to the horrific pictures of the siege of Beirut beamed daily to London and New York by satellite, sympathetic Israeli national icons like kibbutzim and Golda Meir had been replaced by Sharon, massacres, and West Bank settlements. Israel's popular TV advertising jingle, "Come to Israel, stay with friends," was drowned out by Prime Minister Begin's cry, "We don't care what the *goyim* think!"

It was precisely this kind of angry defiance and deep-seated racial hatred—hatred that had turned the Arabs into *untermenschen*—that set the stage for Kahane's remarkable 1984 Knesset victory. Though his dramatic rise from gutter gadfly to Knesset member provoked painful questions in Israel about the fate of the nation's democracy, it also brought Israel's "demographic crisis" out into the open. "To be sure," wrote Israeli philosopher Avishai Margalit in *The New York Review of Books*, "Kahane and his followers are indeed rabid racists and pathologically anti-democratic, but the problem they present—and represent—is different: the problem is their solution to the so-called demographic problem in Israel, which is to expel Arabs. On this point Kahane's support goes far beyond the lunatic fringe that won him his parliamentary seat."

Although Kahane worked hard to woo the mostly Ashkenazi West Bank settlers, who are the bulwark of Gush Emunim, he could never attract them in significant numbers. In 1984, Kach received barely 5 percent of Gush Emunim's vote; most Gush members voted for Likud, Tehiya, and the National Religious Party.

However, Kahane's anti-Arab message found considerable support among Israel's poor, undereducated, and underemployed Sephardim. Ever since moving to Israel, Kahane had recognized the potential for recruiting—and exploiting—disaffected Sephardic Jews who had poured into Israel in the late 1940s and early 1950s from across the Islamic world. As early as 1972, he proposed that the JDL organize tours to Sephardic slum communities for American Jews. "If all the tourists here would stop visiting the *Kotel* [the Wailing Wall] and see some of the poverty houses here, they would see real wailing walls," Kahane wrote to Zweibon. "Tours are money-making opportunities for groups. JDL in America and here would both get quite a bit of money."

Though the poverty tour idea never took off, Kahane continued to focus on the Sephardim as a potential source of revenue and support. "The poverty here is incredible," Kahane wrote in 1972 to Nat Rosenwaser of Long Beach, New York, a nursing home owner and Kahane loyalist who has since moved to a Jewish West Bank settlement. "And it is not only heartbreaking but has terrible political implications. The Left and the Panthers [a left-wing Sephardic protest group in Israel] will use this to incite the poor and the Sephardim and who knows what will emerge. The obvious answer is money to relieve the immediate poverty, buy apartments, etc."

In an attempt to broaden Kach's political base following its 1977 Knesset defeat, Kahane set up religious and ideological study groups in the teeming, crime-ridden Sephardic slums of Jerusalem and Tel Aviv. He tried to attract young people by offering them karate training if they attended his classes in "Jewish values."

"Once we hook them, we emphasize two things," the rabbi told me as we drove through a grim Oriental slum in Jerusalem one night in January 1980. "First, Arabs. They don't like Arabs. They come from Arab countries.

"Second, poverty. When we speak of poverty, we speak of spiritual poverty. The reaction to being poor and how one copes with it is different when one has values. The Jews in Mea Shearim [the ultra-Orthodox quarter in Jerusalem] have twelve kids and live in two rooms and don't go out and commit crimes."

Kahane said that he taught the slum kids to find their spiritual and emotional center in Judaism. He told them to move out to the fresh Judean air and build new settlements. He envisioned the West Bank filled, one day, with proud Oriental Jews.

His greatest pleasure, he told me in 1980, was the discussion group that he conducted on such subjects as Jewish identity, which he led three times a week in the Museum of the Potential Holocaust. The night that I visited, Kahane displayed tremendous rapport with his young followers; they responded to one another with an outpouring of love and good humor. There was an atmosphere of hero worship in the place that Kahane said he considered unhealthy. Therefore, he did not allow photos of himself to be hung in the Museum, even though it was strewn with his literature.

"The rabbi has changed my life," said one young Moroccan slum dweller from Jerusalem who had been rejected by the Israeli army because of his police record—the worst social stigma in Israel. "I don't get into trouble anymore. No more drugs. I study the Torah. The rabbi's influence is growing here."

Kahane is the first to admit that his prospects with the Sephardim vastly improved when Prime Minister Begin left politics following the 1982 debacle in Lebanon. It was the Sephardim who had propelled Begin into power, and when the charismatic Likud strongman faded from the scene, many handed their votes to Kahane, whom they viewed as someone who not only expressed their contempt for the Ashkenazi European Jewish ruling establishment, but would also vent their hatred of Arabs. "Begin could have done anything and the streets would have gone with him," Kahane told me in November 1984, during an interview at the Tudor Hotel in Manhattan. "I used to hear from people, 'If I had a second vote, you would have it.' I knew I couldn't beat Begin. So I patiently waited. I wouldn't attack Begin [though in fact he often did] because it was foolish to attack Begin. But his leaving was good for me and it was certainly good for the Jewish people.

"I am an Ashkenazi Orthodox Jewish rabbi leading a mass movement, which is predominantly Sephardim," Kahane boasted. *"I have the streets!* That's what frightens the Left."

As the Kach movement rapidly expanded in the aftermath of the 1984 Knesset elections, Kahane put into leadership positions the most hardened, socially bitter of these Sephardic slum youth. "They are criminals from Israel's underworld—pushers, pimps, strong-arm men—and politically more extreme than Kahane," says Nachum Barnea, an influential Israeli newspaper columnist. "He hasn't control over them. They see him more as their friend than their rabbi."

Several of them—with Kahane's blessing—set up a shelter in Kiryat Arba for Jewish women fleeing Arab husbands. The shelter received funds from the Kiryat Arba Town Council and the

Ministry of Interior, but closed down in the wake of a scandal, in which several of the Jewish women publicly accused Kach men of coming to the shelter and demanding sexual favors.

Kahane, who had promised his supporters that he would drive the Israeli establishment crazy once he got into the Knesset, certainly did not disappoint them. His very presence in Arab towns—where he often traveled under the cover of parliamentary immunity to exhort the Arabs to leave Israel—was enough to provoke riots. In the Knesset he seldom failed to slip in an anti-Arab statement, no matter what was being discussed. During a debate on crime in Israel in January 1985, for example, Kahane jumped up to the podium and announced that Arab criminals should be sterilized.

"This is racism," Shulamit Aloni of the left-of-center Citizens' Rights Movement Party shouted at Kahane. "I ask that this be stricken from the protocol."

"This is the way they spoke in the German Reichstag, not in Israel," cried Yossi Sarid, who belongs to Aloni's party.

"You're a sick man. Get out of here," said Mapam's Elazar Granot.

Three ushers forcibly removed Kahane, as Knesset members screamed: "Worm, vampire, take him by force!"

Kahane clearly thrived on the excitement. During an interview in New York shortly after his Knesset victory, he boasted that he loved his crazy image. "I get up in the Knesset and say: 'When I'm prime minister no Arab will be hurt by Jewish terrorists because there won't be an Arab left in Israel!' Then everyone rages in the Knesset, and then it's shown on TV, and the attorney general makes his statement condemning racism, then there are demands made all over the place to strip me of my parliamentary immunity. And just when Israeli news editors decide not to give Kahane any more coverage—to keep him off the front pages—I do something outrageous and it's a media event. I'm playing games. . . . Every time I walk into the Knesset, the other 119 members die a thousand deaths!"

Kahane prepared several bills for the Knesset that were shockingly reminiscent of the Nuremberg Laws, which the Nazis had enacted against German Jews nearly five decades earlier. One called for the expulsion of Israel's Arabs. Another would have made it a crime punishable by two years in jail for a Jewish woman to have sex with an Arab. A third would have made it illegal to insult Judaism and the Jewish people. "We state that anyone who declares that any verse or saying in the Bible, the Talmud, or the Commentary isn't true is racist and should be subject to three years in prison," Kahane told me. He also called for confining Israel's non-Jews to ghettos lest they pollute the "authentic Jewish" spirit. As he put it in a speech he delivered in New York in 1984: "The foreigners vomit their sickness onto us, and we swallow it eagerly. . . . Let us vomit them out and purge the Holy Land of all vestige of impurity."

The specter of Kahaneism spreading across Israel like an Old Testament plague spurred the government and some private organizations to pass a number of measures designed to curtail the rabbi's growing influence. Immediately after his election, the army announced an emergency program to teach recruits about the "virtues of democracy." On December 25, 1984, in an attempt to limit Kahane's parliamentary immunity, the Knesset voted to allow the police to bar him from entering Arab villages. It was the first measure ever restricting the movement of a Knesset member. The next day, Kahane sought to violate the order by visiting a West Bank Arab village to urge Jewish women with Arab spouses to leave their husbands. The rabbi was stopped at a military roadblock seven miles from his destination.

Kahane was also banned from entering Israeli high schools and from speaking on radio and television, although he later successfully appealed the media blackout in Israel's High Court. In the autumn of 1985, the Knesset barred Kahane from introducing two bills it considered anti-democratic—one limiting the rights of non-Jews in Israel, and the other prohibiting sex between Jews and gentiles. Kahane again appealed to the High Court. On November 2, 1985, the High Court ordered the Knesset to permit Kahane to table his bills. While acknowledging that the bills were reminiscent of Nazi regulations against the Jews in Germany, the court ruled that Kahane, as a Knesset member, had the democratic right to introduce legislation. The speaker of the Knesset ignored the ruling, forcing Kahane back to the courts.

Kahane also came under fire from the American government, which stripped him of his U.S. passport. The State Department argued that Kahane's immigration to Israel, his acceptance of Israeli citizenship, and his continued residence in Israel evidenced an intent to relinquish U.S. citizenship. The American Civil Liberties Union and the Anti-Defamation League of the B'nai Brith, among others, came to Kahane's defense. The ADL, which wrote an *amicus* brief on Kahane's behalf, said it was worried that the State Department's ruling carried with it a "message that an American Jew cannot be loyal to both Israel and the United States." Federal Judge Leo Glasser overturned the State Department's decision, ruling that although Kahane used his U.S. citizenship as nothing more than a "boarding pass" to America, the "intent to keep citizenship for hypocritical or cynical reasons is no less valid—legally—than an intent predicated on the noblest of altruistic motives."

Kahane's victory in the New York federal courts came back to haunt him. In his affidavit to the court explaining why he should be entitled to retain his U.S. citizenship, Kahane stated that he had never sworn the oath of allegiance to the Knesset as is required by Israeli law. Instead, during the official swearing-in ceremony, Kahane said that he swore his allegiance not to the Knesset but to God, adding a quote from the Book of Psalms. Shortly after I uncovered the court document and revealed his deception in an article that appeared in the Israeli newspaper *Haaretz*, Kahane was stripped of all parliamentary privileges— including his $2,200-a-month salary—until he relented and agreed to take the proper oath of office, which was broadcast live on Israel Radio in June 1987.

At a meeting on democracy in Strasbourg in September 1987, then Speaker of the Knesset Shlomo Hillel outlined some of the steps that the Israeli government had taken to curb Kahane. Stating that Kahane's anti-Arab views evoked the "terrible memories" of the Nazis' anti-Jewish legislation, Hillel explained why, in his view, combating Kahaneism was a moral imperative: "We Jews have suffered throughout history from racial and religious discrimination, and the memory of the Holocaust will remain engraved on our hearts forever. We could not do otherwise.

"We have a two-thousand-year-old heritage from Hillel the Elder, who said: 'Do not unto your fellow man, what you would not want him to do to you.' Moreover, we have learned from the Weimar Republic that a true and viable democracy has to defend itself against those who wish to abuse its liberties to reintroduce racist ideas, neo-fascism, neo-Nazism, and anti-Semitism. Clinging to the values of democracy and shutting one's eyes to the dangers that threaten it, means that we tacitly reconcile ourselves to its failures. The time has come when all must know that only a vigilant democracy, a fighting one, or at least a defensive one, fulfills its duty and deserves our appreciation.''

Kahane's most serious challenge, however, has come from the Israeli Right who compete with him for political power. ''Until 1984, the religious-nationalist camp did not consider Kahane a challenge,'' said Ehud Sprinzak. ''No effort was made to curtail his influence in yeshivot and West Bank settlements. This is no longer the case. Electoral strength in Israel translates into power and money, and there is little readiness to share them with Kahane.'' Ariel Sharon, who his supporters claim is the strongman Israel needs to save it from its enemies, told his followers at a rally in July 1985: ''Our danger is not Yossi Sarid, but rather Kahane, who takes all our votes.''

Ostracized by the government and the press, Kahane took to the road, crisscrossing Israel to speak in public parks and on street corners. In a speech in Haifa on June 28, 1985, Kahane attacked Jews and Arabs equally. ''No one can understand the soul of those (Arab) beasts, those roaches,'' glowered Kahane. ''We shall either cut their throats or throw them out. I only say what you think.'' According to a report in *Kolbo Haifa*, a Hebrew-language weekly newspaper in Haifa, Kahane then directed a stream of obscenities against the mayor of Haifa, Arieh Goral, and left-wing politicians Shulamit Aloni and Yossi Sarid, whom he called ''scoundrel,'' ''dog,'' ''disgusting,'' and ''Jewish prostitutes who employ Arab pimps.''

Kahane concluded his harangue, which was megalomaniacal even by his standards, by promising the audience: ''In two years time, they [the Arabs] will turn on the radio and hear that Kahane has been named minister of defense. Then they will come to me, bow to me, lick my feet, and I will be merciful and will allow them to leave. Whoever does not leave will be slaughtered.''

How successful was Kahane's street corner stumping? Despite the intense efforts by the Israeli government to delegitimize him and his views, a Pori Opinion Poll published in Israel on December 22, 1987, at the beginning of the *intifada*, found that Kahane's support had surged to 3.8 percent of the general electorate—enough to win 4 seats in the 120-seat Knesset. A 1986 poll conducted by the prestigious Van Leer Institute in Jerusalem found that 33 percent of Israel's youth between the ages of fifteen and eighteen (excluding kibbutz youth) supported Kahane's fiercely anti-Arab stance.

Kahane's once taboo views on expelling Arabs even began seeping into the Israeli government. In July 1987, Israel's Deputy Defense Minister Michael Dekel, a Likud senior member, called for the expulsion of Arabs living in the Occupied Territories. And a few months later, Yosef Sapira, then a minister-without-portfolio from the National Religious Party in the Israeli Cabinet, proposed paying Arabs $20,000 each to "voluntarily" leave Israel.

"Well, well, well! And suddenly 'Kahaneism' is bursting out all over Israel," gloated Kahane in a November 1987 column he wrote for *The Jewish Press*. Later, he ran an advertisement in the paper requesting political donations for his 1988 Knesset campaign: "Meir Kahane needs more than your love. Now is the time to help Meir Kahane take a giant step—to the prime ministership of Israel!"

CHAPTER THIRTEEN
Shaking America's Money Tree

At daybreak on April 1, 1987, a dozen FBI agents pulled up in front of the sprawling East Meadow, New York home of Murray Young, a sixty-year-old member of the Jewish Defense League. Acting on an informant's tip, federal agents seized seventeen firearms in Young's home, including several rifles, an Uzi submachine gun and stun guns, as well as JDL bank records, membership lists, and detailed notes made by JDL officials about JDL bombings directed at organizations associated with the Soviet Union. In October 1987, Young was sentenced to five years in prison after pleading guilty to federal charges in connection with a wave of New York bombings between 1984 and 1986, including an attack on Avery Fisher Hall on October 20, 1986, just before the Moscow State Symphony was to appear.

On the same day that Young was arrested on federal weapons violation charges, JDL founder Rabbi Meir Kahane was soliciting donations at his cousin's synagogue, the West Side Jewish Community Center on 34th Street in Manhattan. Kahane did not tell the overflow crowd of enthusiastic supporters that Murray Young—his trusted associate and the man who helped organize his security in the New York area during his numerous fundraising tours—had been arrested for participation in a long line of JDL terrorist incidents. For Kahane, who was not implicated in the charges, it was business as usual. He was free to raise money in the United States for his stridently anti-Arab Kach Party while one of his aides was on his way to jail.

Kahane's amazing political success in Israel has been the result in large part of his ability to raise money from wealthy Jews in America. Amnon Rubinstein, formerly Israel's minister of communications and now a left-of-center member of the Knesset, estimates that by 1987 Kahane was bringing into Israel at least $500,000 a year—enough money to set up more than fifty branch offices around Israel and to buy a sound truck, sophisticated telecommunications equipment, and a printing press that churns out a seemingly never-ending stream of the controversial rabbi's political pronouncements. "Kach spends about $10,000 a week in Israel," Shannon Taylor, an attorney in Manhattan who is a leader of Kach International, one of Kahane's fundraising arms in America, told me in a 1987 interview. "He's opening offices all over the country [Israel]. Kahane can never get enough money."

An investigation into Kahane's political activities in the United States reveals that his support is far broader than the radical, right-wing fringes of New York's Jewish community. What's more, according to former JDL officials, Kach Party activists, and federal investigators, Kahane has set up at least three charitable, tax-exempt foundations in the United States that have sent millions of dollars to his movement in Israel. Many Israeli organizations raise money in the United States for religious, cultural, and educational purposes, taking advantage of tax-free status that allows donors to claim deductions for their contributions. But federal tax codes bar such charitable tax-exempt foundations from using contributions to finance political campaigns.

According to Assistant U.S. Attorney Charlie Rose, as part of an ongoing probe into JDL activities, federal investigators are examining whether tax-free funds raised by Kahane's organizations are being funneled to Israel to be used for political activities in violation of federal tax laws.

Currently, Kahane is overseeing at least four organizations in America to raise money and build support for his party in Israel: Kach International, the Institute for the Authentic Jewish Idea, Jewish Overview, and the Jewish Defense League. The organizations have interlocking board members—all of whom are associated with Kahane. "Kach equals the JDL equals Kahane," said New York State Assemblyman Dov Hikind, the former JDL member and SOIL leader, who is among Kahane's most fervent supporters.

Adela Levy, Kahane's secretary in New York and the person listed on the Jewish Idea's tax return as its director, says the money these organizations raise is used to further Kahane's message in America. When asked if Kahane uses money collected by these organizations for his political activities in Israel, she replied, "Ask the rabbi."

Kahane refused to answer detailed questions about his financial activities. "If they gave out Nobel Prizes for chutzpah," he said when contacted by phone for comment, "you would certainly win one."

Whatever the propriety of Kahane's fundraising activities, his mainstream Jewish supporters in America bear little resemblance to their Sephardic counterparts in Israel. Indeed, one of the best kept secrets in America's ostensibly liberal Jewish community is the considerable support it has given to Kahane. "He has received substantial sums from extremely prominent businessmen, well-known in the Jewish community," says Rabbi Jack Simcha Cohen of Temple Sha'arei Tef'ilah of Los Angeles. Among the wealthy Jews who have generously supported various Kahane organizations is Haagen-Dazs ice cream founder, Reuben Mattus. "If they [the JDL] needed money, I gave it," Mattus told me in 1985, although he says he has not supported Kahane for some time, preferring now to help fund Israel's West Bank settlement drive. Kahane told me that donations to him increased "especially from Jewish millionaires," after his election to the Knesset in 1984. "Everybody loves a winner," he quipped.

Kahane travels to the United States five or six times a year in search of funds. He expertly tailors his appeals to fit the audience. In front of middle- and upper-middle-class groups, he mixes stinging criticism of the "pygmies and dwarfs" that he says run the major American Jewish organizations with Borscht Belt one-liners ridiculing mixed marriages. For Orthodox Jews, he throws in Biblical injunctions against mixing with gentiles and declares that Israel should be a theocratic state. His constant theme is that Arabs must leave Israel because they are a threat to the state's existence. If they do not leave willingly, he says, they should be deported at gunpoint.

Rabbi Gabriel Maza of the Suffolk Jewish Center on Long Island said that Kahane's May 11, 1987 appearance at his synagogue was "subdued and dignified." "He talked about exchange of populations, of the Arab demographic threat to Israel," said Maza, who noted that about one hundred people attended at $50 a head, half of which went to Kahane's movement. Appeals for funds from the floor followed Kahane's speech, and one man handed him a personal check for $10,000, said Maza.

Maza's brother, comic Jackie Mason, who won a Tony Award in 1987 for his one-man performance in "The World According to Me!", drove from Manhattan to hear Kahane. Mason told me during an interview in his dressing room at the Brooks Atkinson Theater in June 1987 that Kahane's analysis of why the Arabs pose a demographic threat to Israel is correct. "Democratic principles shouldn't apply to Israel like they do to America," said Mason, an ordained rabbi who grew up on New York's Lower East Side. "If Arabs multiply to such an extent where they become as numerous as Israeli Jews, they can vote out the Jews and end the Jewish state. Jews would become aliens in their own country. And that's the problem, and that's why Meir Kahane is right! You are stupid, and so are people like yourself who say how terrible we are to the Arabs!"

In March 1987, Mason went on Kach's now defunct Monday evening FM radio program in New York, praising many of Kahane's political views. As early as 1972, Mason performed at a benefit for the JDL Legal Defense Fund at a Queens theater over the protest of his agent. "I was eager to do it," he told me, because the JDL was doing good work defending persecuted Jews. In August 1987, Mason said, he was asked to do a JDL benefit, but he declined because he said he opposes their "violence."

The backbone of Kahane's support in America is unquestionably the Orthodox Jewish community. A 1986 survey conducted by Professor Steven Cohen for the American Jewish Committee, found that 30 percent of the Orthodox Jewish community have considerable sympathy for Kahane, compared to 14 percent of all American Jews. It is not so much the money that he gets from prominent Orthodox Jews as their seal of approval that is so important. His personal appearances in Orthodox synagogues sometimes take on a carnival-like atmosphere. "There is no individual I know who can attract an audience like Kahane," said Rabbi Max N. Schreier, first vice-president of the Rabbinical Council of America, the largest body of Orthodox rabbis in the country. Schreier, whose own synagogue, the Avenue N Jewish Center in Flatbush, has been the scene of frequent Kahane appearances, said that Kahane packs his synagogue when he speaks there. "Once he spoke in my *shul* and it was filled like Yom Kippur!" said Schreier.

Schreier says that Kahane's work with the JDL helped instill a sense of pride in the American Jewish community. "When he urged Jews to stand up to the challenge of the Blacks and to the challenge of anti-Semites, it made a great deal of sense." Schreier agrees with Kahane that assimilation and intermarriage are among the gravest threats to the Jewish people. He said he is alarmed by reports that Arab men are seducing Jewish women on Israeli college campuses. Barriers between the Jewish world and the gentile world must be made stronger, he said. But Schreier, who believes Israel should annex the Occupied Territories, is uncomfortable with Kahane's call to expel the Arabs because "it arouses violent animosity among non-Jews and doesn't enhance the position of Jews in America."

One of Kahane's most stunning successes has been to attract major financial support from the Syrian Jewish community of Flatbush, perhaps the wealthiest Jewish community in the world. Until recently, Syrian Jewish leaders barred Kahane from even speaking in neighborhood synagogues. Opposition to him slackened, however, with his growth in the Israeli polls. One Sunday afternoon fundraiser in the home of electronics magnate Ralph Betesh, Kahane's key organizer in the New York Syrian Jewish community, netted some $20,000. Every major rabbi from the community attended, as well as prominent businessmen. Betesh says that some donors are so worried about being tied to Kahane that they have passed money to him through a sympathetic yeshiva rather than make out checks or give cash to his organizations. According to Betesh, one of Kahane's key supporters is a top executive of the Republic National Bank of New York, which is owned by Raymond Safra, a Syrian-Lebanese Jew.

Kach International, a public stockholding company incorporated in California, is Kahane's principal propaganda arm in America. It was created after Kahane's [1984] Knesset victory because "we felt the Kach name would command more respect than the JDL name among American Jews," said Ken Sidman, Kach's director, until he died of a heart attack on his thirty-seventh birthday on August 29, 1987. The two organizations worked closely together, with many Kahane supporters joining both organizations. "Certainly the JDL's concerns and ours overlap," said Sidman. More recently, Kahane has been ordering U.S. Jews who have approached him about joining the JDL to join Kach instead.

Brett Becker, a twenty-eight-year-old convert to Judaism, took over Kach's Brooklyn office after Sidman died. The former Floridian, who headed the JDL in 1979, was given the task of carrying out Kahane's anti-Arab campaign in America. On December 9, 1987, Becker led about two dozen picketers in front of the Israeli Consulate in Manhattan, demanding that Israel expel its "malignant and growing . . . Arab population." Becker has since resigned from his post.

On May 11, 1988, Kach International held a banquet to raise money for Kahane's bid for reelection at the elegant Beverly Hilton Hotel in Los Angeles. It was attended by more than five hundred persons. "The food was sumptuous, the champagne flowed, and everyone had a night to remember," according to Washington, D.C. Kach official Madeline Abraham, who accompanied Kahane on his West Coast fundraising tour.

The Institute for the Authentic Jewish Idea, Kahane's major fundraising arm in the United States, currently shares office space and a postal box in Brooklyn with Kach International. The Jewish Idea was set up in 1979, after its predecessor, The Jewish Identity Center, dissolved, leaving a $25,000 bank overdraft and pending litigation. According to incorporation papers filed with the New York State Attorney General's office, The Jewish Idea was set up "to educate and enlighten members of the community in order that they may be better informed as to current world problems and their effect on Judaism and the Jewish community." The Jewish Idea was to achieve this goal primarily by serving as a clearing house for Kahane's twelve books, numerous pamphlets, and audio cassettes, as well as arranging his U.S. speaking tours.

The Jewish Idea is currently on the IRS rolls as a charitable, tax-exempt organization that can solicit tax-deductible contributions. According to IRS law, tax-deductible contributions cannot be used to finance, influence, or intervene even indirectly in political campaigns. The law also severely limits political lobbying and the dissemination of propaganda. However, according to numerous Kach donors and other sources familiar with Kahane's fundraising methods, Kahane, in seeking contributions to The Jewish Idea, has unabashedly said that the money would help finance his political movement in Israel. "He's conspicuous about it," said a law enforcement source familiar with the federal grand jury investigation of JDL activities. "He goes to fundraisers and says, 'give me money to advance my political interests in Israel.' Then they write a check and get a tax write-off."

Ed Solomon, head of the JDL in Philadelphia and a Kach Party activist, says that "Donations from the Jewish community [to Kahane] are funneled to The Jewish Idea and that's sent to the rabbi in Israel. . . . It goes to Kach. It's political." Solomon says that a recent fundraiser for Kahane in Philadelphia attended by Orthodox Jewish lawyers netted $50,000 in checks made out to The Jewish Idea. An elderly Kahane supporter from Tucson, who said, "I would give him everything I have," has contributed more than $10,000 in checks to The Jewish Idea. "It's tax-deductible and the money goes to him in Israel."

Several officials of The Jewish Idea acknowledged that money raised by the organization is sent to Kahane in Israel, but they said that the funds are used there for educational purposes.

During Kahane's successful bid for the Knesset in 1984, The Jewish Idea mailed flyers to prospective contributors asking them to mail checks made out to The Jewish Idea in order "to send Kach and Kahane to power in Israel." At a fall 1987 fundraising dinner for Kahane at the prestigious Lincoln Square Synagogue in Manhattan, contributors were told that their tax-exempt donations to The Jewish Idea would help him win ten Knesset seats in the next election, according to Mal Leibowitz, a Kach activist who was on the dinner's steering committee. Kahane raised $40,000 at the dinner, said Richard Propis, Kach International's treasurer.

An internal memorandum drafted by Kahane and circulated among his supporters spells out how to use The Jewish Idea's tax-exempt status as a cash cow for his Knesset campaign. Kahane describes in five easy steps how to organize a house party for fundraising. Kahane even scripted a speech that the host is expected to recite following his talk. "I am sure that we have been deeply moved by Rabbi Kahane's words," the canned appeal for funds begins, according to the memo.

> But being moved will not help him help us. . . . If Rabbi Kahane is to reach Jews with speeches, writings, and activi-

ties and if he is to make the Knesset, WE MUST give him the funds he needs. Rabbi Kahane has made a tax-deductible organization known as The Jewish Idea and all checks made out to it will be tax deductible. I have invited you to my home to hear Rabbi Kahane and I personally ask you to give generously. . . . I would like all of you to now follow me and pledge what your consciences dictate. Rabbi Kahane will answer all questions in a few minutes but first *we* have to give to a man who gives so much of himself. Who will be the next to pledge?

The pitch worked fairly well at a 1989 gathering for Kahane in the posh Lawrence, New York home of Barry Friedman, a well-to-do commodities broker who trades fuel oil on the New York Commodities Exchange. Friedman regularly meets with a discussion group made up of successful professionals who, like himself, have recently embraced Orthodox Judaism. Howard Sirota, an attorney who attended the meeting out of curiosity, says that Kahane made what he considered to be a number of "racist" and "fascist" remarks in a brief speech, then asked for donations, raising about $5,000 from Friedman's guests. "It was incredibly insensitive of these yuppies—who had arrived in their Jaguars from their comfortable homes—to fund a man who is trying to expel a people from their land," said Sirota. "I was disgusted!"

One of Kahane's most fertile hunting grounds is South Florida, home to a large and well-to-do Jewish community. One Jewish Idca activist who has arranged numerous fundraising appearances for Kahane there, says that the rabbi raised more than $100,000 in South Florida in 1988. "He leaves parlor meetings with his pockets literally bulging with bills," says the source, who requested anonymity. He adds that those who want a tax deduction, but are afraid to make out checks to The Jewish Idea, are instructed by Kahane to make them out to the Chabad House, a Hasidic sect with branches in the United States, Europe, and Israel. The Chabad House, which itself has charitable, tax-exempt status, then funnels the tax-deductible contributions to Kahane in Israel. It is a "pass through" technique that is virtually impossible for the IRS to stop because the government is loath to scrutinize religious institutions.

The Jewish Idea received $788,115 in contributions between 1980 and June 30, 1986, according to tax returns. It also has received as much as $10,000 per year from the JDL, which is listed on its returns as an affiliated organization.

On January 19, 1987, The Jewish Idea's director, Adela Levy, sent a letter to supporters informing them that the group had spun off a new, tax-deductible organization called "Jewish Overview," which henceforth would accept all tax-deductible checks for Rabbi Kahane's "struggle." "To start the new tax year off the right Jewish way," she wrote, "If you have not yet given the $100 we need from EVERY supporter of Rabbi Kahane, why not write a check for that now, to JEWISH OVERVIEW? And if you have given already, who says it is forbidden to give more? And where does it say that the maximum has to be $100?"

In pursuit of his political vision, Kahane has even sought funding from right-wing Christian evangelists in America, who, like him, believe that Jews are the Chosen People and that the Messiah's coming is linked to the Jewish return to Israel and the expulsion of Israel's enemies—the Arabs. Kahane accepts the Christians' patronage because he is convinced the Messiah will be a Jew. The alliance between Jewish and Christian fundamentalists is perhaps the ultimate marriage of convenience, with the two groups united to bring on the Messiah and each side convinced the Messiah will be its own.

In May 1984, for example, Kahane traveled to Dallas with Jimmy DeYoung, a born-again Christian, who was then vice-president and general manager of religious radio station WNYM in New York. The two appeared on a television talk show, and later attended private cocktail parties, where Kahane solicited funds from Christian fundamentalists for his 1984 Knesset campaign.

One of the key links between Kahane's Kach Party in Israel and Christian evangelicals is Stanley Goldfoot. The South African-born Goldfoot, a shrewd, rhetorically gifted former member of the Stern Gang, boasts about his involvement in the 1948 assassination of UN mediator Count Bernadotte and the bombing of the King David Hotel, the British headquarters in Palestine during the mandate period. At his palatial home in Jerusalem, he told me there is nobody more courageous or better versed in Jewish religious law than Kahane. "I have a great admiration for him and his movement," said Goldfoot. "His views are very sound. I think he is the only Israeli politician that has real guts."

Encouraged by Kahane, Goldfoot formed the Jerusalem Temple Foundation with Douglas Krieger, a lay minister from California, and Terry Risenhoover, an Oklahoma gas and oil millionaire. (Risenhoover was recently sentenced to four years in prison for selling worthless oil exploration leases in remote sections of Alaska, bilking approximately three thousand investors out of about $25 million. Krieger, an assistant vice-president of Risenhoover's company, was not indicted.) By the mid-1980s, the Israeli Labor movement's respected newspaper, *Davar*, was reporting that Goldfoot's group had raised $10 million, which it planned to donate to West Bank settlements, and to use to purchase Arab real estate in the Muslim quarter of East Jerusalem with the intention of turning the Old City into a Jewish domain—the prelude, the group members believe, to the Messianic Age and the Redemption of Mankind.

Though Kahane's vision of Israel and the means he advocates are abhorrent to the majority of American Jews, he has a surprisingly large, affluent cadre of supporters who through their donations keep him in the thick of Israeli public life. "We are very much impressed with his integrity and we believe his program is a Torah program which has every chance of succeeding in Israel," said Rabbi Abraham Hecht of Brooklyn, one of the prominent rabbis from New York's Syrian Jewish community who has enthusiastically endorsed many of Kahane's views. "We believe that while some of his preachments sound very radical, they are not contrary to what an Orthodox Jew should believe."

CHAPTER FOURTEEN
The End of the JDL

~~~~~~

"Jews need a crazy image now," said Victor Vancier, the brash, tough-talking twenty-nine-year-old whom Rabbi Meir Kahane appointed to head the JDL in New York in November 1984, shortly after his Knesset victory. "One reason Nazis bullied Jews was because Jews were easy targets. To put it bluntly, crazy Jews live longer."

Vancier—a small, slight, boyish-looking man who carried a three-foot-long black metal flashlight that he used as a truncheon—told me during a 1986 interview in a Manhattan coffee shop that "craziness" helps Jews in a lot of ways. And Vancier, who drove Bonnie Pechter to the brink of a nervous breakdown, knows a lot about craziness. "If the Soviets are afraid that their diplomats in the U.S. will be killed, that their offices will be blown up, and that we will take other actions that will disrupt Soviet-American relations, they'll realize that they are better off letting the Jews go."

Dressed in jeans, a faded flannel shirt, and a pale blue parka covered with grime, Vancier said that a crazy JDL would also liquidate neo-Nazis and American Arabs who support the PLO, whom he called the "proponents of the New Holocaust, the New Genocide." He even talked about silencing Edward Said, a prominent Palestinian-American professor of English literature at

Columbia University who is an outspoken supporter of the PLO. "I think the man is a monster. And that means anything goes. I believe the Arabs are the new Nazis, the heirs of the Third Reich. I don't wish him well to say the least," he said, breaking into peals of laughter.

The professor, however, is not laughing. Several months before I interviewed Vancier, Said's office was ransacked and his apartment building was broken into by a band of young Jewish thugs. For all his swagger, Vancier said he did not know who was behind the break-ins, but called them "Jewish patriots."

The JDL—built on a doctrine of desperation that warned American Jews they would be engulfed in a second Holocaust—was itself on the verge of extinction when Vancier took over the group. "Our best boys have gone to Israel to be with the Rabbi," Irwin Block, the head of the JDL in southern Florida told me in a 1986 interview. "All that's left here are old men." Indeed, the JDL's membership had dropped to well below one thousand by the end of 1985, and it had less than $3,000 in its national treasury. In December 1985, Fern Rosenblatt, then the JDL's executive director, closed the organization's national office on Kings Highway in Brooklyn for lack of funds.

The JDL was not only broke, but it was also in total disarray. Kahane's prolonged absences from America, along with his frequent feuds, created a vacuum that over the years had nurtured the growth of competing bands of right-wing warlords, united only by Kahane's legacy of violence and Jewish machismo. It is a legacy that has ultimately turned the JDL into a fratricidal movement, in which its members spend more time plotting against each other than against their gentile enemies. So violently factionalized had the JDL become that in December 1985—not long after Kahane named Vancier East Coast JDL boss at a convention at the Penta Hotel in Manhattan—turmoil erupted within the movement. Walter Berkowitz, the JDL's sixty-five-year-old national treasurer who opposed Vancier, confiscated the organization's bankbook and membership list and turned them over to Fay Lloyd's son Yaacov—a young hothead from Queens with visions of becoming another Kahane. The two men proclaimed themselves the heads of the "New JDL," though Yaacov told me that they did not have a single follower. In December 1985, a pipe bomb exploded under Berkowitz's car, shattering windows throughout his quiet Queens neighborhood. In February 1986, Berkowitz's car was totally destroyed by a firebomb.

Within this labyrinthine world of Jewish militancy—where virtue is measured by how much money one gives to right-wing causes in Israel—there have been many pretenders to Kahane's throne.

The most serious challenge to Kahane's control of the JDL—and ultimately of the militant, right-wing Jewish community in America—came in the mid-1980s from Murray Wilson, a forty-eight-year-old Bronx-born Jew who has a soft spot for Las Vegas crap tables, Mafia movies, and radical right-wing Jewish politics. Wilson says he has contributed more than $350,000 in cash and equipment to the JDL (although he broke with Kahane for several years in the early 1970s after the rabbi allegedly expropriated money meant for the JDL school in the Zion Hotel). Wilson publicly broke with Kahane again in August 1984, after the rabbi wrote a column in *The Jewish Press* calling for the liquidation of "Hellenist, spiritually sick" (liberal) Jews who "threaten the existence of Judaism."

Wilson told me Kahane's violent rhetoric against Jews whom he opposes, combined with his neglect of the JDL while advancing his political career in Israel, eventually turned him against the rabbi. "He never gave a shit about American Jews," Wilson said from his tenth-floor suite in the Empire State Building where he oversaw his many business interests, including an import-export firm and a now defunct kosher restaurant in midtown Manhattan, Le Difference. "He cares about Meir Kahane. If he cared about American Jews, he wouldn't have gone to Israel. Now that he's there, let him stay there!"

So deep was his hatred of Kahane that in September 1984, Wilson hired private detectives to follow the rabbi while he was in New York raising funds. One night, Wilson told me, Kahane was tailed to a safe house in an Irish neighborhood in Queens, which he rented under an assumed name. While the rabbi slept, the men broke into Kahane's car and stole his briefcase. Several days later, Kahane's car was broken into again. This time clothing and religious articles were stolen. Bertram Zweibon and two ex-JDL goons sat in a parked car as Wilson spray-painted Kahane's Hertz rental car with the slogan: "Nigger get out of America."

That same week, the JDL's Brooklyn office was broken into and the JDL's files were stolen. On November 4th, four men were arrested for carrying concealed weapons outside the Fort Lee, New Jersey synagogue where Kahane was speaking. The men were bailed out of jail by Wilson. Kahane later complained in a letter to the FBI that Wilson was responsible for burglarizing the JDL office. He also accused Wilson of attempting to have him assassinated—a charge that Wilson flatly denies.

In October 1986, Wilson brought together a group of Jewish militants to discuss "forging a united militant Jewish front" that would co-opt the JDL and take it firmly out of Kahane's orbit. Seated with him around a corner table at Lou G. Siegel's kosher restaurant in Manhattan's garment district were: Bertram Zweibon, who had been waiting for a decade to get even with Kahane; Chaim Stern, the Queens furniture manufacturer to whom Kahane and Paglin had addressed a crate of weapons following the Munich Olympics massacre; Mordechai Levy, head of a small JDL mutant offshoot, the Jewish Defense Organization (JDO); Sammy Watenstein, a hulking former head of the JDL's "chaya" squad; and Los Angeles JDL chapter head Irv Rubin, who was selected by Kahane in August 1985 to be the JDL's national director.

"We agreed to carve up the U.S.," Wilson told me. "Rubin was to get the West Coast [where he has about sixty hard-core followers], Levy the East Coast; a JDL representative would have a desk in Levy's New York office, and a JDO representative would have a desk in Rubin's office in L.A."

Rubin said he agreed to the arrangement because Kahane was exploiting the JDL. "After all these years of promoting Kahane-ism, we're entitled to something. Kahane gets all the money and headlines," he said, "yet we don't even get enough money to go to Kansas City to hassle Farrakhan.'"

The sit down at Lou G. Siegel's was notable if only because it brought together Rubin and Levy, who had been bitter enemies. Levy once belonged to the JDL chapter in Los Angeles. But, according to Rubin, the independent-minded Levy had a habit of launching violent actions on his own. Rubin claimed that he finally beat up Levy so severely that Levy had to spend two weeks in the hospital.

Meanwhile, by his own account, the scruffy-looking Levy spent much of the early 1980s leading a double life. In Los Angeles, he was a maverick JDL activist. During the same period, he would sometimes turn up in New York, reincarnated as a security agent for the anti-Semitic conspiracy group headed by Lyndon

LaRouche. Of Levy, LaRouche once said: "I think of him as my son." Nevertheless, Levy claims that he did not join LaRouche, but rather infiltrated the group and shared what he learned with the Anti-Defamation League of the B'nai B'rith and other Jewish organizations. "His role was enigmatic," Irwin Suall of the ADL, told *The Washington Post.* "I was as certain as I could be not to give him information that would be useful to the LaRouche people. I thought he was playing some sort of complex game." Levy later became a federal informant gathering evidence on LaRouche, who was subsequently convicted for loan fraud. In 1984, Levy changed colors again and founded the JDO—which, like the JDL, has been dedicated to a campaign of often violent harassment against its enemies.

Word of the October 1986 Lou Siegel meeting quickly leaked to Kahane in Israel. "He was horrified when he found out," Rubin later told me. "He thought I'd gone over to the enemy camp." A few weeks later, Kahane sent Rubin a threatening letter written on Knesset stationery. "Dear Irv," the letter began, "I was really distressed to hear you're involved in dope smuggling from Mexico. Give my regards to Murray and Bert. P.S.: Bob Manning also sends his best. . . . I will decide what to do with you when I see you in L.A."

Rubin phoned Wilson in a panic. Not only was Kahane threatening to smear him with what he claimed were baseless charges, but Bob Manning, a former middle-weight boxing champion in the U.S. Army, was one of Kahane's most feared enforcers.

"If he [Kahane] died tomorrow, I'd be happy," Rubin whined to Wilson. "I would not sit *shiva.*"

"Now you know what kind of garbage you're dealing with," Wilson replied. "And you wouldn't let me do what I wanted to do."

"Murray, do whatever you want to do," said Rubin.

Nevertheless, Kahane, ever the master of manipulation, put down the revolt. He let Rubin keep the JDL's West Coast chapter as his private fiefdom, as well as the title of JDL national director, in return for a promise to stay away from Wilson. "Kahane threatened to take away Irv's JDL T-shirt if he didn't behave," snorted Wilson, whose opposition to Kahane slackened when the Justice Department's Organized Crime Strike Force in Las Vegas began to investigate him on racketeering charges.*

Rubin, meanwhile, has since made up with Kahane ("He just sent me a letter saying I'm doing a good job"), although he still makes noises about trying to distance himself from his former mentor. "It is my purpose to break away from Israeli politics and establish a viable, independent JDL" that is not weighed down by "the negative baggage that surrounds Kahane," said Rubin. "If Kahane becomes prime minister, there will be a civil war in Israel, and Jews will die. That's my greatest, greatest fear. I never joined the JDL to fight Jews."

In the spirit of détente, Rubin forged an alliance of sorts with JDL New York boss Victor Vancier. Vancier, in turn, established an uneasy truce with Levy, even though they competed for money and recruits. Meanwhile, Vancier set out to rebuild the JDL on the East Coast.

Vancier, a waif-like man who speaks with a slight, effeminate stutter like Kahane, was determined to leave his mark on the JDL. In December 1985, he dispatched squads of JDL members armed with stun guns that deliver powerful electric shocks to attack members of a religious cult called Jews for Jesus, who were pamphleting Manhattan street corners. "We cleared them off the streets in a week," bragged Vancier. Also that December, the JDL rolled stink bombs into a Palestinian solidarity day meeting on the Queens College campus. In January 1986, forty JDL members picketed the Pan Am building in Manhattan to protest against the airline's alleged hiring of neo-Nazis for top management positions. In April 1986, two churches in North Bergen, New Jersey that actively proselytized Jews were broken into and vandalized. Graffiti spray painted on the walls read: "This time we write, next time we bomb."

---

* On June 30, 1989, Wilson and his sidekick Sammy Watenstein were convicted by a federal jury in Las Vegas of conspiring to defraud the Dunes Hotel and Casino of millions of dollars in a complex confidence game. The government argued that Wilson had arranged for dozens of Russian Jews from New York to receive credit from the casino to gamble, knowing that they had no intention of repaying the loans. The government's star witness against Wilson was Zvi Hagar, an ex-JDL thug who testified that he helped Wilson cash in hundreds of thousands of dollars in casino chips that had been obtained on credit by the Russians that Wilson brought to the Dunes. According to court testimony, Hagar, the son of a prominent Hasidic rabbi from Crown Heights, New York, turned against Wilson and Watenstein after they drove him to an abandoned warehouse in Secaucus, New Jersey, where he was stripped and beaten for allegedly stealing money from their office.

Under Vancier the JDL, which had small chapters scattered throughout the New York Metropolitan area, offered boxing classes at synagogues in the Chelsea section of Manhattan and Kew Gardens, Queens. Vancier also had a weekly half-hour TV show on Manhattan Cable called "The JDL Speaks." He described the show as "just a half-hour of me raving."

But Vancier focused much of his considerable energy on finding "qualified" Jewish activists to join the JDL. On a bitter cold January day in 1986, Vancier introduced me to five men he called the JDL's "New Wave"—professionals with families who had belonged to the JDL in their youth, left it for successful careers, and then rejoined. The men, who represented JDL chapters in Greenwich Village, Staten Island, Flatbush and Brighton Beach, agreed to be interviewed in a Chelsea bar as long as their identities were kept secret.

"Ronnie," a soft-spoken, bearded father of two young children, ran a consulting firm in New Jersey. He moved to Israel in the mid-1970s but found economic conditions too harsh and moved back to New York. Now he has a yuppie income and a co-op in Greenwich Village.

Four months before we met, Ronnie told me, he helped the JDL enter the computer age. He and a friend set up a nationwide JDL computer network by renting lines from American Peoplelink, a large Chicago telecommunications firm. "Using home computer terminals," Ronnie said, "Irv Rubin in L.A. and Ken Sidman [then local JDL-Kach head] in Boston can communicate with each other at the touch of a keyboard. The 'conversations' can be encrypted so that even if the FBI was on the line, they'd need to break the code to understand it."

Ronnie said that the system could also be used as an electronic bulletin board to provide news about upcoming JDL demonstrations or Kahane's latest political pronouncement. He said about seventy JDL members around the country were plugged into the network.

Ronnie claimed that JDL hackers have also used the system to break into a similar network set up by a neo-Nazi group in North Carolina. He said the JDL has left threatening messages on the Nazis' bulletin board and is trying to electronically steal the group's membership list.

I asked Ronnie if he condoned a violent Jewish underground that murdered Arab-American supporters of the PLO and alleged Nazis.

"It's a tough question," he said. "I've often thought about whether I could kill a Nazi or Arab who supports the PLO. I don't know if I could. I do know there is no difference between Hitler and Arafat—between a Nazi in Germany and an Arab in America who supports the PLO."

"Marty," who appeared to be in his late forties and who claimed to work for New York City, said that violence against Nazis and American Arabs is necessary, but only as a defensive rearguard. "There is no future for Jews in America. I have no individual retirement account. I have a valid passport. I have my money as liquid as possible, and I urge every Jew to do the same."

"Alexei," a recent émigré from Odessa who headed the JDL's fifteen-man, all-Russian Brighton Beach chapter, said that a violent Jewish underground is an acceptable way to combat anti-Semitism. "I don't lose sleep over murdered Nazis or American Arabs who support the PLO. They have been responsible for the deaths of so many people."

Alexei claimed that his group, some of whom were soldiers in the Red Army, occasionally practiced with automatic weapons in the Catskills. "There is a Puerto Rican underground, there is a Cuban underground, why shouldn't there be a Jewish underground if it helps our cause?"

Alexei, an engineer, said he first heard about Kahane in Odessa. "The Russian media denounced him daily as a 'Zionist hooligan,' " he said. Although Alexei believes that Kahane is responsible for bringing tens of thousands of Russian Jews to America, there was no support for Kahane or the JDL in Brighton Beach, a predominantly Russian Jewish enclave of Brooklyn. "Now with Kahane in the Knesset it's different. Last year when he came to Brighton Beach he spoke to overflow crowds. I won't lie and say the majority in our community favors Kahane. The majority of Russian Jews in the United States are politically apathetic. But there is a growing minority who support Kahane and the Jewish underground."

Vancier's career was finally upended in November 1986, when the FBI nabbed him in front of the Penta Hotel in Manhattan at 2 A.M. cradling a firebomb. Within days, four of Vancier's colleagues were arrested, and subsequently pleaded guilty to a series of firebombings in New York City between 1984 and 1986, including a tear gas bombing during the opening performance of the Moiseyev Dance Company at the Metropolitan Opera House, in which twenty people were injured. While Vancier awaited sentencing, he worked on the staff of New York State Assemblyman Dov Hikind as a researcher on Soviet Jewish affairs. Hikind and Vancier had been co-leaders of SOIL, a front group set up by Kahane to protest Israeli government peace initiatives that might jeopardize "Greater Israel." On October 26, 1987, Vancier was sentenced to ten years in federal prison. "You don't go bombing people, innocent people, to make a point," lectured U.S. District Judge Leo Glasser. "That is just not acceptable behavior in civilized society." Shortly before Vancier's sentencing, his co-defendant Jay Cohen died of a drug overdose in a Catskills hotel room. A New York City police investigator said that Cohen committed suicide apparently because he "couldn't handle going to prison." Kahane spoke at Cohen's funeral, calling the young militant a "hero." The New York chapter of the JDL, which for years had beaten with a faint heart, expired at Cohen's funeral. Kahane henceforth ordered U.S. Jews who approached him about joining the JDL to join instead Kach International.

CHAPTER FIFTEEN
Who Killed Alex Odeh?

▼▲▼▲▼▲▼▲▼▲▼▲▼▲▼▲▼▲▼▲▼▲▼▲▼▲▼▲▼▲▼

While Meir Kahane's cadres in America were busy bickering among themselves, the rabbi was laying the groundwork for a terrorist underground in the United States that the FBI says carried out a string of bombings in 1985 that killed two persons, including Alex Odeh, the forty-one-year-old Western regional director of the American-Arab Anti-Discrimination Committee who was blown apart by a pipe bomb attached to his office door. Kahane had long dreamed of forging a Jewish underground that would spread fear and shatter the souls of his enemies. Now, just a year after his Knesset victory, he had professional assassins roaming America. Not surprisingly, the FBI discovered that the terrorists' tracks led back to the ultranationalist settlement of Kiryat Arba, which a confidential Justice Department document I obtained describes as "a haven for right-wing Jewish extremists."

For Andy Green, a large teddy bear of a man with a scrawny beard and a sly smile, the road to Kiryat Arba and ultimately, says the FBI, to Alex Odeh's office door began in the Bronx, where he joined the JDL. Like many Jewish kids in New York in the early '70s, Andy grew up in a transitional, middle-class neighborhood, where he was surrounded by what he perceived to be gangs of tough, hostile Puerto Ricans and Blacks. An indifferent student with a poor self-image, Andy used the JDL as a way to escape a melting pot of limited possibilities.

"Andy was like a lot of kids who joined the JDL," said Gary Moskowitz, the New York City cop who was a karate instructor at the JDL Catskill Mountain training camp. "They had lots of problems and were looking for direction. Kids from good, middle-class homes who joined the JDL stayed with it for a while, then went to college. Guys like Andy, who only had a high-school education and limited job opportunities, tried to make a career out of Jewish activism."

Green moved to Israel in June 1975, the day after he graduated from high school. Kahane convinced Andy that the action was on the West Bank—that in Israel, guys who murdered Arabs were heroes. "Irgun leader David Raziel planted a bomb in an Arab market in 1939, killing fifteen or twenty Arabs," Andy told me. "And do you know how many streets are named after Raziel in Israel? If it was all right for him, how come it's not all right for us?"

Green joined the West Bank settlement of Elon Moreh, near the ultranationalist Arab city of Nablus. Built in defiance of the Israeli government, Elon Moreh was legalized by Prime Minister Yitzhak Rabin after two years of intense lobbying and violent clashes between Israeli army troops and the settlers. The settlers' victory opened the way for massive land expropriation and Jewish settlement in the heart of Arab Samaria.

When Andy arrived at Elon Moreh, "there were about seven or eight families living in tents on top of a hill above an army camp," he recalled. "The conditions were very bad. On one side of us was the Arab town of Kaddum, where Farouk Kaddumi [head of the PLO's political department] is from. It was not a friendly town to say the least."

The settlers were a volatile mixture of Gush Emunim members and a small band of recently arrived, pro-Kahane Russian and American immigrants. The two groups clashed repeatedly about how to treat the local Arabs.

"Somehow the Gush people felt we could buy them out—improve their economic conditions under Israeli rule so they'd accept us," Green said. "I felt Kach had more respect for the Arabs than that. I don't think you can buy Arabs' national aspirations.

"The Arabs have no claim to the land. It's our land, absolutely. It says so in the Bible. It's something that can't be argued. That's why I see no reason to sit down and talk to the Arabs about competing claims. Whoever is stronger will get the land."

Green adapted quickly to the rigors of pioneer life. He joined the Israeli army in 1976, changing his name from Andy Green to Baruch Green, and then Baruch Bar Yosef. "There were always a lot of things going on in Kaddum," he said. "There were Arab riots. Then we'd go into Kaddum and show them we weren't going to take it in stride."

Shortly before Green joined the Israeli army, Kahane began to lay the groundwork for an anti-Arab terrorist underground. The organization was named TNT—Terror Against Terror— Kahane's version of a Latin American right-wing death squad. Its members were mostly young Jews who had belonged to the JDL in New York. Israeli police sources say Kahane was very careful not to become directly involved in the planning or implementation of a terrorist act. "He created the climate for his supporters to act in," said an Israeli police official. In May 1975, TNT struck for the first time, firebombing an empty Arab bus in East Jerusalem. One month later, four Kach men were caught firebombing an East Jerusalem mosque. In the next few years, according to Israeli police sources, TNT committed hundreds of terrorist bombings and beatings, as well as several murders.

Green eagerly joined TNT's anti-Arab pogroms. In January 1978, he was arrested for the TNT bombing of an Arab bus in East Jerusalem in which three Arabs were seriously injured. Green denied the charge. Less than a month later Green was arrested for conspiring to bomb the Arab Student Union in East Jerusalem. He spent forty-five days in a military stockade for supplying army grenades to the other conspirators.

After Green's release, he was transferred to an army unit on the West Bank. But when the company commander heard that Green was boasting about plans to steal a tank and blow up the West Bank city of Jericho, he kicked Green out of the unit.

While the army tried to figure out what to do with him, Green was sent on extended leave. He started working full time as Kahane's chief aide. There was a lot to do. Prime Minister Menachem Begin was about to leave for Camp David and President Jimmy Carter was scheduled to come to Israel to speed peace negotiations between Egypt and Israel. Shortly before Carter's arrival, Green, Kahane, and dozens of other right-wing troublemakers were arrested and detained until Carter had safely left the country. When Green got out of jail he was exiled to a unit in Sharm el Sheikh, at the southern tip of the Sinai. "The army wanted to keep me away from Kahane," Green said.

By the late 1970s, TNT attacks had grown more frequent and deadly. The group even firebombed the cars of U.S. Embassy officials in Israel, according to documents obtained from the Secret Service under the Freedom of Information Act. Begin ordered Shin Bet to step up its surveillance of Kach. But the JDL kids from New York who made up the group's core were wary of outsiders. "Every time an intelligent non-American wanted to get involved, we suspected a Shin Bet agent," Green recalled.

Despite pressure from the Begin government, Andy and his friends in Kach continued to act with relative impunity. Then one day the Arabs hit back hard and it left not only Kach, but Israel, reeling. On May 2, 1980, a storm of machine gun fire and exploding hand grenades cut down six young settlers as they walked out of a synagogue in downtown Hebron following Friday evening prayers. One of the victims, James Eli Mahon, Jr., a thirty-two-year-old American Christian convert to Judaism, was Andy's best friend—not to mention Kahane's most skilled assassin.

* * *

James Eli Mahon, Jr.'s journey to the West Bank began on U.S. military bases in New York, West Germany, Pennsylvania, and the Philippines, where he was raised to believe that only an unshakable belief in God and country could save the world from communism. His mother, Sonny, was a Bible-thumping, born-again Christian, who tried to have three presidents impeached. His father, James Sr., a colonel in Air Force Intelligence who learned to speak fluent Russian at Columbia University's Russian Institute, devoted a lifetime to fighting the "Red menace."

His parents' red-white-and-blue extremist views inspired James Jr. to serve his country. In Vietnam he was the point man in a squad that crawled into VC tunnels looking for Charlie. He liked it so much that he signed up for two tours of duty. And twice he was evacuated to America after sustaining horrible injuries.

He won a Silver Star, a Bronze Star, and a Vietnam Gallantry Cross and was recommended for the Medal of Honor.

After returning to America in 1969, James was hired by the FBI to infiltrate the radical Weatherman Underground. He piled up eleven arrests in four states while on the FBI's payroll for offenses that included the shotgun slaying of a member of a Washington, D.C. motorcycle club called The Vipers. His father told me the shooting was part of his son's job. "In order to get into the role," said Colonel Mahon, "he had to submerge himself in the underworld of the Washington, D.C. community. To stay there, he had to do the things that looked natural. This came to a climax when he had to kill one of the people he was associated with." Though the charges against James were eventually dropped, Colonel Mahon said the FBI let his son twist slowly in the wind. "He was allowed to face the opprobrium—trial by media—similar to what Oliver North is going through. He left the Washington, D.C. area in the early 1970s extremely bitter.

"Here was an extremely idealistic young man barely twenty-one years old," Colonel Mahon continued. "The two objectives that had guided his life were service to God and country. And he was betrayed by his country." Nor did his belief in Christianity sustain him any longer, says his father.

James Jr.'s obsessive need for action drew him to Israel at the outbreak of the October 1973 Yom Kippur War, expressly to fight Arabs. He eventually joined an elite Israeli army unit renowned for its deep penetration raids behind enemy lines. Following his stint with the Israeli army, where he went on numerous commando operations inside Lebanon, he married an Israeli woman, converted to Judaism, and joined Kach, changing his name to Eli Haazev—the Wolf.

In no time the Wolf became head of one of Kach's roving death squads. Often when a West Bank Arab disappeared under mysterious circumstances the Wolf would privately take credit. "The guy is, was, a psycho, and he hung out with psychos," an American-born West Bank settler told David Shipler of *The New York Times*, shortly after the Wolf was killed. "Physically, he reminded me of a German Shepherd—a very tense watchdog. He'd come into a room and his eyes would be everywhere. He wouldn't sit generally, he'd be up prowling, just prowling. He gave off the strangest vibes, this guy.

"He used to come over regularly, which was a real pain because he scared everybody. We'd all be sitting and smoking dope, listening to music, relaxing, whatever, he'd be here prowling around.

"He once took a couple of guys outside and showed them how to kill people with bare hands, ripping off nostrils, fingers in eyes, ears, like an Indian scout gone wild."

In 1979, the Wolf was arrested at Ben-Gurion Airport by Israeli security for reportedly planning to assassinate a PLO official touring college campuses in America. The Israeli police found various disguises in his luggage, including an Arab headdress. After a month in jail he moved from Jerusalem to Kiryat Arba, the sprawling settlement on the parched Judean hills above Hebron that is home to thousands of Gush and Kach zealots. On May 26, 1979, he was sentenced to ten months in prison for breaking into the homes of Arab villagers, smashing their furniture, and physically assaulting them. Avigdor Eskin, a Russian Jew who had translated Kahane's book *Never Again* into Russian before immigrating to Israel, was also convicted with the Wolf. About three weeks after the Wolf's release from prison, he was killed by Arab gunmen.

Kahane learned about the Wolf's murder while serving a short prison sentence for inciting a riot in the West Bank city of Ramallah, where he had led several hundred demonstrators on a march to protest against the arrest of four Kach men who had earlier smashed scores of windows there with hammers.

Kahane was released from jail to attend the Wolf's funeral. As the funeral procession passed through Hebron, Kahane stood on top of a car exhorting the settlers to violence. "Our son's widow pleaded with him not to start another brawl," Colonel Mahon told me. " 'Let us have the funeral,' she begged. 'Please don't incite the crowd.' " But Kahane shrugged and continued his harangue. After his graveside speech in Hebron's ancient Jewish cemetery, some of his followers "went on a little binge," Kahane later told me. They raced through Hebron stoning Arab homes. "We rampaged through the city hot and excited to strike," said Andy Green, still aglow from the memory of Arabs cowering behind their shutters.

Several days after the graveside riot, Knesset member Chaika Grossman of Mapam presented a resolution to make Kach an illegal party; the ensuing debate raged through the day, but Kach was not outlawed.

Meanwhile Kahane and Green, intent on avenging their fallen comrade, plotted to blow up the Dome of the Rock Mosque in Jerusalem. Built on the site where the Jewish temples of Solomon and Herod once stood, the mosque is the third holiest shrine in Islam. But Shin Bet got wind of the plan. On May 12, 1980, in an unprecedented action, then Defense Minister Ezer Weizman ordered Kahane and Green to be detained for six months under the 1945 Emergency Powers Law promulgated by the British Mandate in Palestine. The law has been used extensively by Israel against Arab terrorists, but had not been used by Israel against Jews since the early days of the state.

In prison Kahane wrote his classically racist, anti-Arab tract—*They Must Go*. Green worked out with weights. Together, they were a caricature of Kahane's dictum that a Jewish mind should be combined with a Jewish fist.

Rabbi Shlomo Kahane of New York remembers going with Sonia to visit his cousin Meir in prison. The Arab inmates had rioted that day so the Kahanes were not allowed inside to see him. They stood in a parking lot and talked to him through a barred window. "It was the first time I had seen him with a beard," recalls Shlomo. "He looked horrible—like a caged monkey. I was crestfallen. Sonia said, 'I'm glad Charles isn't here to see this.' I went behind a car and started to cry. But Meir laughed, and started talking about the political speeches he would make when he got out. I figured, if he's laughing and he's happy—no more crying."

After Andy was released from jail, he began to shuttle back and forth to America on missions for Rabbi Kahane. Then in August 1983, Green moved back to New York with his Moroccan-born wife and three children. "I felt very tense in Israel," he told me. "I felt that if I stayed, I'd wind up doing something crazy. The Shin Bet was all over me."

Kahane appointed Green to head up the New York branch of Kach, which was slowly supplanting the JDL. But because the rabbi was running a pay-your-own-way organization, Green was compelled to develop a career outside Jewish activism. Having learned something about surveillance techniques from his years in Israel with Kahane, Green opened an unlicensed private inves-

tigation firm in New York with Robert Manning, a Kiryat Arba
resident originally from Los Angeles, who, according to the FBI,
replaced the Wolf as Kahane's premier bombmaker and strong-
arm man.

Green and Manning first worked together on a child custody
case in which they kidnapped three children in Texas and took
them to live with their father in Israel. "The children were Israeli
citizens," said Green. "There was nothing the mother could do
because there was equal custody. As we got better known we
started handling deprogramming cases."

Before long Green and Manning were snatching youths from
cults across America. After forcibly deprogramming them, the
Kach men extorted large sums of ransom from their parents—
who were so grateful to have their children back that they seldom complained to the authorities, according to law enforcement sources. Besides kidnapping kids for hefty fees, Green and
Manning found another lucrative sideline: kidnapping Hasidic men
who refused to grant their wives a divorce and holding them
until they would agree to the proceeding. Under Orthodox Jewish law, a woman generally cannot obtain a divorce without her
husband's permission.

Green told me that it was Rabbi Kahane who taught him the
importance of reclaiming Jewish souls from "crazy cults."
Though Green followed Kahane blindly, he never appreciated
his own cult-like obsequiousness to the Kach leader.

On February 20, 1985, police detained Green and Manning
outside the Suisse Chalet Motor Lodge in Warwick, Rhode Island,
which they had been using as a base for their deprogramming
activities since October 1984. During a search of the men's rental
car, police found sophisticated eavesdropping equipment and
Kach and JDL literature, as well as a detailed log of prominent
Black leader Jesse Jackson's movements. The motel rooms used
by Green and Manning had been rented by Leonard Leitner, a
member of Kach International's executive board. Previously,
Leitner had been arrested in Tauton, Massachusetts, and charged
with two counts of assault with a deadly weapon and cocaine
possession. Federal authorities speculate that cocaine was being
used to facilitate the deprogramming and may have been a possible source of revenue for the Kach men.

Federal officials also suspected that some of the money that
Green and Manning made as deprogrammers financed their activi-

ties on behalf of Kahane's front group, Jews Against Jackson, which, according to press reports and Secret Service documents obtained through the Freedom of Information Act, conducted a campaign of violent harassment aimed at disrupting Jackson's 1984 presidential campaign. At a Manhattan press conference that year, Kahane called Jackson "a vicious fraud," "a Jew hater," and "a stain on the Democratic Party," and announced that he was unleashing "truth squads" to harass Jackson. (During the 1988 presidential campaign, Jews Against Jackson held noisy demonstrations while Jackson was speaking in Los Angeles, New York, and elsewhere.)

Green and Manning apparently had more on their minds than harassing Jesse Jackson and working as deprogrammers. During a five-month period in 1985, federal authorities say, the men carried out as many as seven terrorist bombings.*

Just how deadly Kahane's shadow army had become was apparent on August 15, 1985. At 4:29 that morning, Tscherim Soobzokov, who had been a member of the Nazi Waffen SS, was killed by a pipe bomb when he opened the front door of his Paterson, New Jersey home after being awakened by a neighbor and told that his car was on fire. Soobzokov's neighbor was slightly injured. Soobzokov's name had appeared on both JDL and JDO hit lists. Moreover, JDO boss Mordechai Levy had denounced Soobzokov in a speech on August 7 in front of fifty people at a Passaic, New Jersey synagogue. "Whoever did it, did a righteous act," Levy later said of the bombing. Rabbi Kahane, who was in New York at the time of the blast, said: "I can only cheerfully applaud such action." Soobzokov had worked for the CIA in the Middle East before the agency helped him enter America on forged documents.

On September 6, 1985, at approximately 4:30 A.M., Elmars Sprogis of Brentwood, New York, a sixty-nine-year-old former Latvian policeman who had been cleared on charges that he helped Nazis kill Jews during the Second World War, was slightly injured when a pipe bomb placed on his front steps exploded.

---

* A Justice Department report on domestic terrorism published in January 1986 says: "Kahane has advocated and encouraged the use of violence, to include the use of bombings and incendiary devices, against groups or individuals that the JDL has deemed to be anti-Semitic and/or overtly supportive of Arab endeavors determined not to be in the interest of the State of Israel. At least two persons have died as a result of these attacks (in 1985). The Kach Party . . . is the embodiment of his (Kahane's) militant and terrorist principles."

The blast blew off the legs of Robert Seifried, a young rock and roll drummer who tried to put out a fire on Sprogis's porch, which apparently had been set to draw Sprogis outside. About twenty minutes after the bombing the Long Island, New York newspaper *Newsday* received a telephone call with what sounded like a recorded message: "Listen carefully. Jewish Defense League. Nazi war criminal. Bomb. Never Again!" JDL official Fern Rosenblatt called the Sprogis bombing "a brave and noble act."

On October 11, 1985, in Santa Ana, California, ADC official Alex Odeh was killed when a booby-trapped bomb wired to his office door from the inside exploded. At least seven other people were injured by the flying debris from the explosion. The previous night, in the middle of the *Achille Lauro* affair, Odeh had appeared on a local TV-talk show to deny that Arafat had any connection to either the ship hijacking or the murder of Leon Klinghoffer, a Jewish passenger aboard the ship. "My tear ducts are dry," Irv Rubin later said of Odeh's murder. "I'm too busy crying over Odeh's victims." *

Within hours of the Odeh bombing, the charred ADC office was swarming with FBI and Treasury agents and members of the Los Angeles Anti-Terrorism Task Force and the Santa Ana Police Department. "The names of [JDL member Keith] Fuchs, [Andy] Green, and [Bob] Manning were mentioned as the bombers while we were still in front of the bombed-out building," said a police official who requested anonymity.

According to police sources in California directly involved in the investigation, federal agents had followed Green and Fuchs,

---

* During this period a spate of other attacks on American Arabs prompted then FBI chief William Webster to warn that American Arabs had entered a "zone of danger" and were prime targets of "Jewish extremist groups." The day after the Soobzokov bombing, for example, a pipe bomb placed in front of the ADC office in Boston exploded in the faces of two bomb disposal experts, injuring one critically. ADC members received countless threatening phone calls and telegrams from the JDO and the JDL. One telegram said: "We have Bassam Shaka's legs," referring to the West Bank mayor who was grievously injured in 1980 by a car bomb planted by Jewish terrorists in Israel.

The ADC's Washington office was also the scene of noisy demonstrations led by Rabbi Kahane and Mordechai Levy. On January 7, 1986, two ADC staff members were forced off the road on their way home from work by a car which sped away. On June 30, 1985, a nineteen-year-old woman was beaten and raped in a suburban Tucson parking lot by two men who carved a Star of David into her chest with a knife, according to *The Arizona Daily Star*. The woman had reportedly been dating a Palestinian college student known for his support of the PLO. No arrests were made.

who was traveling on Manning's identification, from New York to St. Paul, Minnesota, where, on October 10, 1985, they changed planes for a flight to Los Angeles. The men were later observed leaving the plane in Los Angeles, where the feds lost their trail. One of the men was spotted flying out of Los Angeles at 7 A.M. the next day, two hours before Odeh was killed. "The information that Green and Fuchs had flown out [to Los Angeles] on Manning's credit card was available that first day," said the police official.

The FBI was impressed by the sophisticated nature of the pipe bomb that killed Odeh, a trip wire device rigged inside his office door. "A timer on the bomb gave the terrorists one minute to set the device and close the door," said the police official. According to the FBI, the bombings of Odeh, Sprogis, and Soobzokov were carried out with similar devices. "Other characteristics that were similar in the three bombings indicate either the bomb-makers had the same teacher or the same group or person did it," said former FBI official Thomas L. Sheer, who headed the Joint FBI/NYPD Task Force on Terrorism. "Each bomb has a signature," he explained. "Do you remember how in *The Little Drummer Girl* the terrorist twisted a wire inside the bomb in a certain way? That was his signature. These bombs have signatures too."

The FBI quickly created a JDL task force in California and New York to investigate the bombings. At its head was Larry Wack, an unconventional agent in a rigidly conservative profession, who has worked on a series of sensational international terrorist cases, including the search for the assassins of Orlando Letelier, the former Chilean ambassador to America who was blown to bits on September 21, 1976, in a Washington, D.C. car bombing. (In 1976, Wack also received his first exposure to the JDL when he was assigned to monitor the phone calls of Steven Rombom, a seventeen-year-old leader of the JDL terrorist faction known as the Jewish Armed Resistance. Remarks that Rombom made during wiretapped conversations led to the arrest of the entire JAR underground.)

Wack soon learned that, like Andy Green, the other JDL suspects in the 1985 bombings were no strangers to police investigations. Robert Steven Manning, a thirty-six-year-old high-school dropout from Los Angeles who was discharged from the U.S. Army for emotional instability while learning to become a demolitions expert, is a veteran of JDL terrorist bombings. Manning and Phil Zweig, now a chiropractor in Los Angeles, were convicted in 1973 in connection with bombing the home of accountant Mohammed Shaath, a Palestinian immigrant to America whom the JDL alleged was a member of Black September, a Palestinian terrorist group. Flying debris from the bomb narrowly missed the man's sleeping two-year-old daughter. Manning subsequently received a small fine and a three-year suspended sentence after disavowing the JDL in court. Sometime in the early 1980s, the FBI believes, Manning moved to Kiryat Arba. Prior to his departure, there had been a rash of similar JDL bombings in Southern California of American-Arab-owned businesses, cars, and several residences, as well as attacks against alleged Nazis, according to Secret Service documents that I obtained under the Freedom of Information Act.

"Before he joined the JDL Manning was a Hell's Angel type of a character," said Alex Sternberg, Kahane's former bodyguard who now owns a karate school in Forest Hills, Queens. "He was a pool-hall fighter and a general no-goodnick who got involved with the JDL and used the 'cause' to justify his violence. In fact, it gave him a license to beat up people. He's a big, tough guy who follows orders and intimidates people."

One story Sternberg likes to tell is about the time Manning rescued a woman who was being menaced by a drunken mob in front of a pool hall in Los Angeles. "He waded into the crowd and carried her away on his shoulders," said Sternberg. "He had a cue stick that he broke in half. He dared people. He was probably foaming at the mouth. Kahane finds people like that."

Keith Fuchs, a third suspect in the JDL bombings, is younger than Green and Manning but no less of a fanatic. Bearded and wearing a skullcap on his close-cropped red hair, the American-born Fuchs was sentenced to thirty-nine months in an Israeli prison in July 1983 for standing in the middle of a West Bank highway and drilling a passing Arab car with his Soviet-made AK-47. Fuchs later said that he did a *tova* (Hebrew for an act of kindness) by not killing the Arab driver. Funds for Fuchs's legal defense were raised by the head of Kiryat Arba's town council, as well as by many of Gush Emunim's leading rabbis, including Moshe Levinger and Eliezer Waldman, a Knesset member from the Tehiya Party. On December 27, 1984, Fuchs was released early from prison, taken to Ben-Gurion Airport in handcuffs and placed on board a jet bound for New York. Israel's Supreme Court decreed that Fuchs was not to return to Israel until such a time as he would have completed his original sentence.

Samuel A. Abady, a New York lawyer who represents the three JDL bombing suspects, told me that the FBI was hounding JDL members because it is opposed to the group's political views. "Kahane believes his followers are being targeted by the FBI because of his philosophy," said Abady, who added that no one has been indicted in the bombings, "because the government doesn't have a case."

But on August 9, 1987, Wack wrote to Manning in Kiryat Arba, warning him that the FBI had a very strong case against him and his colleagues. His letter to Manning appears to have been written in an attempt to pressure the Kach men into cooperating with the FBI. "Our investigation has uncovered numerous areas of interest to both state and federal law enforcement surrounding your activities and the activities of your associates," the letter said. "In addition to allegations of bombing/murder, attempted murder, and bombings in general, there are now allegations and evidence available revealing a pattern of racketeering activity which is covered under the Federal RICO statute. There are *severe* penalties for anyone convicted of violations of this statute."

Wack boasted about the Joint Terrorist Task Force's prowess, saying that it has an "extremely incredible record for putting domestic terrorist groups out of business." Assuring Manning that the FBI was "not in the business of sending innocent people to prison, or in this case to death row," he nevertheless warned that "the fact that Jewish extremists resorted to murder in 1985 in this country has intensified the investigation. I wonder what the Jewish community will say when the truth about the activities of their 'patriots' finally is exposed?"

Wack may have been venting his own frustrations as much as trying to scare Manning. According to internal FBI memoranda that I obtained, the FBI's efforts to prosecute the JDL have been hamstrung because of the reluctance of Israeli authorities to assist the United States in following up investigative leads that point to Kahane and his followers in Israel and the Occupied Territories. One document written in August 1987 charged that Israeli government responses to repeated FBI requests for information about JDL murder suspects now residing in Israel "have been untimely, incomplete and in certain cases no response was rendered," Floyd I. Clarke, assistant FBI director for investigations, wrote to his boss, Executive Assistant Director Oliver Revell.

The Justice Department document states:

> Numerous leads have been forwarded through FBIHQ to the Israeli Secret Intelligence Service (ISIS) in Washington, D.C. Response to these leads is crucial for the solution of the twenty-five terrorist incidents and other criminal activity perpetrated by the JDL. Lead requests were for telephone subscriber information, criminal background information, arrest records, prison contacts, associates, residence status, and travel documentations. . . . The Terrorism Section has had numerous meetings with ISIS representatives in Washington, D.C., during which our concerns relative to their handling of our requests were raised. Although these discussions have sometimes resulted in a temporary "flurry" of activity on their part, no sustained improvement in the flow of information has been realized.

Justice Department officials that I talked to accused the Israeli government of deliberately protecting Kahane and his followers. "We know Kahane has high-level support in Israel," said a Justice Department source familiar with the impasse between Israel and the United States. "It is important to know if that connection reaches over here. Is there a control factor? Is the arm of the Israeli government reaching into Brentwood? We don't know. There is an underground operating out of Kiryat Arba with false papers. The gap in information is as wide as the ocean."

Generally, there are close U.S.-Israeli links in intelligence-gathering and sharing of counterintelligence activities. Recently, for example, security police in Caracas arrested Mahmoud Mahmoud Atta, a naturalized U.S. citizen who was allegedly recruiting terrorists for Abu Nidal in the United States. Atta is currently being held in a federal detention center in New York, fighting extradition to Israel, where he is wanted in connection with the machine-gunning of a civilian bus. According to *The Wall Street Journal*, Israeli intelligence and FBI agents worked together to help track Atta down. (A federal magistrate ruled in June 1988 that although there seemed to be sufficient evidence to convict Atta, he could not be extradited to Israel because the crime was political in nature.)

Israel, the largest recipient of U.S. aid, advertises itself as a bulwark against terrorism in the Middle East, and has often chastised America for not combating Arab terrorism vigorously enough. But Israel's apparent lack of cooperation with the FBI in the JDL investigation calls into question its sincerity in prosecuting the war against terrorism when the terrorism emanates from Israel itself. An Israeli Justice Ministry spokesman in Jerusalem declined to comment about U.S. government allegations of non-cooperation. Complaints about Israel's inadequate cooperation in another criminal investigation also arose in the case of Jonathan Jay Pollard, a U.S. Navy intelligence analyst convicted of spying for Israel and sentenced to life in prison.

U.S. government sources and analysts in Israel cite several reasons why the Israeli government is dragging its heels on the JDL investigation. To put it simply, many Israelis view Jews who kill Nazis and PLO supporters as heroes, not criminals. During a time of heightened tension between Israelis and Palestinians in the Occupied Territories, there is widespread public sympathy for Jews—even those associated with Kahane—who have struck down Nazis and PLO sympathizers, regarded by many Israelis as one and the same. "It would be very, very controversial here to extradite young American Jews for killing Nazis," said Danny Rubinstein, veteran Arab affairs correspondent for the Israeli daily newspaper *Davar*. Rubinstein noted that following the Second World War, both the Haganah and Hashomer Hatza'ir partisans set up hit-teams to kill SS and Gestapo officers in Europe. These men and women are considered heroes in Israel.

Rubinstein also pointed out that following the conviction of the twenty-eight-man Gush Emunim underground, which for several years in the early 1980s terrorized West Bank Arabs, a huge public relations campaign directed by Israel's "nationalist" camp, made up of prominent Knesset members in the Likud, Tehiya, and religious parties, pressured the government to release the prisoners. Of the twenty-eight who were tried, convicted, and sentenced in April 1985, nearly all are out of prison; several have prominent public positions. One currently directs efforts to settle Jews in Hebron.

Even William Nakash, a Paris-born Jewish underworld figure convicted of killing an Arab in France before escaping to Israel, where he successfully battled extradition for nearly two years before being handed over to French authorities, was enthusiastically supported by the religious community in Israel, including the two chief rabbis. "Jews should never be handed over to gentiles under any circumstances," said right-wing Knesset member Rabbi Eliezer Waldman, who has lobbied for Nakash, Keith Fuchs, and the Gush Emunim terrorist underground. Waldman's sentiments were so pervasive in Israel that then Prime Minister Begin passed a law in 1977 prohibiting the extradition of Israeli nationals, effectively overturning a key feature of the 1962 extradition treaty between the United States and Israel. "It has to do with two thousand years of Jewish history, of Jewish persecution at the hands of Gentiles," said a senior Israeli government official.

Israel may also be concerned about not enraging New York's large, wealthy, right-wing Jewish community, which has been supportive of JDL terrorism in America. New York Assemblyman Dov Hikind unabashedly told me that he supports a Jewish underground that assassinates Nazis and American-Arab supporters of the PLO. "If it is a group that is made up of people who are intelligent professionals and their goal is to execute those clearly responsible for killing tens of thousands, then I would have no trouble with that."

To be sure, Israel is not totally to blame for the FBI's failure to apprehend the JDL murder suspects. The 1985 bombings came at a time of relative JDL quiescence, catching the FBI without wiretaps and informants in place. Further complicating the FBI's investigation has been the reluctance of potential witnesses to testify before a grand jury. One reason for this reticence is that a number of grand jury witnesses have been threatened, making it hard for the FBI to persuade them to come forward, according to government sources familiar with the investigation. The FBI is said to have one informant whose testimony can link Kahane to planning sessions that took place before two of the 1985 bombings, including the murder of Alex Odeh. The informant, however, refuses to testify publicly.

Nevertheless, the FBI has had several major breakthroughs. It has slipped informants into at least four JDL-Kach cells operating in the United States, Canada, and Kiryat Arba. The Bureau also uncovered a JDL plot to assassinate ADC founder James Abourezk. According to Abourezk, a former U.S. senator from South Dakota, the FBI told him about the plot after foiling it. In addition, the FBI thwarted a plot by a Kach member from Israel who was in Los Angeles allegedly recruiting militant Jews to kidnap two Israeli Arab businessmen working in California. In order to avoid an embarrassing trial that could damage U.S.-Israeli relations, the Kach man was quietly bundled off to Israel in the summer of 1986, according to law enforcement sources.

One of the most dramatic developments in the JDL investigation occurred on June 22, 1988, when Robert Manning's forty-eight-year-old wife, Rochelle, was arrested in Los Angeles as she disembarked from a plane arriving from Israel and was charged with conspiracy in the mail-bomb slaying of a California woman in 1980. Robert was later indicted for the murder. According to court documents, fingerprints of both the Mannings were found on a cardboard box that contained the bomb, which was addressed to Brenda Crouthamel, owner of Prowest Computer Corporation, in Manhattan Beach, California. Disguised as a new invention, the bomb exploded when a secretary, Patricia Wilkerson, plugged the device into a wall socket. Police officials who have investigated the 1980 bombing say they are convinced the bomb was intended for Ms. Crouthamel and does not appear to have been politically motivated. In August 1988, William Ross, a multimillionaire Los Angeles real estate broker and JDL supporter, was the third person indicted in the Wilkerson murder. Federal officials say that Ross was involved in a dispute with Crouthamel over real estate, and contracted the Mannings to carry out the bombing. A Los Angeles federal grand jury investigating the case has subpoenaed other JDL members to testify before it, including Steve Smason, one of Kahane's top fundraisers and the head of Kach International.

On January 20, 1989, a federal judge declared a mistrial in the case against Manning and Ross after the jurors announced that they were hopelessly deadlocked. After five days of deliberations, which some jurors said disintegrated into a shouting match, the jury announced that it was split six to six on Ross, and was leaning ten to two in favor of convicting Manning. Prosecutors subsequently dropped the charges against Ross and Manning. Assistant U.S. Attorney Nancy Widen Stock later said that she would seek Robert Manning's extradition from Israel to stand trial for the murder of Patricia Wilkerson. "If we get him back [from Israel] there will definitely be a new trial," a Justice Department spokesperson told me. Robert Manning's lawyer, Samuel Abady, said that Rochelle's arrest and trial was nothing more than an attempt by the government to lure Robert to the United

States to face charges for terrorist bombings that the FBI has attributed to the JDL.

Meanwhile, FBI agent Wack seems convinced that Manning, Green, and their alleged co-conspirators will not escape justice, even though an extradition hearing in Israel would no doubt be politically messy. "Justice itself is slow. . . .," he wrote to Manning in August 1987, but "please don't believe ANYONE will escape extradition."

Federal grand juries in New York and Los Angeles are investigating JDL bombings, as well as the JDL's other activities, which allegedly have included narcotics sales, extortion, and working as couriers for organized crime. Asked if Kahane is himself under investigation for complicity in the homicides attributed to the JDL, Assistant U.S. Attorney Charles Rose replied: "We are investigating the JDL for homicides, and Kahane's leadership [of the JDL] is being questioned, so you can draw your own conclusions." According to federal law enforcement sources, Kahane was seen in the United States with the suspects not long before two of the blasts, including the Odeh bombing.

Meanwhile, Kahane has not only publicly cheered the recent bombings attributed to his movement but has also called for more. In one of his weekly columns in May 1987 for *The Jewish Press*, he vowed that Kach would set up a "Mossad-type unit" to assassinate perceived enemies of the Jewish people wherever they reside: "Let the Nazi groups that have arisen in the United States and Canada and France and Britain and Latin America know that they are on the cross hairs of the Israeli gun."

CHAPTER SIXTEEN
The Golem

∧∧∧∧∧∧∧∧∧∧∧∧∧∧∧∧∧∧∧∧∧∧∧∧∧∧∧∧∧∧

On the eve of the November 1, 1988 Knesset elections, Kahane's popularity was surging at the polls. The *intifada*, which began in December 1987, had driven tens of thousands of Israelis rightwards, and Kahane's violently anti-Arab Kach Party appeared to be a major beneficiary. On October 2, 1988, a front-page article in *The New York Times* quoted respected Israeli pollster Hanoch Smith predicting that Kahane would win at least three seats (or 60,000 votes), thereby giving him the balance of power between Labor and Likud, which were in a stalemate at the polls. Smith told the *Times* that if Likud did not invite Kahane into a right-wing coalition, it would be unable to form a government.

Professor Ehud Sprinzak, an expert on extremist groups at Hebrew University, told me that if Kahane got the votes of five to six percent of the electorate (or about six seats) as several Israeli polls predicted,* he would be the head of the third largest bloc of voters in Israel. "That would almost certainly mean Kahane would get a cabinet post if there were a Likud government," he said. "Kahane wants the Ministry of Defense. He would never get that. They would give him the Ministry of

---

* A poll conducted by Modi'in Ezrahi for *Ma'ariv* during the second week of September 1988 indicated that Kach would win six seats.

Interior. He would be in charge of civil rights and minority affairs. Can you imagine what that would mean?''

To prevent that from happening, the Knesset's Central Election Commission banned Kach from participating in the elections on the grounds that it is a racist and anti-democratic party. The commission based its ruling on an anti-racism law that was adopted by the Knesset (by a vote of 57 to 22, with 7 abstentions) in August 1986. Kach's banishment was spearheaded by Likud's Yitzhak Shamir and Tehiya's Geula Cohen, who had no intention of sitting back and watching Kach become a right-wing juggernaut. Although Shamir and Cohen clearly had much to do with turning Kahane into a potent political phenomenon, they wanted nothing better than to destroy his career and siphon away his tens of thousands of supporters.

On October 18, 1988, Kahane appealed the Central Election Commission's ruling to Israel's Supreme Court, arguing that he grounded everything he did and said in pronouncements from the Torah and other Jewish religious writings. (Significantly, most Knesset members from the religious parties had voted against the anti-racism bill because, as Rabbi Haim Druckman of the Morasha Party put it, under the bill, "maintaining the *Halakhah* will make us all criminals.") Nevertheless, a five-member Supreme Court panel unanimously upheld the ban, declaring that Kach's proposed treatment of the Arabs is "shockingly similar" to the horrible crimes "which the Jewish people experienced." Outside the packed Jerusalem courthouse, frenzied Kach supporters lifted Kahane onto their shoulders chanting "Kahane, King of Israel!" Several Kach women who had recently emigrated from the United States were in tears as they described the court decision as an abomination. "It's a black, black day for Israel!" said a frazzled-looking young woman from America, who tore at her clothes in a sign of mourning. "If my bill that would have criminalized intermarriage and sexual intercourse between Jews and non-Jews is racism," Kahane screamed, "then take out your Torah and Talmud and burn them all! Right now, thousands of Jewish women are married to Arabs. That's democracy! Do you want that?''

Kahane may be out of the Knesset, but he is hardly out of the public eye. And his ideas continue to gain momentum throughout the Jewish state. In the ancient port city of Acre, the 1988

Likud candidate for mayor, David Bar-Lev, ran on a platform to transfer the Arabs out of the city. In Ariel, a sprawling Jewish West Bank settlement of sleek, ultra-modern homes and apartment complexes carved out of the stark Samarian hills, Mayor Ron Nachman proposed a law in 1989 requiring the town's Arab workers to wear an identification badge, reminiscent of the yellow Star of David that the Nazis made Jews wear during the Second World War. In Kiryat Arba, where Kach shares power on the town council, Kahane's party pushed through a resolution in 1986 prohibiting the city from hiring Arab workers. The resolution was declared "null and void" by Israel's attorney general, who called it "discriminatory" and "racist."

On the West Bank, following a rampage by thirty yeshiva students through an Arab town that ended in the shooting death of a thirteen-year-old Palestinian girl in July 1989, the yeshiva's dean, Rabbi Yitzhak Ginsberg, justified the murder, telling an Israeli court that "it should be recognized that Jewish blood and a goy's blood are not the same. The people of Israel must rise and declare in public that a Jew and a goy are not, God forbid, the same. Any trial that assumes that Jews and goyim are equal is a travesty of justice."

In Or Yehuda (Light of Judea), a grimy, working-class suburb at the edge of Tel Aviv, the Palestinian uprising has been answered with hate and gasoline. In the fall of 1988, a group of Israeli teenagers soaked a wooden shack with gasoline, threw a match, and ran. Two Palestinian workers sleeping inside burned to death. A third ran out into the road like a human torch. According to reports in the Hebrew press, passersby refused to douse the flames and the Arab died. "What does it matter if an Arab burns?" Shuki Khalif, a sixteen-year-old Israeli friend of the Jewish arsonists, asked an Israeli reporter. "What does an Arab matter at all? It's not a human being. I wouldn't care if more than two thousand burned." His friend Reuven Alayev added, "I would burn five thousand more."

Some Jewish religious scholars have quietly argued that there is nothing wrong with using genocide to eradicate the "Arab problem." In 1984, Rabbi Moshe Segal, who was aligned with the Irgun during the pre-state period, wrote a letter on behalf of a committee that was collecting legal defense funds for the Gush Emunim terrorist underground, in which he compared the

Arab residents of the Occupied Territories to the Amalek tribe, which had been destroyed by the ancient Hebrews. "One should have mercy on all creatures . . . but the treatment of Amalek—is different. The treatment of those who would steal our land—is different." Then, quoting Numbers 33, Segal wrote: "You must drive out all the inhabitants of the land as you advance . . . and settle there, for to you have I given the land to possess it. . . . But if you will not drive out the inhabitants of the land as you advance, any whom you let remain shall be as barbed hooks in your eyes, and as thorns in your sides. They shall continually dispute your possession of the land in which you dwell. And what I meant to do to them, I will do to you."

Israeli liberals criticized Segal's letter as being tantamount to advocating genocide. But Segal's is not an isolated case. Recently, Rabbi Israel Hess, a noted scholar at Bar Ilan University, published an article in the university's official magazine entitled, "The Genocide Ruling of Torah," which also compared the Palestinians to the Amalekites, whose extermination was mandated by the Torah.

As anti-Arab passions burn bright in towns and cities across Israel, the *intifada* has given Kahane's concept of expelling the country's Arabs urgency. According to the Israeli newspaper *Yediot Aharonot*, Israeli Deputy Foreign Minister Benjamin Netanyhu told students at Bar-Ilan University in November 1989 that, "Israel should have taken advantage of the supression of the demonstrations in China, while the world's attention was focused on these events, and should have carried out mass deportations of Arabs from the territories. Unfortunately, this plan I proposed did not gain support, yet I still suggest to put it into action."

Kahane, who often attends the funerals of Israelis killed by Arab terrorists looking for recruits, continues to preach that expulsion is holy. At a rally in downtown Jerusalem the day after the July 6, 1989 attack in which a Palestinian seized the steering wheel of an Israeli bus and sent it plunging into a ravine, killing sixteen, Kahane cried: "Give me the power to take care of them [the Arabs] once and for all!" Hundreds of Kahane's supporters applauded wildly and chanted: "Death to the Arabs and their [Jewish] leftist friends." An explosion of hateful fury followed. Dozens of innocent Arabs were injured in reprisal attacks across Israel and the Occupied Territories. "Our God is a god of vengeance," said a Kach bulletin distributed in Jerusalem. "It's nonsense to assume vengeance is not a Jewish concept."

In the wake of the bus attack, Kahane and his followers have increasingly turned their wrath on Jews. Throughout Israel one can find wall slogans calling for the death of various liberal politicians and signed with a Kach logo—a clenched fist exploding through a black Star of David. Kach goon squads have attacked peace activists, assaulted homosexuals and Jewish women who have had relations with Arabs, and threatened left-wing politicians, artists, and journalists. In 1989, a shadowy underground called the *Sicarrim* firebombed the homes of a number of prominent left-leaning Israelis. They even firebombed the home of a pollster who conducted a survey that showed that a slim majority of Israelis would consider trading territory for peace with the Arabs. Following an arson attack on Petah Tivka Mayor Dov Tavori, the Hebrew daily newspaper *Yediot Aharonot* received this message: "We, the *Sicarrim*, are responsible for setting fire to the house and car of Petah Tikva's mayor. We identify with the Kach movement."

In a July 14, 1989 column in *The Jewish Press*, Kahane blamed fellow Jews for the horrifying Palestinian bus attack earlier that month. "Who murdered them?" Kahane asked, referring to the sixteen Jews who died in the terrorist incident. "Who are the partners, the accomplices in the murder of these Jews? Whose hands are stained with their blood? Whose souls will forever be marked with the guilt, the sin, the *crime* of the murder of Jews?"

The answer, Kahane wrote, is: "Every Jew who worships at the altar of gentilized, Hellenized foreign culture. . . . Every Jew who ever babbled about 'racism' and 'fascism' and who obscenely compared the call for expulsion of Arabs who would murder, massacre, and exterminate Jews to the acts of the Nazis. Every Jew who ever called Kahane a 'Nazi'. . . . The American Jewish Establishment with its condemnation of Kahane. . . . The American liberal and leftist Jews, suffering from the [*Tikkun* editor] Michael Lerner disease . . . The UJA Federation . . . the temple rabbis. . . . The American Jewish news-media. . . . The Jews of Silence. . . . the [Israeli] right wing and the nationalists who joined in condemnation of Kahane."

In one *Jewish Press* column, Kahane even called for the liquidation of Jews whose views he finds pernicious. On August 31, 1984, he wrote:

In order to save Israel, the Torah says to burn out the evil from our midst. Indeed, the rabbis of the Talmud bring down the verse, "and thou shalt love thy fellow Jew as thyself," in order to explain why we must kill the Jew who is deserving of death in a humane way.

Love of Jews? Of course. And sacrifice for them; by all means. But when a Jew rises to challenge fundamentals of God, Jewry, and Israel, that Jew must be stopped. And indeed, the punishment that we bring on the wicked Jew goes a long and necessary way to atonement for him in the world to come.

Kahane named some of the Jews that he thinks must be stopped:

If Yossi Sarid and Shulamit Aloni [members of the Citizens Rights Movement Party in the Knesset] and Mapam [a left-wing labor party] and Meir Vilner [the secretary general of the New Communist Party and a member of the Knesset] and the whole host of Hellenists, spiritually sick, move to threaten the very existence of Judaism, Jewry, and Israel—there is nothing moral about tolerating it. To the contrary, it is the most immoral and evil of things. Their evil threatens every Jew; their sins will sink the Jewish ship which carries every Jew. If [Alexander] Schindler [head of the Union of American Hebrew Congregations] and Reform Judaism split Jews into two separate camps and threaten the very definition of Jew with their ignorant arrogance, are we to be "tolerant" and "moderate"?

It takes great strength to love Jews so much that one fights for them. It takes, perhaps, even more strength to love Jews so much that one fights Jews who would destroy them. The pity is that they neither love nor hate enough. They remain indifferent and "pareve," seeking to hide from responsibility. But the truth remains that we are in need of the strong Jews. Those strong enough to love and hate and wise enough to know when to do what. "Any scholar who is not as strong as iron is not a scholar." Where are the scholars? Where is the strength?

According to Professor Sprinzak, Kach is reminiscent of the European fascists in the '20s and '30s before the Nazis came to power: "They are openly violent and they are proud of their violence. Unfortunately, he [Kahane] is not *Halachicly* isolated." Indeed, Sprinzak said that one of Kahane's most ardent supporters is the Sephardic Chief Rabbi of Israel Mordechai Eliyahu, who had been a member of a small, right-wing religious extremist group that was crushed by the Shin Bet in the early 1950s. "He's very radical and he's Kahane's personal rabbi," said Sprinzak. "He agrees with Kahane's *Halachic* interpretation of everything."

Sol Margolis, a Rockville, Maryland lawyer, believes that Kahane is one of the greatest figures in world Jewry today. "I read Kahane's book *Why Be Jewish?*, and it was so much on target it hurt," said Margolis, the former treasurer of the Greater Washington United Jewish Appeal who recently became head of Kach International. "When I saw him, I was very impressed, and he was surrounded by articulate and intelligent people. . . . Kahane addresses painful issues that people don't want to hear because it's holding a mirror up to themselves. But anyone who gives him a fair hearing will come away stimulated by the process." A February 1989 parlor meeting for Kahane held in Margolis's home and attended by seventy people netted the Kach leader some $15,000, according to a report in the *Washington Jewish Week.* "Kahane has a much greater following than anyone in the United States will admit," New York Assemblyman and Kach enthusiast Dov Hikind told me in May 1989. Hikind said that establishment Jewish leaders condemn Kahane "because they are jealous."

* * *

Kahane has good reason to be optimistic about the future. His banishment from the Knesset has not wiped away his constituency. In the past, his power and strength have grown as Israeli society has become more deeply polarized along ethnic, social, and political lines. The last time Kahane granted me an interview, in November 1984, a time when he was still flush with the high from his Knesset victory earlier that year, he predicted that he would soon be the leader of the second largest political party in Israel. "I always knew I'd get a [Knesset] seat," Kahane told me. "And if they hold elections in a year, we will get many, many more seats. If unemployment in a year is as high as we think it will be, and if inflation in a year is as high as we think it will be, and if Ronald Reagan—who of course is a disaster for the Jewish people—pressures the Israeli government to trade land for peace—and there are more Arab terrorist attacks on Jews—it's completely conceivable that we will have eight to ten seats. . . . The worse it gets for Israel the better it gets for me!''

Political and economic conditions in Israel today are far worse than Kahane had imagined. The *intifada* has raged since 1987, and the United States is speaking to the PLO, striking fear into the souls of proponents of "Greater Israel." As the crisis in Israel continues, weakening the country's democratic institutions, the demagogues on the Right will undoubtedly try to take over. Thanks to the animosity of his former friends on the Right, Kahane will never be the one to run Israel. But he will fan the flames of hatred and destruction—paving the way for a strongman like Ariel Sharon to step in and put the house in order.

Ultimately, the Israeli Right is angry with Kahane because he *says* what they *think*: that the Jewish state should annex the Occupied Territories and expel all of Israel's unruly Arabs. And declaring that openly is not good public relations. Kahane is not a golem forged from the anxiety of a tormented diaspora—as the propagandists on the Right would have us believe. To a great extent, he is the creation of Israel's "respectable" (secular) Right, and despite their differences with him, Kahane is the logical culmination of Shamir's and Cohen's uncompromising nationalist views.

Of course, Kahane is more than merely an extreme version of Shamir and Cohen. He is also a voice of Orthodox Judaism, which increasingly has become a bastion of religious intolerance. Kahane's unique fusion of right-wing secular Zionism, which attributes supreme value to the concept of nation, land, and race, and militant religious nationalism, which is guided by a Messianic quest for redemption, has helped spawn a virulent form of racism that is spreading across Israel.

For all his religious posturing, Kahane is a con man whose considerable contempt for his fellow Jews has been evident since childhood, when he would stand in his father's synagogue disparaging the congregants for not being "Jewish" enough to suit him. His tireless pursuit of money and power has been clear since he was a teenager and tried to divert funds from Betar. His opportunism is best illustrated by the ease with which he transferred his hatred of American Blacks to Israel's Arabs, caring little if his backing came from the CIA, the FBI, Mossad, or the Mob.

Although he attempted to pass legislation in Israel that would have made it a crime punishable by a prison term for Jews to have sex with gentiles, Kahane drove one gentile mistress to suicide. Even now, when he is in New York on fundraising tours, there is a house that he uses to bed his young supporters, as brawny Kach members stand guard, according to several of those who have been posted outside his bedroom door.

The Jewish people have been beset by many false prophets during their long and turbulent history. If Kahane can trace his political roots to Jabotinsky and the Old Testament, then the taproot leads directly to Sabbatai Zevi. Born in Smyrna, Turkey in 1626 to an upper-class family, Sabbatai claimed that he had heard a voice from God, who told him to redeem Israel. Sabbatai, a cabalist, proclaimed himself the Messiah, and was soon hailed as the saviour by hundreds of thousands of pogrom-plagued Jews from Morocco to the Ukraine. Sabbatai was arrested by the Turkish Sultan for subversive activities not long after he appeared in Palestine, where he was embraced by the Jews as their long-awaited Messiah. When given the choice of converting to Islam or facing the sword, he donned a turban and became a gatekeeper in the sultan's bordello. News of Sabbatai's conversion threw the Jewish world into turmoil. A fanatical cult of extremists preserved a movement named the Sabbateans until the beginning of the nineteenth century.

A cult is unlikely to develop around Kahane when he passes from the scene. Kach is a one-man show, and it will die with Kahane. But he will leave behind a legacy of hatred and violence that will trouble Israeli and American Jews for some time. In Kahane's words one can hear the echo of Nazi viciousness. His call for transfer is a call for genocide. Sadly, Kahane already has achieved a prominent place in Israel's popular culture. A new computer game inspired by Kahane, called "*Intifada*," is sweeping the country. Invented by electronics wizard Michael Medved, a Soviet Jew who was formerly a member of the JDL in Brooklyn before moving to Israel, the game places a player in a West Bank village, surrounded by *keffiya*-clad, rock-throwing Arabs. The player is given the choice of using tear gas, rubber bullets, plastic bullets, or live ammunition to quell the "uppity" Arabs. The score is based on the number of Palestinians wounded, killed, and hospitalized. If the player is killed, the words "You are another victim of Arab terror" flash on the screen. If an Arab is killed, the screen reads, "The state thanks you! Continue the good job!" When a player reaches the highest score possible, Rabbi Meir Kahane's smiling face fills the screen and a message declares that the Kach leader has been named defense minister of Israel. The computer award may not be what Kahane had in mind when as a boy in Flatbush he fantasized about becoming prime minister of Israel, but it is certainly a testament to his continuing influence on public life in the Jewish state.

AFTERWORD
The Kahane Legacy

〰〰〰〰〰〰〰〰〰〰〰〰〰〰〰〰〰〰〰〰

Jewish Defense Organization Chairman Mordechai Levy was an accident waiting to happen. By his own account, the paunchy, twenty-seven-year-old loner had spent more than a decade moving in and out of the often violent world of radical fringe groups, supplying information to intelligence agencies and Jewish organizations, including the FBI and the Anti-Defamation League. But throughout the summer of 1989, nothing obsessed Levy more than his increasingly bitter feud with two rival Jewish militants—West Coast JDL boss Irv Rubin and convicted JDL terrorist Steven Rombom. When these two—together with Allan Klebanoff, a bearded, hulking, twenty-seven-year-old Israeli army veteran from Haifa—came to the JDO's fortresslike Greenwich Village headquarters to serve Levy with court papers stemming from a libel action, something in the tightly wound Levy apparently snapped.

"Mor-dy, Mor-dy, we've got something for you," the militants sang in taunting voices described by eyewitnesses as something out of the movie *Nightmare on Elm Street*. Levy, who had an arsenal of licensed weapons in his office, scrambled to the roof and sprayed the street with a burst of semiautomatic rifle fire, wounding a retired air conditioning repairman as he sat in a parked van. "They were really provoking the guy," said repairman Dominic Spinelli, who was taken to the emergency room at St. Vincent's Hospital in Manhattan. Spinelli said that the three men knocked at Levy's door and, after receiving no answer, began to throw stones at the windows and to shout " 'Come on Mordechai, we know you're in there.' I guess the guy just got mad and started shooting.''

Around midnight on Wednesday August 9, 1989, just twelve hours before the shoot-out in Greenwich Village, I received a call from Levy, with whom I have discussed Jewish militant activities over the years. "I'm sorry to call so late but it's an emergency,'' he said, panting into my phone answering machine. "Pick up. Listen, Rubin is in New York with Rombom. They are fucking looking for you.'' Levy, more hyperkinetic than usual, said that the men had staked out *The Village Voice* offices, where I sometimes work, waiting for a chance to "teach me a lesson'' for writing a book about Meir Kahane that they were sure they would not like. "Rombom is armed,'' warned Levy. "They are looking for you. Call me any time, day or night.''

Both Rombom and Rubin were later to tell me that Levy's midnight call was just one more delusion produced by a very, very sick mind. And they say they posed no threat to Levy when they were met with rifle shots from a Ruger Mini-14.

Moments after the shooting, Bleecker Street, where Levy lived and worked, looked like a war zone. Dozens of heavily armed police, backed by an armored personnel carrier and a bomb disposal robot, had cordoned off the neighborhood as the JDO leader was holed up in his office, phoning friends for advice. FBI agent Larry Wack finally convinced Levy to surrender.

As Levy, looking sad and extremely frightened, was led in handcuffs to a waiting unmarked police car, he told reporters, "They were trying to kill me.'' Wild as it may seem, he's not alone in that belief. "I think Rubin and Rombom went to Levy's to rub him out,'' said a well-known Jewish militant in New York.

But FBI sources investigating the shooting are more skeptical: "These guys cry wolf so much you never know what's really happening,'' said an FBI official. "Think of what *might* have happened: Rombom and Rubin could have left Bleecker Street in a body bag.''

Levy is currently awaiting trial for the attempted murder of Rubin and Rombom. Not surprisingly, Levy's attorney is none other than Bertram Zweibon, JDL co-founder and now one of

Meir Kahane's bitterest enemies. If the shooting on Bleecker Street has the overtones of comic opera, it is also just one more example of Kahane's soiled legacy. Ostensibly founded to defend Jews, the JDL has degenerated into little more than a racketeering enterprise made up of warring, brutish loons who use anti-Semitism as an excuse to sow fear in the Jewish community and to raise money for themselves.

Several weeks after Mordechai Levy ran amok, I encountered still more evidence of Kahane's influence on New York City's political scene. On a late summer afternoon, I interviewed comic Jackie Mason, who was New York City's Republican mayoral hopeful Rudolph Giuliani's honorary campaign manager. I had interviewed Mason in 1987 for *The Washington Post* about his admiration for Rabbi Meir Kahane, whose call to expel Israel's Arabs Mason enthusiastically endorses. Now Mason was endorsing Giuliani for mayor of a city that has been rocked by horrible incidents of racial bias. I thought that they were an improbable pair: Mason, the *very* Jewish comic whose biting, ethnic humor is suddenly in vogue, and Giuliani, the pallid, deadly serious ex-prosecutor who pursued media coverage as zealously as he pursued the Mob. But when Giuliani began reeling at the polls after his strong early showing, media magician Roger Ailes, who served George Bush so well, cast Mason in several Giuliani commercials that attacked Democrat Ed Koch as a turkey of a mayor. Mason brought a little glamour to a campaign that had been run into the ground by Giuliani's bland inner circle of stuffed shirt lawyers.

But Ailes and Giuliani got far more than they had bargained for. Perhaps they did not know—or care—that Mason had been a fan of the JDL since its founding days when the organization was little more than an anti-Black protest movement obsessed with combating Black demands for better jobs and decent housing. In 1969, the JDL had made Black-Jewish relations a bitterly divisive issue in the mayoral campaign, targeting Mayor John Lindsay for defeat, because, as far as Kahane was concerned, Lindsay was far too sympathetic to Blacks. Now, some twenty years later, the JDL's race-baiting politics were being brought to the 1989 mayor's race courtesy of funnyman Jackie Mason. (Another ghost from the 1969 mayor race turned up in the middle of the 1989 mayoral campaign to haunt Democratic candidate David Dinkins. Leslie Campbell, who now calls himself Jitu

Weusi, resigned as co-chairman of African Americans United for David Dinkins after the ADL revealed that Weusi had read a poem on WBAI radio in 1969, which began: "Hey, Jew Boy, with that yarmulke on your head, you pale-faced Jew boy—I wish you were dead." The poem, recited during the height of tensions stemming from the New York City teachers' strike, sparked one of the JDL's first public demonstrations.)

There was nothing funny, however, about what Mason had to say to me when I interviewed him for *The Village Voice* concerning Giuliani's Democratic rival, David Dinkins, an African-American. Echoing charges first made by Kahane in the 1969 mayoral campaign, Mason said that Jews, especially in New York's outer boroughs, lie awake at night in fear of Black street crime. As far as Mason was concerned, Dinkins was inadequate to the task of stopping his rampaging Black brothers. "When there is a war going on you need a general," said Mason, referring to the rising tide of crime in New York, which he said has destroyed the city. "You don't need a guy like Dinkins, who spends his whole life putting on shirts and jackets and parting his hair. Dinkins looks like a Black model without a job."

Mason went on to say that if Dinkins beat Giuliani, it would be because liberal Jews, sick with guilt complexes, reflexively voted for a Black man. "There is a sick Jewish problem of voting for a Black man no matter how unfit he is for the job," said Mason. "All you have to do is to be Black and don't curse the Jews directly and the Jew will vote for a Black in a second. Jews are sick with complexes. They feel guilt for the Black predicament as if the Jews caused it. Jews have always marched for the Blacks. Jews have always supported all their hospitals, their causes. A big percentage of the money the United Jewish Appeal collects goes to the general fund which is directly responsible for funding Black organizations of every kind, like anti-drug centers, alcoholic centers, food distribution centers. The Jews are constantly giving millions of dollars to Black people. Have you ever heard of a Black person giving a quarter to a Jew? I never heard a Black person say we have to help the poor Jews. There are plenty of poor Jews in the world. . . . I'm not saying Blacks should be giving to the Jews, but Jews don't owe anything to Blacks."

In the firestorm that followed Mason's published remarks, Giuliani bounced the comic from the campaign. "Mason *is* the sick Jewish problem,'' cried Ira Silverman of the American Jewish Committee in one of many rebukes from the Jewish establishment. But just a few days after the Mason interview, Giuliani placed a racially divisive ad in a Jewish newspaper in Manhattan that stressed Dinkins's link to Jesse Jackson, who had openly called for a West Bank-Gaza Strip state for Palestinian Arabs alongside Israel. Like Mason's comments, the ad was denounced by liberal Jews.

Indeed, there does not seem to be much difference between Mason's diatribe against liberal Jews and Kahane's views on the subject. In a 1984 newspaper column, Kahane railed against the liberal "born-by-accident Jews who are riven with schizophrenia over their identity and riddled by self-hate and desire for self-destruction.'' In the same column Kahane went much further than Mason when he called for killing these Jews, though "in a humane way.''

Now, just as twenty years ago, Kahane's invective can be read in *The Jewish Press**, where he pollutes political discourse and heightens racial tensions. Even for him, Kahane's racist shtick has reached new heights of irresponsibility during the *intifada*. On August 25, 1989, in *The Jewish Press*, Kahane openly called for revolution in Israel because the Israeli government "is incapable or unwilling to protect to the utmost, and in every way possible, the lives of its citizens.'' Because, in Kahane's view, the only way to absolutely protect Israeli Jews from the stones of the *intifada* is to expel each and every Arab—something that the Israeli government is not yet prepared or willing to do— Kahane says that the government "loses every legal and moral right to rule. . . .'' Magnanimously, he offers Israeli leaders two choices: referendum or revolution. "Failing [referendum], there is only one other [choice]: revolution by bitter and frustrated Jews who know what the Arabs would do if they could. . . . I urge this government to choose referendum. Let the people decide. For the alternative is the bitter one of revolution.''

How has Kahane gotten away with his vicious campaign of criminal incitement, his call for revolution, his divisive racial

---

* New York's abrasive ex-mayor, Ed Koch, also wrote a regular column for *The Jewish Press* while he was in office. On occasion, his mug shot peered across the page at Kahane's brooding, bearded visage. Koch, who is decidedly not a Kahane supporter, once publicly called the rabbi a "scum." "Koch is not a happy man," responded Kahane. "He's *gay*, but he's not happy."

tactics, the terrorist violence? In America, had Kahane been a Black militant, there is no doubt in my mind that he would have been prosecuted and convicted for his myriad crimes and sentenced to jail for a very long time. In Israel, had he been an Arab and called for revolution, the government would have put him on the next taxi crossing the Allenby Bridge into Jordan.

Obviously, he has substantial subterranean support in Israel and America, and not just from the Jackie Masons and the Mordechai Levys, but also from the Dov Hikinds, the Barry Slotnicks, the wizened Orthodox rabbis, and all the other scared, angry Jews who see in Kahane a chance to stick it to their perceived enemies—as if Kahane is somehow an antidote to their feelings of inadequacy or, perhaps, a megalomaniacal manifestation of their dreams of Messiahs, rebuilt temples, and Jewish empires.

Beyond that, Kahane often has been a useful tool for a number of intelligence agencies, which are now responsible for policing his activities. The FBI breathed life into the JDL when J. Edgar Hoover used Kahane in his COINTELPRO against the Black Panthers. Now the very same agency, which is attempting to investigate Kahane's terrorist underground, is complaining that its probe is obstructed by Israeli intelligence, which itself employed Kahane in the late 1960s and the early 1970s to violently publicize the plight of Soviet Jewry. (Ironically, now that hundreds of thousands of Soviet Jews have a chance to leave for Israel and to populate the West Bank as Yitzhak Shamir and Geula Cohen had planned, many are opting for Brighton Beach, a seaside community in Brooklyn.)

One wonders if these police and intelligence agencies, having once worked so closely with Kahane, are now unwilling or unable to pull the plug on the rambunctious rabbi. Perhaps most difficult to understand is why the Internal Revenue Service, the most powerful government agency in America, never investigated Kahane. "If the IRS had audited Kahane, the JDL, or any of our front groups, we would have been finished," said Bertram Zweibon. Two other former JDL officials told me that Kahane has long had a close friend who is a high-ranking IRS official, a charge that was impossible for me to verify.

For four years, I papered government agencies with requests for information relevant to the JDL and Kahane. And for years I got a bureaucratic runaround. On July 21, 1987, for example, I wrote a Freedom of Information Act request to the CIA (where Kahane once worked on contract during the Vietnam era) for information on various Jewish organizations and individuals connected to Kahane. On September 15, 1989, as this book was nearing completion, the CIA denied my request, stating in a letter that the documents found pursuant to my request, "are classified because their disclosure could reasonably be expected to cause exceptionally grave damage to the national security." No wonder the rabbi is laughing at the establishment; it is protecting him even while he is trying to bring it down.

Critics say that Kahane is a marginal figure, that his following is small, that his impact is limited. But Kahaneism has had anything but a limited impact in Israel, where the government has striven mightily to delegitimize him. And even though Kahane has been banned from the Knesset, his ideas have taken root and have become "respectable." Rahavam Ze'evi, a retired major-general and former Labor Party member, now sits in the Knesset at the head of the right-wing Moledet Party whose single issue is "transfer." As the *intifada* continues, "transfer" will become the preferable solution for more and more Israelis, perhaps giving Kahane's career another of its periodic boosts.

American Jews in particular, even on the liberal-left, prefer to think of Kahane as an aberration. But Kahane comes out of the broad stream of the Orthodox-Zionist Right. Though he may be an emotionally disturbed individual, he learned his philosophy at his father's knee. It is a philosophy that is a product of the Begin-Jabotinsky ethos melded with a strain of *Halacha* that is as disturbing as it is racist.

What does Rabbi Meir Kahane really want for his people, humanity, the globe? "A horrible world war is coming," Kahane once told me, his black eyes steaming under thick arched brows. "Tens of millions will die. It will be the Apocalypse. God will punish us for forsaking him. But we must have faith. The Messiah will come. There will be a resurrection of the dead—all the things that Jews believed in before they got so damn sophisticated. The amount of suffering we endure will depend upon what we do between now and the end.

"That's up to us—it's not up to God."

Between now and an apocalypse that Kahane could well trigger, world Jewry should come to terms with how powerful a force Jewish fundamentalists like Kahane have become, and then do something to stop them before they destroy Israel and poison the future of the Jewish people. That, too, is up to us.

ACKNOWLEDGMENTS

I received ecumenical support for this book from Jewish groups and individuals across the political spectrum, as well as from prominent American Arabs. Distaste for Rabbi Meir Kahane may be one of the few things on which many Jews and Arabs agree.

I received encouragement, support, and invaluable editorial advice from many people. I would especially like to thank: Micah Sifry and Victor Navasky of *The Nation*; Bob Silvers of *The New York Review of Books*; Murray Polner of *Present Tense Magazine*; David Ignatius and Larry Meyer of *The Washington Post*; Steve Leibowitz, formerly deputy director of the Israeli Government Press Office in Jerusalem; Danny Rubinstein of *Davar*; Yehuda Litani of *The Jerusalem Post*; Nachum Barnea of *Yediot Aharonot*; Professor Edward Said; Professor David Garrow; Professor Kenneth O'Reilly; former Senator James Abourezk; Larry Cohler; Jim Zogby; Philip Weiss; Marc Frons; Rabbi Abraham Zuroff; Victor Kovner, and Ramsey Clark.

I found great value in the work of the following writers and journalists: Shlomo Russ, Sol Stern, and *The New York Times*'s Michael Kaufman.

The following organizations assisted me in the research of this book: The Alicia Patterson Foundation; The Fund for Investigative Journalism; The Anti-Defamation League of the B'nai B'rith; The American-Arab Anti-Discrimination Committee; Americans for Middle East Understanding; The American Jewish Committee; The Foundation for Middle East Peace and its president, Merle Thorpe, Jr.; and The Center for Constitutional Rights, especially Michael Ratner, Margaret Ratner, Ann Mari Buitrago, and Frank Deale.

In particular, I would like to thank Bertram Zweibon for lending me portions of the Jewish Defense League archives from 1968 to 1974. Even though our political views could not be farther apart, I came to respect his commitment to his political ideals.

Finally, I would like to thank my family, most especially my wife, Christine Dugas, an excellent journalist, and my mother. Without their love and support I could not have completed this project.

A final word about Rabbi Meir Kahane. I first interviewed Kahane in Jerusalem in 1979 for *Present Tense Magazine* and *The Los Angeles Times*. My last interview with Kahane was in November 1984 in New York City. Soon after, Kahane stopped talking to me because, as he put it, my reporting about his movement was too critical.

INDEX